Rattled!

Broadway Books
New York

Rattled!

A Memoir

Christine Coppa

BROADWAY

Published in the United States by Broadway Books, an imprint of the
Doubleday Publishing Group, a division of Random House, Inc.,
New York.
www.broadwaybooks.com

BROADWAY BOOKS and its logo, a letter B bisected on the diagonal,
are trademarks of Random House, Inc.

STORKED! is a registered trademark owned by Advance Magazine
Publishers, Inc.

Book design by Songhee Oh

Library of Congress Cataloging-in-Publication Data
Coppa, Christine.
    Rattled! : a memoir / By Christine Coppa.—1st ed.
       p. cm.
    1. Pregnancy, Unwanted—United States. 2. Unmarried mothers—
United States. I. Title.

  HV700.5.C67 2009
  306.874'32092—dc22
  [B]
          2008045955

ISBN 978-0-7679-3082-6

PRINTED IN THE UNITED STATES OF AMERICA

10 9 8 7 6 5 4

For Jack Domenic,
You are the light of all of my days.

"The child must know that he is a miracle, that since the beginning of the world there hasn't been, and until the end of the world there will not be, another child like him."

—Pablo Casals

The Positive Sign

*F*alse *A-larm* I think as I tear open the box and dump the contents, a folded pamphlet of paper and a capped stick, into my hands. I've never taken a pregnancy test before in my life. I'm twenty-six, but suddenly I feel like a scared fifteen-year-old hiding out in a bathroom stall somewhere. My hands shake as I read the directions, which say to remove the cap and place the stick in the direct stream of my urine. It's a black-and-white statement but I read it four times because I am certain I am going to screw this up and cook this wrong. My toes are burrowing through the fuzzy lavender rug; my thong and leggings are slouched at my ankles. *You're not pregnant, Christine,* I assure myself as I swim the stick between my legs. I peer around the small, white bathroom. The tub is lined with half-empty bottles of products that smell like honey and jasmine and citrus (the perks of living with a beauty editor) and the toilet is plastered to the floor on a weird corner angle that I'm just noticing for the first time. I pull the stick out from under me, placing it on the counter as I inch toilet paper off the spool with my fingers. *Maybe I'm supposed to get my period next* *week,* I think—no, *pray. Dear God, next week, right?* I suppose I should start noting my cycle in red ink on the calendar like my sixth-grade health teacher recommended nearly fifteen years ago. I suppose I should buy a calendar. Maybe I should just get on the pill. *Yeah, I'll get a prescription from Dr. Collado,* I think, reassuring myself this is clearly a false alarm that will go down in history as a "Remember when" story I'd rehash to my girlfriends over cocktails—or, better yet, one that would talk one of *them* off the ledge: *I was late once, too—it was fine—relax . . . another round of drinks, on me!*

Cold air is pushing through the closed window behind me. The thin blue curtain gently balloons and relaxes. It's January and frozen outside. The streets are white, washed in salt, and the sky is just starting to light up with the bright, morning sun. A wave of nausea rolls over me—again, but I don't fall to my knees and palm the sides of the bowl. I swallow the dizziness. *The flu. I have the flu. It's flu season. Everyone has the flu. My cycle is messed up because I'm sick,* I think as I comb my fingers through my hair, collecting it into a tight bun. As I wrap the elastic around the lumpy knot, I try to process the fact that we *did* have unprotected sex. Once. The stick is sitting next to the sink. I find it with my eyes, but quickly look away. *Deep breath, Christine.* I say it out loud, like I'm kneeling down before myself holding my own hand. I reach for it, quick, but cautiously pull back. What if I am pregnant? A and I haven't exactly been together that long—almost three months, in fact. I don't know his middle name. Does he have one? I just admitted to some of my girlfriends that I might want to break up with him—and that I might *not*. Our relationship happened at warp speed.

I take a deep breath, close my eyes, and feel for the stick. I open my eyes and my face wrinkles up in scared anticipation like a firecracker is about to go off in my hand. I see it— two blue lines. I fold my body in half and let my hands touch the tile floor. It's cold to my fingertips and assures me I am awake, not dreaming this scenario from my bed, about to wake up relieved. I sit there for a moment before darting my eyes back to the stick and willing the appearance of a negative symbol. I pinch the stick between my thumb and forefinger, squint, squint harder. I scramble for the box's directions, but after reading them again, twice, the paper just wrinkles in my fist. My stomach feels like the roller coaster just dropped. A surge of panic fills me. I think my throat is closing up, but it's not. I pull my underwear and pants up in one tug, run into my room, and shove the stick into A's hand. He's sitting on the edge of my bed with my roommate's oversize coffee mug in his hand, watching ESPN.

"What does it mean?" I insist, glaring hard at the stick, pursing my lips together, stressing the question more. I know what it means.

He irons out the crumpled-up directions on his thigh and runs his finger down a paragraph of text. Looks at the stick. Then the text again. I need another set of eyes to confirm what I *didn't* see. I must've read it wrong—that's all.

"You're pregnant," he says, and he looks up at me.

I stand at the edge of my bed looking at him like I'm waiting for someone to translate what he just said. *I'm what?* I think as I turn from him and press my palms against the windowpane. The sun is filtering through the trees in the square courtyard and even though every day I look out at this cocoon lined with rusty fire escapes, it suddenly seems very unfamiliar.

"Okay," I say and turn to A.

"Okay," he repeats.

"I need to lie down. I feel sick," I say, slumping on my bed.

He lifts the covers for me and I slide under, pulling the comforter up to my chin. I turn over and stare at the wall, which is discolored with splotches of plaster. He sits on top of the covers, against the headboard, and I hear him breathing, digesting the news and tapping his teeth against the mug.

"What do *you* want to do?" he wants to know.

Me? The question makes me shift uneasily under the covers. What do *we* want to do, he means. Obviously.

"Ya know what, the test is probably wrong. I bet it's been sitting on the shelf for eighteen years all dusty and picked around," I say, not turning over. After a couple of weeks of dating, A and I got into a deep phone conversation at midnight and he told me about how someone close to him had an abortion and how at first she wanted to keep the baby, but then since the guy wasn't exactly onboard she made the decision to . . . A didn't ask what I would do in that situation, but I felt inclined to tell him that I respected her choice, but I probably wouldn't have an abortion. I think the conversation changed to where we were meeting for dinner the following evening. We didn't need to talk about such heavy stuff, anyway. I close my eyes and start to panic in silence: *I don't think I can have a baby. Can I? Should I?*

Then I realize it's Saturday morning, and on Monday I am scheduled for my yearly checkup. The coincidence of the appointment is unnerving, but Dr. Collado will give me a "real" test and fix this . . . *misunderstanding.* So the commercial calls it the "Most Accurate Test on the Planet"—so what? I hate the commercial.

"This is fuck-ing crazy," I blurt out, breaking the silence between us.

"I know," A says.

We haven't even said "I love you," because although we've been exclusive the last few months, who really knows where this is going? I don't know if I love him. Wait, does he love me?

We met at a bar on the Lower East Side one night when my friend Claire pushed me into him and winked. Alcohol influenced the breezy flirtation between us. He had kind eyes. They looked a little sleepy and when he smiled the skin under them folded a bit. He bought me a beer. The next day we convened at a small café on the Upper East Side where we shared a bottle of wine and a plate of grilled calamari in a pool of lemon sauce. The waitress thought we were a couple, I guess because we got on so well. We talked about movies and work. I told him I was a writer and he told me he was a runner. It was easy. After that he pretty much started living at my apartment and in the beginning I didn't mind it. I liked the company. It had been a long time since I let someone hold me while I slept. By now, basically, we're spending every waking minute together, but only in the last month or so have I realized how present he is in my life. His spare sneakers are perpetually on my bedroom floor and his neckties are flung over my desk chair. Come to think of it, I don't believe I sat down at my desk once since I met him. I should have told him how I was feeling, but I didn't. When he first put his toothbrush in my cup, I remember wanting to throw it out the window, then I felt like a psycho and just let it go. See, I wasn't exactly ready to play house and I don't think he was, either. He had moved to New York City from the Midwest a few months after breaking up with his long-time girlfriend and decidedly declaring his independence. Having sex with him sans a condom was like getting on a roller coaster at Six Flags and not buckling my seat belt. You don't do it. We're not supposed to be pregnant. We're sup-posed to be eating dinner, screaming conversations at each other at loud, overcrowded bars, communicating via cheesy text messages. I feel so defeated lying here like this. It's not even like the condom broke or I fucked up and forgot to take the pill. I turn over to find A, slumped in the pillows, sleeping, and I study his face, thinking, *Everything has changed now.*

A couple of hours later, I wake up from napping. It's af-ter one p.m. now. I bet the girls are still drowning in mi-mosas at brunch downtown. I turn over into A's neck. He's wide awake, staring at the ceiling.

"Hey there," he says.

"Hi," I say.

"We're going to be okay. This is fine. Babies are a blessing," he says. He sounds like he's been awake, thinking about this while I slept off the nausea and then woke up and fake-slept for the past twenty minutes, my mind racing. He sounds excited, even.

"Right," I say. "This *is* fine." I love babies. I want babies.

"Should we tell our parents?" he says. My stomach drops. *Tell our parents?* This is really happening.

"Let's wait until after I talk with my doctor," I say.

"Sure?" he asks.

"Yep," I say, realizing I could just about burst into tears. I get up and take a shower instead and cry behind the curtain, the *shhh* of the water covering up my sobs. I lean against the tiles, or risk toppling over from the sporadic waves of nausea. If I could stay in this curtained cocoon until Monday, I would. The rest of the day happens in slow motion. The television is on, but we're not watching it. We're sleeping in the afternoon but we're not tired. A goes out to buy dinner and I sit pushed against the headboard wondering if he's going to come back at all. He does. I nibble on a cheese quesadilla and decide I'm not hungry. All I know is that I can't have an abortion and I'm not exactly ready to be someone's mom—am I?

Two Heartbeats

It's Monday now. I feel like it took one year and not one day to get here. A nurse calls my name and takes me into an examination nook. She asks me to raise my sleeve so she can take my blood pressure. She squeezes my arm and it tingles until it hurts.

"I might be pregnant. But I'm not," I nonchalantly announce.

"O-kay. I'll give you a test, then?" she asks.

"I mean, I took a drugstore test over the weekend and it says I am," I say, looking past her at a big pink model of a vagina.

"Those tests are pretty accurate and a lot like the ones we give here," she says.

"Really?" I say and pull my sleeve down and feel my stomach flip-flop. *Crap*, in a low muted whisper, tumbles from my lips.

"What?" the nurse says. I look up and half smile, shaking my head.

She tells me my blood pressure is normal and asks me to step on the scale. *Mother fucker*, I think as the scale reveals my weight. *Why am I two pounds heavier?* Next, she opens a drawer stacked with pregnancy tests and hands one to me.

"Put it in the direct stream of your urine," she says and points to the restroom across the hall. Sounds way too familiar.

As I sit on the toilet yet again, I examine the package before tearing it open. It's the exact same test I took in my apartment. I'm screwed. Alone in this tiny, impossibly clean bathroom that smells a little like medicine and mouthwash, I hear my internal dialogue loud and clear: *You're in there, Baby, aren't you?* I hand a little paper cup with the stick in it to the nurse and linger in the doorway. There's a bulletin board on the wall tacked with baby pictures. One baby is naked, plopped in an oversized flowerpot, and the card says: "Thanks for bringing me into the world!" People need to stop putting their kids in flowerpots. I'll never do that. The nurse is writing something in my chart. She looks like America Ferrera from *Ugly Betty*, except her nose is narrower.

"Am I pregnant?" I ask her, with hair hanging in my face.

A phone is ringing. "Doctor's office, please hold," the woman behind the counter sings. The nurse pulls the tube from the cup and cocks her head. I fixate on her face, thinking how for the rest of my life I'll never forget how Ugly Betty in green scrubs held my fate between her fingers.

"You are," she says and leads me to a room that has an exam table with stirrups cupped in purple socks that advertise some kind of birth control, of course.

I'm pregnant. There is no misunderstanding here. I start to panic. What does this mean? A and I get married? I get fat, I crave things; I become someone's mother in nine months? Nine months? Nine months from now the start-up magazine I've been working on for almost two years will have launched. I'm supposed to be promoted to Senior Associate Editor—and, wait, six months from now I'm supposed to be in Spain with my girlfriends.

"Undress from the waist down. The doctor will be in shortly," she says.

"O-kay," my voice cracks.

I hop onto the table and try to imagine what A must be thinking. He has to be freaked out. Though, right at this moment, he's probably standing in line waiting for his coffee, or eating a soggy premade sandwich from a chain deli. Even though he seemed okay with the news, it feels like we're in different galaxies, or like we're about to break up over e-mail. But we can't just break up. We share something real. I can't just throw his toothbrush out and buy new sheets. Maybe he'll ask me to marry him. *Maybe I want to marry him?* I examine the statement for a minute.

Knock-knock. There are urgent knuckles at the door.

My gynecologist, Dr. Collado, enters with my chart.

"I see," she says and sits across from me on a little backless chair with wheels.

I feel my cheeks spread with red and I look up at her with tears welling in my eyes.

"How's your Nanny? I see her all the time in her black outfits, taking short walks on her block," she says and smiles kindly. "She waves to all the cars, you know. She's like the mayor."

How's my Nanny? Seriously?

"Good," I say and it occurs to me I'm going to have to tell people I'm pregnant, people like my eighty-seven-year-old grandmother, who constantly asks about my "love life" or when I'm going to get married.

Dr. Collado tells me to lie back so she can examine me. From under the sheet, I hear her say, "I feel six or so weeks along." Now she wants to send me to an ultrasound technician to get a read on a heartbeat to be positive. She says she'll send me for bloodwork, too. I hate needles.

"Be positive? You mean there is a chance I'm *not* pregnant?" I urgently ask.

"A heartbeat can sometimes be detected at this stage," she says.

"So, if there isn't a heartbeat?" I persist.

"Let's just take this one step at a time," she says. "Are your breasts tender?" she asks, feeling around under my armpits.

Yeah, they are. This can't be happening, is all I can think as she scribbles the order for a transvaginal ultrasound. After she's done writing she looks up, meets my eyes, and says, "You know you have options, Christine."

She tells me it's still early enough to take RU-486, otherwise known as the abortion pill. The name freaks me out a little. It sounds so official. She does not administer this pill, nor does she perform "procedures," but tells me she can refer me to someone if I decide to "terminate the pregnancy." Terminate. I turn the word over in my mind. *Terminate* is etched in stone. I once vowed to be a vegetarian, but two weeks in I suddenly got a craving for a strip steak and a dirty martini—so I ordered them. Not once did I wince in disgust as I sliced into the rare meat, while blood and marinade collected along its edge in a little pool I then sopped up with bread. I change my mind a lot. I know better than to get a tattoo—that's way too permanent for me.

Dr. Collado has striking cheekbones and her hair is set in soft, loose curls. She tells me I would take the first pill in a doctor's office. This pill would begin to slow then stop the hormones that sustain pregnancy. I never noticed how pretty she was, or the spray of freckles barely dotting her nose. She's got on panty hose and pretty shoes with a kitten heel. I imagine a doctor I don't know, his hands sheathed in blue rubber gloves, switching my pregnancy off like it never existed at all. Dr. Collado continues explaining that I'd go home and take a second pill, sometimes in the form of a "vaginal suppository," and wait—wait for the "cramping and bleeding." As she continues to tell me my options, I envision myself alone in my tiny bedroom while the rest of the world carries on. People hail yellow taxis just outside my apartment; my roommate clanks dishes in the sink.

One minute something is there and the next it is gone. Gone with no second chances to get it back. Gone without warning of how I might feel afterward. Except I know how I would feel, I think—in half. For the rest of my life, looking over my shoulder like there might be someone's hand to hold, or like I forgot to do something, until I remember I didn't forget a thing—everything is in order except it isn't. Like throwing the dice in the air unable to predict what will turn up in mere seconds. I don't like that breathless feeling.

I know it well. It's like having a bad dream, except you're awake.

I feel a dizzying mix of panic and fear and then something different: Excitement? Happiness? Yes, I think so. I tug at my lip, thinking, *This is my baby.* I wish I had my little reporter recorder with me so I could tape this moment, because I know I will need its reassurance in the months to come.

"Got it?" Dr. Collado asks.

It's too early. If this was a normal day, I'd be thanking the Starbucks lady on Fiftieth and Second right about now, cursing myself for not wearing my commuter sneakers instead of stilettos, grabbing a copy of the *Daily News* and standing on the platform waiting for the late A train to whisk me to the George Washington Bridge, where I hop a two-second bus to my New Jersey office.

"Got it," I say.

Before leaving me to dress, Dr. Collado touches my shoulder gently. She's known me since I was fifteen. She gave me iron shots every week before I had an epic spinal surgery to correct an aggressive case of scoliosis (not fun). She told me to relax when I was seventeen and having my first pap smear, and she assured me I was just having "classic quarter-life" panic attacks when I thought I was going crazy a couple of years ago. She hands me the ultrasound order along with a sample pack of prenatal vitamins (and a prescription for more), and I lay back on the table, a tear streaming down my cheek. Before she leaves, she says, "Things happen for a reason," and I believe her.

As I make my way to the strip mall where the imaging of-

fice is, I think how easy it would be if there *isn't* a heartbeat—
if there is nothing there at all. I could resume my day as usual
and just dip into the office late because I was "covering an
event." Oh, yeah—*an event, alright, Christine!* I chuckle to
myself. I know this sounds rather contradictory, since moments ago I was resigned to the fact that I do want my baby—
but what if there's not a choice to make? What if the two tests
and physical exam are wrong? It's not like a miscarriage *or* an
abortion—it's just a kink in the system, a big misunderstanding that would all of a sudden be a nonissue. As I pull into the
lot, I thought I'd find a relieving comfort in my reasoning, but
then it hits me, I might well be disappointed if *Baby* isn't
there. As I drag myself into the office with my thoughts see-
sawing wildly back and forth, I realize how emotional I am—
I'm definitely pregnant and my hormones are right on time.

I sit, slouched, in a chair in the corner and keep my sunglasses on. There's an old man with gray nose hair nodding
off in the corner. His leg is propped up on the chair opposite
him and his foot is bandaged in a blue air cast. A woman in
green scrubs calls my name and I cower some in the chair,
because even though I could very well be getting my big toe
scanned, I feel like there is a word bubble floating over my
head that reads: "KNOCKED UP." She leads me to a small
room where she tells me to undress from the waist down, and
that a technician will be with me shortly. I step out of my
jeans and my underwear, yet again, and leave them carelessly
crumpled like an accordion on the floor. There's a poster on
the wall of an interior cross section of a pregnant woman's
womb and I close in on it. At about six weeks, the embryo

looks like a limbless blob blooming with buds. I palm my stomach, wondering if that is in fact inside of me.

I sit on the table with a disposable blanket draped over my bottom half and wait. My legs dangle, limp and heavy. I need a pedicure. I run my fingers through my hair and stare straight ahead at the door, thinking how stupid I was to have sex without a condom, and with a guy I'd only been dating for a few months. Who does that? *Idiot, Christine—you're an idiot,* I hear myself say. Then I think how stupid he was to just come inside of me, and I feel better blaming him. But who am I kidding? I could have kicked him off of me.

A woman with short, dark hair enters the room. She has on a scrub jacket dotted with little bears and toy blocks—*perfect.* She says hello, introduces herself as Pam in a Polish, no, German accent, and starts going over the test. I'm looking at her and her perfect bob. Her lips are moving, but I'm thinking about all the wine I consumed with my friends Lo, Ashley, and Stef just one week ago, during our girls' trip to the Napa Valley. That can't be good. We spent New Year's Eve in San Francisco at Lo's parents' house and her dad got me loaded on a concoction called Holiday Bombs that he served up in chilled martini glasses every evening. If I am pregnant, I wonder if my embryo is okay and make a mental note to Google "alcohol & fetus" when I get home. That gets me thinking about the last time I ate sushi. *Crap, SF,* I think. And why is there a sign outside of the steam room at the gym that says pregnant women should not enter? I did enter. *Three mornings ago!* I panic. My God, how much damage have I already done? I'm starting to realize why I was so tired in SF—it wasn't jet lag.

I hadn't felt like going out our very first night in SF and Lo couldn't understand why I was lying on the couch with an afghan pulled up to my nose, contemplating another serving of her mom's awesome chicken-and-artichoke casserole. It was the first time my girlfriends had to pitch "going out" to me. Lo especially knows how uncharacteristic it is for me not to be donning some glitzy top and heels, clutch in hand. I met Lo, a carefree redhead with great taste in bags and shoes, when we were both working at *First* magazine in 2005. I admittedly noticed her classic Louis Vuitton bucket purse and black Gucci heels with gold stems. She was new to the beauty department, and even though I worked in the "Real Life" department, I often pitched in and covered events for the fashion editor, Brian. Lo and I started showing up at the same open-bar parties and leaving with the same stuffed goody bags, like the Everlast event at chi-chi Marquee, where we bonded over vodka shots. We became fast friends—e-mailing during work to decide where Happy Hour would convene and sending each other links to scandalous industry stories on Jossip.com. As I sit here and think back to our vacation in SF, I recall a friend from work telling me how "wiped out" she was in the first trimester, or, as she called it, "T-1." Suddenly I feel like a private eye, putting pieces to a very easy puzzle together.

Pam says, "Got it?" but I have no clue what she just said, and suddenly she's holding a long dildo-ish thing sheathed in what looks like a condom and firing up the ultrasound machine. "Yes, thank you," I lie. She tells me to lie back. I don't want to, but I collapse and a mess of brown hair sprays around me. My fingers fold into one another and I rest my hands on my chest.

She sits at the computer and begins typing information from a chart. I have a chart. It says that I'm "six or so weeks along." I stare glassy eyed at the tiny specks of black that pepper the ceiling tiles. I'm thirsty—my tongue feels like a sweater—and my teeth are chattering but I'm not cold. How the hell did I get myself into this situation? One minute the girls and I are planning a summer vacation to Spain over eggs and mimosas, the next—I'm half naked on this exam table. My legs are locked at the knee and my mind goes back to that night last month when A and I both had too much champagne at a holiday party and felt, well, impregnable. I think how easy it would have been to hit PAUSE before our clothes fell to the floor, run to the twenty-four-hour bodega across the street from my apartment building, and buy a pack of condoms. And then I'm back to blaming A. He has the penis. He should have the condoms. In fact, penises should just come with condoms. Do I buy tampons when I have my period? Yes. Well, he should have bought condoms. Don't all guys keep a condom in their wallet or is that just in the movies? He knew I wasn't on the pill (that was a conversation we had early on after too many beers and the how-many-people-have-you-slept-with talk) and he could have stopped himself! Or I could have stopped him. We're two college-educated adults and we should have known better. I learned about the birds and the bees in junior high health class for Christ's sake, or come to think of it, on HBO when I was nine.

"Open your legs, dear," Pam says. I inch them open and

my arms fall to my sides; my hands clench the sides of the table; paper rustles and my knuckles look whiter.

"Wider," she persists.

I let my legs frog open, exposing myself. Pam's scary dildo slides in and begins to probe. The room is dark, except for the glow of the computer screen. I think about a little boy I saw the day before. A and I were having breakfast at the diner. I tried to eat a grilled cheese sandwich, but anxiety had quashed my appetite, so I just sipped a Diet Coke with lemon. My father was picking me up after breakfast and giving me a ride to my childhood home in Jersey. For all he knew, I was just coming home for Sunday dinner (which I did every now and then) and to raid the cabinets for nonperishables to stuff in my duffel bag to hold me over until payday—not announcing he was about to be a grandfather. How was I going to tell him? My mom? Uh, my brothers? The girls? What would they think? At the diner's counter, A sat next to me and shoveled thick pieces of French toast soaked in syrup into his mouth, topped off his coffee cup, too. There was this boy, maybe two or three years old, sitting on his father's lap on my other side. His tiny hand was wrapped around a chubby sausage link and he took bites too big for his mouth that ballooned his cheeks. I felt alone in that diner, or like everyone was frozen with forks of pancakes midair. Seeing that little boy made me think of my own child and how I'd sit across from him someday and cut his food into tiny little pieces and make airplane noises. The thought was very complete and visceral and I suddenly found myself smiling at the tiny stranger.

The truth is, I've always loved kids. I worked in a day care after school when I was in high school. I was unfazed by smelly diapers and pants wet with oval stains of urine, attached to shy little faces with red cheeks. I even got private babysitting jobs on the weekends from parents of the kids in my classroom. One little boy was notorious for flinging his bowl of dry Cheerios off the table. It never, ever bothered me and I actually remember laughing on my hands and knees as I swept up the mess with my hands and listened to him giggle "Ut-oh!" with his hands cupped over his mouth. His mom had an important job and was often late to pick him up. She was partially deaf and constantly yelled at him in a voice that sounded like she had food in her mouth. He was a frustrated little boy and often cried when his mother came to collect him, even when it was past his dinnertime. Sometimes I wanted to take him home with me and camp out in the family room under a pillow fort. A coworker routinely told me I could send him to her classroom because she knew how "difficult" he could be, but I didn't think so, he was just two. He usually just sat in my lap and turned the pages as I read to him. It's not like I don't have experience with kids. I could diaper one in the dark. That's reassuring.

"Scoot down," Pam says from under the paper blanket covering my bottom half.

I let my butt slide down the foam hump I am propped on.

"More." She rolls the chair to the side and looks at me.

Uh, okay, Cranky. I decide I hate this woman. I close my eyes and feel the thick probe enter me again, and I resist it.

"Relax," she says.

I take a deep breath and rub my eyes. I keep hearing Dr.

Collado's voice. "If there isn't a heartbeat, the pregnancy is not viable."

"Is there a heartbeat?" My voice cracks.

"I need to get a read of your uterus first," Pam says, squinting at the screen.

I stare at the ceiling tiles, then the clock on the wall. It is now one thirty on a Monday. I should be at my desk with a half-eaten salad to the right of me, editing something. I turn back to the monitor.

"Now? Is there a heartbeat? What do you see?"

"Am I inside of you? I can't seem to find your uterus," she says.

Uh, is this a skit for *Saturday Night Live*? You can't "find my uterus"? I assure her I have one. She doesn't even look at me.

The tool inches side to side in me until she stops and clicks on the mouse several times.

"What are you doing? Is there a heartbeat?" I raise my head, straining my neck to see the frozen picture on the screen. My face wrinkles up because it makes no sense to me. All I see is a chaotic mess of black and white and gray; an underwater universe of sorts. She rolls her chair over to the screen and points at a small black circle.

"This is the sac. You see it?" she says as she circles her finger around it.

"Yes, but is there a heartbeat?"

She squints at the screen and coaxes me with her hand to come closer.

"See this dim flickering?" She points to something pulsing. I push myself up to sitting.

I see it, but barely. It looks like a little asterisk on fire.

"This popping, faded white light?" she continues.

"Mmm, hmm," I hum and know I am staring at my child.

"Well, this is your baby's heartbeat," she says with delight, pulling her gloves off and folding one into the other.

I'm suddenly not so brave and fearless anymore, like I was in Dr. Collado's office. There is a heart beating under mine. I'm pregnant. I reach for a breath and feel my face fall into my hands. I'm crying now, immediate tears staining my palms, hot breath pulling in and out, its wild heaving warming my nose and mouth. I open my eyes and see my feet hanging a few inches off the floor. Pam touches my shoulder, crouches down, then looks up at me nodding in assurance.

"Baby is a good thing," she says handing me a box of tissues.

"I know," I say pulling a tissue from the box, spreading it over my face. "I know," I nod urgently and sniffle, sniffle again.

Breaking the News

I leave the imaging center with a red face and bloodshot eyes. My lips are cracked and bone-dry now. I pass a few people on my way to the car and a guy in baggy jeans with a hook for a hammer almost knocks me over. There is a cell phone attached to his head and he has two cases of beer pressed up against him, under his chin. *Watch out, I'm pregnant,* I think, as I shuffle past him. *I'm pregnant?*

My fingers search for the keys in my purse and for a moment I'm back to *that night,* remembering searching, half dressed, for a condom in my nightstand. No condom. I slide into the car and slouch like a rag doll. The collar of my sweater is suddenly very itchy and very tight. The inside of my car is cold; the steering wheel feels frozen as I trace my finger along its rim. I squint at the bright white sky. It seems it could open up into a brilliant snowstorm at any second and I wish it would. Snowed in, suspended in this moment, I could be just Christine, while the snow covers my car and dresses the trees in soft, crystal lace. I stare up at the sky and will it to swallow me up, but it doesn't.

I start the car and a gush of cold air spits out from the vent. I smack it down and turn the dial all the way to the red side. I'm cold and debating whether or not to call A. *Why hasn't he called me?* I think as I punch his number in.

"Hello," he says.

"I'm *really* pregnant," I say.

"What are *you* going to do?" he asks.

"Keep my baby," I say unflinchingly.

"Good. That's what I hoped you would say," he says.

There's a defining pause of silence—I listen to the whir of the running motor. A says he has to get back to work, so I hang up and sit in the car, warming my hands at the vents, taking a long, deep breath. I always imagined my husband and I jumping up and down for joy like in the movies when we discovered I was "expecting." We'd call our parents next and our chins would bump because we'd both be talking into the same phone. My husband and I would have a house with a mortgage we couldn't really afford, a dog we'd give a little onesie to so she could sniff it, adjusting to the baby we would bring home. Then we'd stab a big stork cutout on the front lawn and gender-appropriate balloons would line the porch. I wanted my career to be far more established by the time I had kids so I could write from my home office, breaking to host Girl Scout meetings and bake things for school fund-raisers. My husband and I would sit on the back deck and drink wine while our kids ran around barefoot trying to catch fireflies. But it's not playing out like that now—it's not supposed to be happening *now*. This is all supposed to happen after I conquer my magazine career, tour around Europe some more, have many more nights to party without reservation until four a.m. . . . . I sit in my car with the motor running, feeling sorry for myself, then incurably selfish, until tears break from my eyes. I take a breath, hoping it will dissolve the uncertainty I am feeling about A. He's fun and deliriously handsome (I believe my friend James asked me if he was a model when they first met), but I just want more time to not be pregnant and date him. I need to know him better. I wasn't done feeling him out and now we're life partners even if we don't end up together. *This is exactly why you practice safe sex, Christine. Exactly why you get married*—then *procreate*, I think, running my finger along the chain of my necklace. My feelings are erratic and scaring me; part of me just wants to curl up in his arms and the other part is stepping cautiously away. I call the office. There's no way I can go to work this afternoon. I use the "food poisoning" excuse again. My boss, Maria, asks about the lip-gloss samples I was supposed to call in from the PR executive at Tarte. I tell her everything is in, locked in my desk drawer, and that I'll e-mail her the credit info this afternoon.

As I pull out of the parking lot, I suddenly don't know what to do or where to go, so I drive around aimlessly, wondering how to break the news to my parents. I wonder what my brothers will think, too. They're both extremely protective of me, like papa bears. When I moved to Manhattan two years ago, they thought I was being ridiculous, and I'm sure more than a little indulgent. After all, I had approximately zero dollars saved, almost two thousand in credit-card debt, and was pretty much going to be living paycheck to paycheck. But moving to New York City had always been a dream of mine and sooner or later I knew I'd make it come true. After living in Center City Philly for four years during college, in an apartment sandwiched between a smoke shop called Wonderland and a dildo store called The Pleasure Chest (my father loved that!), I made a pit stop back to my hometown in New Jersey instead of moving onward to Manhattan. It was a hard transition being back under my parents' roof after living on my own, but an *easy* decision to make. My then boyfriend, Keith, lived in Jersey, so that was motivation enough. After he had trekked back and forth to Philly for over a year, I was excited for us to be in the same zip code. Oh the things we do for love. Only, at the time, I had no idea what that would *really* mean.

I come to a red light and look down at my stomach. I don't look pregnant. "Hello," I hear myself say to my belly. "What's going on in there?" The light turns green and the car behind me honks. I have to tell my parents.

I pull into a quiet shopping strip, park, and dial my father's cell phone, then quickly hang up before it rings. I feel so out of sorts, like I'm almost awake but still paralyzed in a dream, fighting to open my eyes so I can take a breath and wipe the sweat from my brow, get some orange juice and crawl back under the covers. I turn off the heat, take a deep breath, and dial my father again.

"Hello," he answers.

"It's Chrissy. I'm pregnant, Dad."

My father's a pretty relaxed guy, and he's used to me

dropping the bomb every once in a while. He's also used to talking me down from the ledge. A month or so into college I called him and told him I was dropping out and to come get me, but really I was just wigging out because my roommate was a Jesus freak (whose father coincidentally ran an online porn store) and everyone had paint on their pants and sang in the dorm hallways like in *Fame*. After living in the Wayne, New Jersey, bubble for eighteen years, I just wasn't used to such an eclectic, urban environment. So he drove down to Philly that night and took me out for a steak dinner at Ruth's Chris, and I went to class the next day. Then there was the time when I was a senior in high school and I begged him to let me have "a couple" of friends over for New Year's Eve and one hundred showed up, or the time I got thrown in the drunk tank (not my finest hour) in Belmar Beach for being "publicly drunk." Still, I don't think anything could have prepared him for this news.

I'm not sure what I expected. Maybe silence, or the opposite—a torrent of questions too fast to answer—but his response is something different. He immediately tells me he'll "love the baby more than anyone else in this world." That is his first reaction. Um, okay, Dad. But did you hear me? I think. I'm knocked—I'm *pregnant*. He heard me, because then I hear him sniffle and I realize he's crying. He wants to know if we're getting married, because he can "pull a wedding together 1-2-3—I'll call Tommy at The Brownstone," he says, urgently. Right, Dad. And I'll call Vera (Wang) at the showroom. Better yet, let's call Lo on three-way—she *is* an editor at *Brides*, after all.

"Jesus, Dad, why don't you just send me away to a convent for nine months, or Italy!" There must be a Coppa making pasta in a small village somewhere, with a spare room.

As I lower the phone from my ear to click it off, I hear him apologize. I tell him it's okay and that I am going to call my mother at home. I sit alone in my car and take a quick swig of the Diet Coke I bought this morning. It's warm and fizzy and when I feel it tickle my tongue I pinch my lips together and frantically reach for the door handle. My hand rattles and bangs at the handle until I realize I need to unlock the door. I look like a mad woman trapped in a box. Tears stream down my face as I hang my head out of the car. My body folds up and the soda spews from my mouth as I remember what Dr. Collado said about watching my caffeine intake. I already had a coffee this morning. One swig wouldn't have hurt, right? I need to buy a book. There has to be one listing all of the rules. The pavement is powdered in crushed salt—still no sign of snow, though. I call my mother.

It's almost two in the afternoon now. She could be doing any number of things: folding laundry, packing Christmas ornaments away, chasing her brand new poodle, Max, as he whips around the coffee table at warp speed with something life-threatening like a walnut in his mouth (just move the damn nut bowl!). Speaking of surprise additions to our family, Max was one. My older brother, Carlo, and I decided to give Mom an impromptu gift a couple of weeks ago. Our golden retriever, Brandy, had died last February and this was going to be our first Christmas without her. I couldn't imagine the holidays without her chewing on ribbon, nosing through wrapping paper, and incidentally gagging on a bow I would have to pull from her throat with my fingers while Carlo forced her mouth open and Brian, my younger brother, held her resistant body. Of course there would be a middinner quarrel at the table because Nanny would throw a meatball—a whole meatball—on the carpet for Brandy to nosh on, then stone-cold deny she had done it. "Not me," she'd say, shaking her head, "pass the grated cheese." I'm such a softy—I still tear up when I think of Brandy's little face on my lap, or how her paws always smelled like dirt and grass and a little like corn chips. When Carlo suggested we surprise my mom with a new pup my response was "yes," and instant—characteristically, I didn't think twice about the gift. It didn't occur to me the puppy would require training and neutering and attention—attention from my mom and not three little Coppa kids. We were all grown up . . . and now I was "knocked up." Or that adorable little Max is a neurotic dog who refuses to go to the bathroom outside and prefers to poop in shoes and chew on Christmas tree branches, threatening to topple the tree to the floor. "No, Max!" and "Christine, what the hell possessed you to buy this thing?" quickly became the holiday refrain.

Actually Max wasn't even the first new puppy I sprung on my unsuspecting mother. When I was in college I charged a puppy on my Discover card (why anyone in their right mind gave me a credit card with a two-thousand-dollar line, I have no idea) and gave it to her. My grandparents (her parents) had just died, two months to the day from each other. My mom could have starred in a Paxil commercial at the time, given that she hardly left her bed and literally wept in her hands. I thought a new little friend would cheer her up. Brandy was still alive and the dynamic between her and the new pup was not cute. The two dogs did not share a string of spaghetti and curl up by the fireplace. My dad made me re-turn her—as in, "Hi, I'd like to return this. Here's the re-ceipt—and the dog." The breeder was sympathetic to the situation—and I also turned on the water works and success-fully got my card credited. Well, those furry surprises seem insignificant to the news I'm about to drop in her lap now.

My mom often jokes about how she's itching for a grand-child, though I imagine she'd first like me to drag her around, trying on fifty wedding gowns, like I did when I searched for my prom dress and ended up with what I call these days an unfortunate hoop dress in a celery hue.

The leather seats in my car are cold and I feel their chill through my jeans.

"Mom?" My voice cracks.

"Christine? What's the matter?" she asks. She knew I saw Dr. Collado this morning and she's probably thinking some-thing scary like uterine cancer or an STD. *Hey, at least I don't have chlamydia—or genital warts.*

I pull at the finger of my glove and bite it off. Here goes.

"I'm—pregnant, Mom." My eyes burn with tears yet again.

"What?" Pause. "What are you going to do?"

What am I going to? My lips quiver.

"Hav-ing my baby," I say in between sobs as I pet my stomach to reassure *Baby* these are happy tears (mainly) not scared shitless ones.

"Okay, okay, well of course you are," she says, not a hint of sarcasm. I can feel her digesting this news. Maybe she's even smiling on the other end of the phone, making a mental note to buy yellow yarn for a baby blanket she'll attempt to knit herself but never finish, like the infamous "blanket I'm making you for college." She crafted four squares of green and never knitted them together. Rather, she bought me a blanket from JC Penney and wrapped my dorm bed in it. It can't be this easy. Why are my parents okay with this? I'm not married. They haven't even met this guy. The fact that everyone is so calm is really starting to freak me out. The *Twilight Zone* music should start playing right about now.

"And what about A? Is he with you now?" she asks. I completely ignore her question.

"Mommy, what am I going to do?" I sob into the phone and wonder where that "mommy" came from. *Mommy?* I've never once called her that. In fact, I mostly call her Ma or even "Jack," short for her name, "Jackie." She says she can't tell me what to do. But I need her to tell me what to do. Someone needs to tell me what to do, or at least reassure me that I'm not crazy, that everything will be okay. I hang up with my mom, telling her I'll call her when I get back to Manhattan. I dial my father back and ask him what I should do. He tells me to "look inside my heart." Thanks for the poetic solution, Dad. My parents aren't on the best terms and will probably be legally divorced by the time I give birth, since they've been pretend-separated for the past . . . too many years.

I smooth my hands over the crown of my head, then pull

the visor down, finding my reflection in the mirror. I've always wanted to be a young mother—have a kid by thirty, maybe two. *You're twenty-six, Christine, not twelve. Thirty will be just three years away by the time the baby arrives.* But I always hoped I'd be more prepared, financially, emotionally, pretty much in every single way imaginable. . . . I should tell my brothers.

Carlo is twenty-seven and lives in Connecticut. He has an important job. It came with a badge. When we were in high school together he sabotaged my first weekend away from home by setting up surveillance at the hotel in Wildwood, New Jersey, where my friends and I were staying. He booked the room right below mine, and he and his buddies set up camp for two and a half days. I remember him barging into my room and finding a box of condoms on the dresser—and promptly calling my father. They weren't even mine. I went down to the shore a virgin and came home one, too: It was a time in my life when I felt like the last virgin on the planet. Funny how back when I was a teenager there was a stockpile of the little rubber disks when I didn't need them, but not one when I was a grown adult in a relationship. The phone rings.

"Car?" I say.

"What's up?" he says, cheerfully.

"You're not going to believe this."

"Did you get into an accident? Again!" he demands, imagining I crashed my car and need help.

"No," I say.

"New job?" he asks.

"Car, I'm—pregnant," I say.

"Okay, Christine!" He laughs.

"Car, seriously," I say.

"Are you a fucking idiot?" He seriously wants to know.

"No, I mean . . . yes." I start to cry.

"You're so stupid. Big city girl!" he says. He's mad.

"I have to go."

"What the hell were you thi—?" he says.

I click the phone off and catch my face in my hands. I should be mad he's being such a jerk, but he's right. Here I was, finally on my own in New York City and look what happens. If Carlo was here right now, he'd be waving his finger at me, declaring: "Told ya so!" But Brian won't react like that. I'm his big sister. Everything I do is genius. He's twenty-three and is a chef at a fancy place that hosts weddings. When he was in high school I took him to parties at this place called The Bottle Factory (it was really an abandoned parking lot). We drank cheap vodka (or sometimes the good stuff we hijacked from our parents' stash) and ice tea out of Snapple bottles—it was *so* cool. We have a more laid-back relationship than Carlo and I do. Brian is a deep guy. We can talk about life and love and times, whereas Carlo is just matter-of-fact. Bri's always eager to call me with revelations at four a.m. and tell me about his next big idea, like the café he wants to open. When I tell him my latest news, he doesn't want to know what the hell I was thinking. He wants to know about A—whom he met once.

"I don't know," tumbles from my lips. "He's happy?" I say it with a question mark. *But I'm not in love with him*, I want to blurt out, but don't.

"So, I'm going to be an uncle?" He sounds excited. "I hope it's a boy. Girls are annoying, ya know? If it's a boy I'll totally take him camping and play ball with him," he says.

"O-kay." I try to process this.

I stare down at my stomach. Part of me is waiting for Ashton Kutcher to pounce on my car. I'm being Punk'd, right? Dad's planning an off-white wedding and little brother is off to buy a Nerf ball.

As I turn the key to start the car, a gush of flurries sprays across my windshield. Suddenly there is a wild frenzy of snowflakes all around me. It's no blizzard, but it will do just fine. I step out of the car and lean up against the door. Pinches of snow collect on my eyelashes. I stand here for a while and allow myself to be suspended in the moment, because for now it's finally snowing. The wind picks up and suddenly it looks like I'm standing in the middle of a snow globe, far away from everything and everyone. I squint out into the white, listening to my shallow breath, seeing it float from my mouth in a barely-there cloud . . . *Still breathing*, I think, closing my eyes.

3

Paralyzed

I decide I can't deal with public transportation so I'm cruising down Route 80 East, in pursuit of the George Washington Bridge and then my apartment, in my sporty two-door Accord that's been sitting in my parents' driveway since I moved to the city. *I'll shoot back tomorrow and take the bus to work the following day*, I think as I come to a peak right around the exit for the city of Hackensack. I wince at the exit ramp because my gynecologist mentioned she practices exclusively at Hackensack University Medical Center, which is notorious for its private maternity suites that feature state-of-the-art plasma-screen televisions, twenty-four-hour room service (with really good cheesecake), and amenities like in-room pedicures. They deliver babies there, too, and apparently will deliver mine—in September, according to some little paper dial Dr. Collado twisted around. When the nurse at Dr. Collado's office handed me a pamphlet, "Postpartum Depression: Know the Signs" (gee, thanks for having so much faith in me; do I get a prescription for Prozac too?), she also mentioned that I'd have my twelve-week sonogram at HUMC and then started raving about the place as if it were the Union Square W Hotel.

All of a sudden the New York City skyline is hanging in the sky. I approach a lull of stop-go traffic with the city stretched out in front of me, and the hospital where my baby will be born literally three minutes off the highway. I squint up at the late afternoon sky that's threatening to fade into night. The snow lasted just a moment. The tiny flecks barely touched the pavement. *So much for a blizzard*, I think as I creep toward Manhattan. I feel my eyes fill with heat again. I can't cry anymore. I shut the radio off and hang on to the steering wheel. The woman in the car next to me is shaking popcorn from a snack bag into her mouth. I bet her life is impossibly perfect at the moment.

I keep playing A's and my relationship in my head like a movie. Here we are eating Mexican food for free (since I was reviewing the restaurant) and talking about our favorite movies. Running side by side in Central Park, bickering at the foot of the stairs in my apartment building, eating eggs on the couch while watching *The Goonies*. My friend Nic repeatedly reminded me I was in a relationship and the first couple of times she said it, I shrugged her off and diverted the conversation to her fabulous Gucci shoes. But the more mornings I woke up next to him, tapped my foot on my bedroom floor waiting for him to get out of *my* shower, and the more times I met him after work for dinner, forfeiting the gym or drinks with the girls (yet again), I realized that I certainly was. A pristine image of a box of condoms floats full frontal in my brain. I can't get this song off repeat: Who the hell has sex sans any protection? I really want someone to say: "Everyone does, silly!" I think about calling Nic, my wing woman. We met when we were twenty-one and eager Gucci interns. We spent our lunch breaks talking about our boyfriends and how we loved them so much and were going to marry them and how our daughters were going to be BFFs like us. Fast forward two years and we were both single, living in New York City. It was perfect. *Was.* As I'm scrolling through my phone for her number, it rings, displaying "Jr." I call Carlo that sometimes, and he hates it, but he *is* a Jr.

"Hi," I answer with hesitation in my tone, pulling the phone from my ear, because he's probably going to start screaming again.

"Okay. Processed everything. Plan?" he says. *Ah, there's the Carlo I know. Thank God*, I think, letting out a sigh of relief.

"Plan? Car, I'm like four minutes pregnant," I say.

"You sound too calm," he says.

"Everything is going to be fine," I say, half-believing myself.

"Okay," he says. "But this guy, A, what's going on with you two?"

"I don't know," I say.

"You don't know? Do you love him? Does he love you?" he asks. *Carlo, Carlo, Carlo*, I think.

"I don't know," I say.

"Okay. Well, either way he's going to be a father," Carlo says. "He will do right by the baby . . . Christine. Aren't you at all freaked out by how . . . how drastic this is?"

I really have no idea what to say to him and this becomes clear when I open my mouth, but stop midthought. I don't even have anything sarcastic to say, which is pretty crazy—

I'm the queen of one-liners. I tell him I have to hang up and blame it on the fact that I'm driving on the highway, when actually I'm in dead-stopped traffic.

Right now I'm just trying to put my pregnancy into perspective and it's not that bad. This is not cancer. No one is dying. This is a baby. *A baby!* I think and smile. The fact is I am no stranger to sudden upheavals in my life. Things *do* happen, no matter how much you think: *That'll never happen to me.* Maybe that's why I'm taking this in stride and not in the fetal position on Dr. Collado's floor. And "it" always happens when you least expect it. The ironic thing is I moved to New York City in the aftermath of the last major curveball of my life. I was so set on getting my life back on track and not even two years later here I am, back here, in this place where everything changes in a split-split second.

I shudder from the chill coming through the car window and the recollection of *that* afternoon. August 23, 2003, when my then-boyfriend, Keith, was injured in a motocross accident. I should mention that as a result I absolutely loathe the month of August. I wish it would fall off the calendar. It's thirty-one days when I feel bad things are destined to happen. And the city air is so thick and sticky. I just hate August. Thank God my baby is coming in September. Having an August baby would make me too superstitious and I'd spend the majority of my pregnancy with a fortune-teller, wondering, "Baby is okay in there, right?"

I was living at home that summer after graduating from the University of the Arts, nursing impossible dreams of working at *Vogue* (or any magazine, really). For as long as I could remember I had envisioned myself trapped in their fashion closet, up to my neck in high-end samples. I watched fashion shows on television and convinced myself one day I would be in the real trenches, like all the editors in the folding chairs with their little spiral notebooks. I was ready and willing to work the grueling hours, fetch coffee, and network—that was the best part. I'm such a people person—I make friends with everyone. So I perfected my résumé and took informational interviews after graduation. I pitched editors stories, got rejected, and pitched them again. I was determined to make a career for myself, but life and love had other plans for me.

The night of Keith's accident, I was lying on my bed with a mess of wet hair tucked under a towel. I was in jeans and a bra, flipping through the channels, and eyeing the alarm clock as the big minute number flicked again and again, thinking, *He's late.* Brandy was chewing on a rawhide bone and, in between bites, licking her paw. I loved that dog. Talk about true love—when my door was shut, she would sit pressed up against it and wait. There were six doors on the top floor and she chose mine every single time. I was waiting for Keith because we were going to pick up his new truck at the dealership, then go out for a generic dinner at Applebee's or Outback.

Earlier that day I had been with my mother at my cousin's wedding shower. As I drank mimosas and picked through the buffet line I couldn't help but wonder if Keith and I were headed down the aisle next. If maybe I'd be sitting in the big chair while my friends plopped an unfortunate paper plate of bows on my head. I daydreamed about us getting married, having kids, living happily ever after. My cousin seemed so happy and content up there, peeling through boxes of pretty wrapped gifts and holding linens up for everyone to see while her mom took pictures from all angles. My cousin and I are the same age and sometimes I wondered how she got there before me—if I'd ever get there at all. I spent most of the party sitting cross-legged with a finger in the air, signaling the waiter for another. I checked my phone obsessively that day assuming the wave of laughter and on-cue meowing when my cousin held up the sacred lingerie for the, er, "big night" (yeah right) would drown out the ringing. But there was no missed call. I ate my cake and the frosting flowers of my mom's piece and really didn't give it much thought. Keith was riding. I'd see him for dinner that night.

But it was a weird time in our relationship. After a couple of years of being inseparable we were considering a breakup and, in fact, had just the night before made up after a week-long trial separation that somehow dissolved over a few beers at the Greenhouse bar in our hometown of Wayne. I had gone to the bar with an attitude and my girlfriends, but when he showed up an hour later with his friend, it took one smile from him and I was hopelessly back in love. We decided to give it another try (because that's what we did: We fought. We made up. We were just a couple of twenty-two-year-old kids) and I stayed at his place that night. In the morning when he dropped me off I leaned in to him and felt his scruff on my cheek when he kissed me. He smelled like soap. We exchanged "I love you"s. I did love him.

And then twelve hours later the phone rang. I should

note I'm a bit weary of ringing phones, too. Even at work when my phone rings every day around noon, I wonder, Is it my tuna sandwich from Evergreen Café or is someone dead? I reached for the phone thinking it would be Keith telling me he was running late, that he'd be over in twenty minutes, which would really mean an hour.

Sure enough, I saw his pet name, "Moobear," display and I instinctively picked up in a huff: "Where are you? I hate when you go riding and don't call me!" But it was Keith's brother, Bobby, telling me that Keith was in the hospital, with dirt from the track still on his face, in a blue neck brace. His brother told me the doctors thought he "broke his neck" and that he might "never walk again" in one sentence. Before I hung up with him, he told me that Keith said to tell me he loved me. When I got off the phone I literally ran around in circles until I realized I needed a shirt and shoes and to find my car keys. It was like I was in a foreign bedroom, not the one I grew up in, because everything was happening in slow motion and although everything was in fact in place: shirts in the drawer, keys on the dresser—nothing seemed to be in its spot. I drove to the hospital alone and in silence, except for the whoosh of air rushing through the sunroof. The whole time I kept thinking that this had to be some sort of mistake (kind of how I would feel years later when I read the positive sign on the home test). His collarbone was broken—not his neck. The line isn't really blue, it's just sort-of blue. Denial was all I had that night, alone in my car. It was the only thing that kept me from veering off the road.

Keith was in surgery when I arrived to find his mom and aunt smoking cigarettes and pacing on the veranda. His brother was sleeping on the couch. I slumped next to him and waited. My parents arrived and sat across from me and Carlo burst in with an urgent look on his face. Brian called and naively told me: "Everything will be okay, Chrissy." I think he was drunk, down-the-shore, at one of those obnoxious clubs where everyone is on Ecstasy and bloated from steroids.

At around two a.m. Keith's doctor robotically explained that Keith's neck was in fact broken in two places and fractured in another. My family and his stood there looking like we'd just seen a ghost or like the doctor was speaking to us in a foreign language. I kept thinking *Huh, wait, what?* I asked if he'd recover and his doctor, in one breath, said: "No. Not likely." It wasn't until I saw him after surgery, lifeless and in traction (with bolts shoved into his skull attached to a hanging weight), that I believed what had happened. My boyfriend, my active, gorgeous boyfriend, was a quadriplegic. He opened his eyes just long enough to know I was there. There was a tube in his throat so he couldn't talk, but I watched as his eyes raced from side to side and up and down. I slipped my hand in his and realized it was limp. I stayed with him for the few minutes I was allowed. Afterward I fell into the hospital chapel. I sat pressed against the wall while Carlo hung in the doorway offering me water or coffee and asking me to "please eat something." Why is it in times of uncertainty people force-feed? I feel a lot of this coming on—especially from my Nanny. There were times that night when I felt like I was looking in on myself from a window. *This really can't be happening* is all I thought as I waited by the ICU door and watched strangers in blue scrubs shuffle in and out, in and out of his curtained nook.

Since I didn't have a job yet, I threw myself headfirst into Keith's care and put the dream of a career in magazines and living in New York City on hold. I liked sleeping in the green vinyl chair next to his bed, changing his socks, and arranging the get well cards on his dresser. I spent all of my time with him, washing up in a sink and eating pretzels for dinner. I fielded questions from doctors at five a.m. when no one else was there. I cursed at my family when they told me I needed to come home. Every now and then it would hit me that I was literally living in a hospital, that I smelled and needed a shower, that my cell phone battery was dead, and I didn't care. Workers in the cafeteria knew my name and asked how my "man" was. There was a bank of steps at the entrance to the hospital and I sat out there often, picking at my nails and people-watching. Then one day a girl called out to me from across the street. It was Jessica, and I've known her since I was three. She was attending Rutgers University at the time, just a few blocks from the hospital. I led her to Keith's room for a quick visit and afterward I watched as she crossed the street in pursuit of her campus, where it would be lively and loud and teeming with students. It was just blocks away from the hospital but seemed like a different time period, as if everything I was experiencing was set in black and white, not happening in real time.

A couple of weeks later Keith was moved from Robert Wood Johnson hospital in New Brunswick to Kessler in West

Orange. I followed the ambulance there in my car. On the parkway I saw the exit for New York City, and as I passed it I felt more of myself slip away with it. By the time I looked in the rearview mirror the little green sign was gone.

Kessler was different from the hospital. It was long-term, but still hopeful. Keith and I sat outside on the patio a lot together and one day it occurred to me it wasn't summer anymore, because there were carpets of leaves everywhere and a constant spray of goose bumps on my arms. The chill on my arms affirmed I was awake and that time was passing, like a constant slide of sand through an hourglass. The rest of the world carried on like that, too. People raked their lawns and bought lattes before going to the office. My friend Liss got engaged and my college friend Kateri was off touring Europe with the proverbial backpack and a couple hundred bucks. Suddenly everything was different. A familiar feeling now.

When a doctor said children were possible, but not a guarantee, I realized this accident wasn't just about Keith and his needs, but mine, too. Before this realization I had ripped up pamphlets about "Caring for the Caretaker." Was this social worker serious? My boyfriend can't move his legs and I'm supposed to digest some bullet points on not giving a crap about myself? No shit, lady. Have you seen my eyebrows? Do you want to see my legs? Compare my weight to what it was six months ago?

Then one day two filmmakers came to the rehab where Keith was living and asked to film him in his daily activities. The "little project" evolved into *Murderball* and earned a

2005 Academy Award nomination for best documentary, but by the time the red carpet was rolled out Keith and I were over. The commercial for the film aired on MTV and there I was, kissing Keith for the entire world to see, only the image was a far cry from actuality. By then my voicemails to him went unanswered. To this day, it's odd to see myself in the film, or to see Keith in a scene, point blank asking his doctor about the potential to have sex with his girlfriend, in other words, me. It was even more unnerving to hear the doctor quip enthusiastically in the scene that the short answer was yes. What was the long answer, doc? Things were too heavy—I wasn't okay with a question mark at the end of sex and baby—I was twenty-three years old. So a year after his accident, I broke up with him and he hated me for it. I would have hated me, too.

I think if the accident hadn't happened I'd still be with him. It's a hard thing to admit to myself. What kind of person breaks up with a quadriplegic? At most I felt like his best friend, a nurse—at times, even a *mother*—but then other times I felt overwhelmingly in love with him, wishing on every star in the night sky as I drove home from the rehab that things would just go back to normal. I'd wake up to my phone ringing and it would be him coming over with coffee. He'd open the door to a restaurant, pull my seat out at the table, order my drink, because he always knew what I wanted—a dirty martini with three olives. He'd wrestle me into his bed, tickling me until I cried. Years later, over too many cocktails at Pravda, I told Nic that when I broke up with Keith it was like I was throwing the dice in the air—I truly had no idea if it was the right decision, but it was one I needed to try out. I wondered if I was confusing fear with contentment, or loyalty with love.

Some people saw me as selfish. I went straight from World's Best Girlfriend to heartless coward in the minds of the same people who breezed in, in their fancy tracksuits for twenty-minute visits every two weeks or so. One of his room-mates in the rehab facility told Keith and I about how his girlfriend stuck around for a couple of months but then broke up with him. I was sitting on Keith's bed at the time, unaware I was cutting off circulation to his catheter bag—I did this often and it became a bit of a joke between us. "She's not like Christine!" his roommate enthused. Such damning words, because I knew then if I ever did leave I'd be stoned. I felt trapped, but I continued on, reaching for a breath, telling myself it was normal to be feeling overwhelmed and scared. The caretaking became second nature—it was like ty-ing my shoelace in the dark. I emerged from the shower stall pushing the rubber chair, with soaked socks and wrinkled fingers, completely unfazed. I managed to get a non-magazine job—three, in fact, but every one ended the same: I just couldn't handle filing things and walking some fancy person's dog when my boyfriend was lying in a bed, watching the clock, waiting for me to return. Even though his nurses frowned on me getting into bed with him, I did, every single day, for one year. Until I realized I was forcing myself to keep on. My spirit was gone. My heart was broken. I was hollow and I didn't even recognize myself anymore.

It was time for me to live again. So I did what I always intended. I moved to New York City with big plans of starting over. I was like a divorcée who had never been married. Carlo said I was running away and he was right, but I denied it with a sure grin. Thing is, we carry our pasts with us. Life is messy. It should come with instructions. My feelings for Keith were immediate and raw and they never went away. They still exist. Even on my first night in my perfect New York City apartment I couldn't help but look around and wish he was there beside me. *He's supposed to be here. We're supposed to get married.* I thought a new apartment and coveted magazine job might make my feelings for him, for us, go away, but in the beginning they just sugarcoated them. For a very long time I hoped to feel that wanted and needed again, like I had that year when I took care of him. A doctor told me it was "classic caretaker syndrome" and something about how parents often feel this exact strain when "the birds leave the nest." He nodded to assure me his fancy degree qualified him to say that. "Great. How do I make it go away?" I asked from a cushy couch.

I threw myself into living for me: traveling, working, going on terrible dates, trying to be a normal twenty-something. I was back to basics. I had no one to take care of but myself. I was focused on my writing and cultivating new friendships. Brunch was an event, and I started to explore New York City and risked looking like a tourist. I started to see things more clearly.

In my wildest dreams I never imagined my life would slingshot me back to a place where everything is sort of stuck in a moment—a nine-month moment. It hasn't even been two years. I feel like I just got ahold of myself. I was planning to return to Europe this summer. I was in France and England last spring with Lo and Kateri. Now I feel as if I'm looking through a wild kaleidoscope of colors with no definitive end or beginning. Everything is just sort of colliding and I feel that familiar rush of anxiety and fear. I've been thinking about Keith a lot lately, too, since the article I wrote for *Glamour* about my experience with him hits newsstands next month. How bizarre is that? I wanted it to be as accurate as possible, so I e-mailed Keith a couple of times during the writing process and we tried to remember conversations we had about his "foreign hands" that no longer moved with ease, our impromptu sleepovers that we never meant to happen but I was too tired to drive home; the way those shower stalls smelled, sort of humid and sweet, like *baby* shampoo. It was interesting to go over these details years later and sort of cool the unspoken heat between us. More so when a fact-checker called me, then him, to go over our lives with us like some plot in a movie. It was so odd hearing someone else tell me how things played out: *So you helped him take a shower?* Yes, I did. It's a strange coincidence this article is coming out now in the midst of yet another life-changing moment, but having that past experience full frontal again, in black and white, does put things in perspective. It certainly reminds me how strong I am—and how eager I was to get on with my life.

Wait until everyone reads *Glamour* and then gets a load of my big news. I can hear them all now: *She broke up with Keith when he needed her the most . . . now she's knocked up!*

Ha-Ha! But karma is not recycling itself here. My baby has nothing to do with that part of my life, unless you count how I agonized over the fact that if I stayed in that relationship I might never be able to have children. My eyes dart around at the boxed-in cars. So what that I'm pregnant! I've always wanted this—maybe not exactly like this. It's a cosmic twist of fate it happened this way, so unplanned, like a special delivery I never could have anticipated. But it happened. Things happen! *Everything will fall into place, Christine. It always does,* I think, creeping toward the GWB, the city lit up in a million little fragments of light.

A couple of days later, over an early dinner at a Mexican place, A gives me a bottle of folic acid. It's a sweet gesture. But what I really want and need is for us to devise a master plan, because I feel like my life is spiraling out of control and he's just ordering a burrito.

"Should we look for an apartment?" I ask him across the table as we wait for the waitress.

"Yeah, I guess," he says.

"But do we want to?" I look up at him with uncertainty in my eyes.

"What do you mean?" he asks.

"I mean we . . . we hardly know each other!" I just blurt it out. There is a pause.

"I know," he says.

"There are things to figure out ... like, financially. Did you know day care in New York City costs sixteen hundred dollars a month?" I look away.

Truth is, I don't think we should pretend to be in love. It's 2008. We can do this together, separately. A shouldn't feel forced to love me or marry me.

"And what about health insurance?" I say. "I have great coverage. Do you have health care? The baby needs to go on one of our plans. Babies are expensive."

The waitress comes over. I open my mouth but then I re-member I can't have a drink—or a Diet Coke.

"Water with lemon," I tell the waitress, then look at A.

"We can talk about this stuff later," he says.

Later feels like nine months from now. My body is already changing. My breasts are tender and I can barely keep seltzer water down. I'm experiencing physical reality I can't ignore. It's not happening to him. I teeter the folic acid bot-tle up and down with my finger. It sounds like a ticking clock and I wonder if A really is up for this, after all. Now that our relationship isn't just movies and beers and sex—it's about. baby and money and religious upbringing and schooling and—*shit*, a college fund.

When I get home to my apartment, I wrestle off my ankle boots and rub my feet (the things I do for fashion) and start making a list of editors I know because I need to start free-lancing, now. My full-time magazine job hardly supports my lifestyle. Let's just say I've learned how to make rice one hundred different ways (when I'm in between pay weeks). And that a Forever 21 top for eleven bucks and a pair of

Theory trousers for two hundred works as a last resort—even *Lucky* mag says so! As I type the list, a sudden calm washes over me. Doing this makes me feel in control. Next, I log on to my health care plan's website and start reading about labor and delivery. I appear to have excellent health care—that's one major plus. Afterward I scroll through a listing of two-bedroom apartments on Craigslist.com, but as I read about "laundry in the building," it occurs to me that I might not want to even move in with A—that he might not want to move in with me. I lie awake thinking about this, watching the time change, thinking how with each passing second I am sustaining life with my own. It's an incredible feeling—and enough to quiet the thoughts in my head, at least for tonight.

4

Dealing

The next week I'm back in Jersey. I have to renew my driver's license, which has been expired for almost a year. I resorted to keeping my passport in my bag at all times, just in case. A couple of months ago a power-hungry doorman at a club in the city claimed my ID was fake. I was drunk and trying to maintain balance in my stiletto boots as I forked over my passport. Now that I'm having a baby, I've decided to be responsible. A new license seems like a good place to start. Then I'm going to attack my credit card bill, which is teetering near fifteen to sixteen hundred dollars, beef up my 401(k), buy some natural toothpaste. I've made a checklist and I run a satisfying red line through each task when it's fulfilled. A says he'll look for an apartment, so let's see if he does. The thing is, all he seems to do is *talk* about things. I'm doing things. And it's actually a little infuriating at this point. I'm the pregnant one—shouldn't someone be holding my hand? Talking my panic attacks down?

The line at the DMV is unforgiving. The man in front of me smells like vinegar. I keep hearing Carlo's voice: *Call Nanny. You—you, have to tell her.* I look at the clock on the wall, then the line, then the person speaking Spanish and the DMV clerk behind the partition responding, "I don't speak Spanish," in English. I dial my Nan.

"Hello," a tiny voice says.

"Hi, Nan!" I say cheerfully.

"Hi-ya, Chris—when are you going to come visit me?" she says.

"Soon. Maybe later. I'm in Wayne now," I say.

"Oh, good. Where's your father? Did you talk to him? He's sick, you know," she says.

My father is Nan's only child. He's not sick, but ever since his cancer scare back in 2003, according to Nan, he's "dying."

"I don't know where he is. Home?" I say.

"I made a tray of white macaroni with egg. Delicious. Your father should pick it up—bring it home," she says.

I hear my heart beating. I imagine her sitting in the green vinyl kitchen chair in the corner of her green kitchen. She's wearing black house shoes, black pants, and a black sweater. The heat is set to keep the house at about one thousand degrees, and she might even have the oven on, its door open but nothing cooking, just to warm the house more. Her long hair is pinned up. She's got her legs crossed; one is twisted behind the other. And she's eagerly waiting for *One Life to Live* to start, maybe eating a Ritz cracker.

"So guess what, Nan?" I say.

"Oh, what?" she says.

"I'm going to have a baby," I say.

"A baby? No," she says over a chuckle. "Come on, now."

"Nan, seriously. I'm pregnant. You're going to be a great-grandma." I say this with enthusiasm like I'm trying to sell her something.

"Okay. Good," she says.

"Okay," I say and move up in the line.

"Does your father know?" she asks.

"Yep," I say.

"Good. You should eat something. A meatball," she says.

Before I can respond she blurts out, "Or a slice of 'piz.' Uncle Carmen made a fresh pie," she says.

"I will," I assure her.

"Oh, this is nice. Very nice," she says.

I'm waiting for her to ask about A, whom she has never met, though she constantly asks me if he is "a nice Italian boy." When she does ask, I tell her I have to go because the line is breaking up. She doesn't know what that means, because she is still trying to wrap her head around cell phone technology. She reminds me again to eat.

An hour and a half later I have my new license in hand and it occurs to me I will, for the next four years, look at this photo remembering exactly how I felt at this very moment. I mean, if there was a word bubble over my head it would read: "Oh. My. God!" I look extremely pale and unassuming—and scared. I look like I did something bad.

Afterward I go to my parents' house for dinner. My father made a tray of chicken parm this afternoon, so when I walk into the house I am first overwhelmed by a thick aroma of baked tomato and garlic—then by that fricken poodle, who promptly begins playing tug-of-war with my shoelace.

"No, Max!" I say and he growls at me like he thinks he's

a Doberman. Carlo emerges on the stair landing and looks me up and down.

"You're how many weeks now?" he asks, staring at my stomach.

"Sev-eight? And I told Nan," I say.

"I know. She thought you were lying. I assured her you weren't. She said to eat a meatball," he says. He's smirking at me like he did when we were little and told my mom something stupid like how I rolled my plaid Catholic school uniform skirt up and the nuns yelled at me.

I kneel down in the foyer and let Max sniff me. I hear my mother and Carlo talking, but I'm not sure what about, probably something like, "I can't believe she's really knocked up." Carlo is waiting for his little sister to look pregnant. When my great uncle Carmen found out from my father that I was pregnant, he called Carlo and asked why he and Brian "let it happen . . . You're supposed to look after her," he said. It's such an old-fashioned, sexist statement, but this is my uncle who grew up slinging pizzas in his parents' bakery, working side by side with Nanny.

My mother is at the stove turning over the sauce, and Carlo is sitting at the table staring at me. I'm furiously peeling a cucumber and dark green strips of skin are collecting in a pile on the cutting board. I've decided to eat more green, leafy things, because the book I'm reading encourages it. I kind of wish *What to Expect When You're Expecting* would update their cover. The "expecting" woman on the cover has mousy hair and looks forty, constipated, and *really* petrified. She's also wearing red pants, brown clogs, and a mustard cardigan set. I think *Glamour* would agree: It's a "don't." I'm determined to still look fabulous for the next eight months and Ms. Mousy is not a good role model. I cut the cucumber into perfect, chubby circles and plop them on a big bed of mixed greens. As I shave a carrot onto the salad I feel Carlo's eyes burning a hole into my forehead.

"What!" I look up at him and accelerate my peeling.

"Nothing. Relax." He's got something to say to me because he's still looking at me, waiting for me to say something like "I'm okay."

"What!" I throw down the carrot and look at Carlo.

"Are we ever going to discuss this?" he wants to know.

"Why are you even here? You live and work in Connect-icut!" I bark back.

"I'm here because I care about you and I want to help you," he says sincerely.

My mother excuses herself to go smoke. My hormones recently demanded that she quit smoking or take it outside away from my baby. Carlo referred to me as "bipolar." I laughed twice.

"Listen. I know you're trying to be brave here, but it's okay not to be. I'm happy with the decision you made, I love babies . . . and I want to help . . . you," he says. His eyes widen like he wants me to respond to his thoughtfulness. I slam a knife through a tomato and it squishes into a mess.

When we were kids, Carlo, Brian, and I used to play "store" and "car." When we played store, I ran the clothing boutique and displayed color-coordinated baby clothes on my bed. Brian owned the supermarket. He set up plastic clumps of peas, misshapen apples, and pink rubber chops from the play kitchen on his dresser. Carlo ran the bank. But a bank isn't a store! Brian and I reminded him. He didn't care. He was in charge. So when we played "car," which translated to us arranging four dining room chairs, one behind the other, in the middle of the living room and draping them with a big, fuzzy rainbow afghan, he obviously got to drive. All. The. Time. He grew up into this type of person, too. He's a problem solver, a *let's-get-this-done-right-now* type of guy. I am not at all surprised that (after his initial shock wore thin), he has been playing an active role in my pregnancy—calling me two times a day to check in, lobbying for America's Next Top Godfather, offering to help me forecast a new budget. The more Carlo steps in, steps up, the more I realize A isn't. Just this afternoon Carlo picked up a new order of prenatal vitamins for me, since I left my prescription in my room in New York City by accident. As nice as he's being, I feel annoyed at the moment. I don't need help. I need some fresh purple onion for this salad and there is none. How could there be three different kinds of milk and eleven kinds of cold cuts in the fridge and not one measly onion? My father lives at ShopRite. The checkout grandmothers who work part time know his name. This is complete bullshit. Carlo hands me a jar of onion powder. Is he fucking crazy? What the hell am I supposed to do with this? All I'm thinking is how I want to hurl this jar out the window. I place it down on the table, take a breath, and look up at him.

I slide the bowl to the middle of the table and wipe my hands on the front of my shirt. Carlo wants to keep talking about where I plan to live, how I plan to afford a nursery, the specifics of my health-care plan, but I can't map out the next eighteen years over pasta. My mom returns to the kitchen smelling like smoke. There's a big sunken bowl of spaghetti on the table and a rerun of *Friends* is muted on the television. Carlo forks a wad of pasta onto my plate and tells me everything is going to be okay. I push my food around, suddenly not hungry, hoping he's right.

It's the weekend. A is in Brooklyn with his friends and he thinks I'm in Jersey at my annual girls' dinner, but I'm actually lying in bed with a bag of microwave popcorn on my stomach watching *Where the Heart Is*. It's like a train wreck—I can't change the channel. The poor thing is having her baby in the middle of a Wal-Mart. Here's hoping my water doesn't break in the Kmart on Astor Place—I'd settle for Bloomies on Broadway, though. I look at the clock and it's already five. I should get in the shower right about now, pick out a fantastic outfit, and hop on a bus to Jersey to meet my high school girlfriends for dinner, but I'm paralyzed in my bed, not ready to tell them I'm pregnant. I reach for my phone and send the five of them a mass text: "Puking. Sorry. Have fun."

Monday at work I'm paging through a look book of spring dresses, flagging pages with Post-its. I'm working with a team of editors on a new weekly magazine and it's set to launch sometime this year. With my luck, the day I give birth. I spent the weekend under my covers, nibbling on saltines, avoiding all forms of human contact. I feel like I'm walking around in someone else's life. How could I be pregnant? This happens to girls on talk shows or twits in movies. It's like there's a big pink elephant in every single room I walk into and only I see it. After all, other than my family, no one knows. They asked the same question over and over: A? *Ah, speak of the devil.* My phone rings. It's him calling to see "What's up?" Way too casual. I tell him I'm just working and he tells me he told his ex-girlfriend in Indiana because he owed it to her. I pull the phone from my ear and wince angrily at it.

I've tried to come around and settle on making things work between us, but when I resign myself to it, A does something mind-numbing like announce he's going to Vegas at the end of August—when I'll be approximately nine months pregnant. "It's for this work thing," A said to me over the phone. He nonchalantly told me I could come. I reminded him I couldn't exactly fly at nine months pregnant—that *our* baby was due on September eighth. Maybe I'm overreacting, but my gut is telling me he isn't the one for me. On the other hand I keep thinking, *Of course* we're going to figure this out, it just takes time, neither of us knows what we're doing here. I push myself out from my desk and stand up like I have something important to do. I make a beeline for an adjacent set of offices.

I walk into my friend Kateri's cubicle and slump into a chair, feeling the color in my face fade to white. It's been so hard not to tell her. I've seen her every day since I found out and every time I went to tell her I said something instead like, "Got a spare quarter for the soda machine?" *For the soda I can't drink.*

"What's the matter?" Kateri asks, almost falling off her chair to reach for my hand.

I met Kateri my freshman year of college. We lived in the same dorm building and took all the same classes. We could sit for hours on the great steps talking about everything, or nothing at all. We lost touch a bit when I was busy on the Keith front and she was traveling through Europe, but we're the type of friends who can pick up from anywhere—even the moon. We work at the same publishing company now. She's a photo editor at one of the teen titles. Coincidentally, her mom got pregnant with her when she was nineteen. Kateri's mom and grandma raised her and she didn't meet her father until she was thirteen. Her hair is ink black and her skin is warm and olive. Her eyes blink and widen, summoning me to spill it.

"I'm pregnant," I say, scanning her cubicle and finding a poster of three boys called "the Jonas Brothers." *Who the hell are they?* It occurs to me that moms would know this kind of shit. Fast forward ten years, my daughter is going to have posters on her wall of guys—boys like this. My dad took my girlfriends and me to New Kids on the Block when we were in fifth grade. We rode in a limo and ate at a fancy Italian restaurant with linen napkins before the show. That was the best ravioli I ever ate. Even the Coke tasted important. My dad wore earplugs during the concert. It was embarrassing.

She cups her hands over her mouth and her eyes bug out in shock.

"Oh. My. God. How pregnant? What are you going to do? What—?"

I cut her off, throwing my palms in the air. I take a breath. "I'm having a baby! I'm about two months."

She looks at me, not flinching. The look of shock is starting to develop into a smirk.

"I'm going to be an auntie?" she says, as a huge toothy smile surfaces on her face.

"Uh, ye-ah." I smile.

"And what about A? Excited?" she asks.

"Um." I don't know what to say.

"Huh?" she asks.

"He's pretty nervous. It's fine," I say. But I think we're breaking up. God, I want to tell her.

"Okay? Well, for now, take a deep breath," she says, and I do.

"Deeper," she says, and blankets her palm over my hand, smiling at me like she's drunk and thinking about touching my belly. She'd better not.

The wheels in Kateri's head are turning and I'm pretty sure my baby shower is half planned, right here. I walk back to my desk feeling confident enough to tell Nic. I dial her office.

"Gucci Group," a young female voice says over her gum.

"Nicole A. In the buyer's office, please."

She says nothing and clicks me off. Punchy club music

plays over a film of static and I imagine a line of pin-thin models, like the kind I used to dress when I interned there, cascading down a runway. I got to dress Liya Kebede, a very prominent Ethiopian model, for a special Yves Saint Laurent preview with a few *Vogue* editors—and Kate Hudson. I've told that story about nine thousand times. In a couple of versions I think I made friends with Kate, but really I just stared at her from behind a thin dressing screen, munching on model food like red grapes and carrot sticks.

"This is Nicole," she answers.

"This is Christine," I sing. It's the standard way we address each other when we answer the phone at our offices, identifying ourselves like robots.

"Hey, wanna go to Dos tonight and get some guac?" she says. She's referring to Dos Caminos, a Mexican place in Soho. Sometimes we consider chips and guacomole—and four frozen prickly pear margaritas—dinner.

"I'm pregnant," I answer her.

Pause.

"Okay," she says.

"Okay," I say.

"Okay," she says again.

"So, I'm having a baby," I say.

"This is fine. This is fine. Totally fine," she says, and I realize she has absolutely no idea what to say to me. She's probably wondering if she should console or congratulate me.

"It is, right?" I really want her to tell me everything is okay.

"Fine. It's fine," she says in an assertive voice. "How pregnant are you?" she asks.

"Like sev—eight weeks," I say. "And don't even ask about A, because I just don't know."

"Two months. Okay. But when you say you're not sure about A and I know you've been feeling confused lately, what does that mean?" she asks.

"Nic, I don't know. It's a shock for him, too," I say. "I don't think I want to be with him—like—marry him."

"Christine," she says, then pauses. "If you guys break up, you're going to be a single mom. Do you know what that means? Do you get it?" she asks.

"We share custody?" I say, questioningly.

"Yeah, do you know what that *really* means? Are you pre- pared to be single, I mean, a single mom?" I pass a paper clip down my fingers and back again.

"No. Yes. I don't know," I say in one thought. I'm so con- fused.

My other line is beeping and I hang up with her and let it go to voice mail. I check my e-mail and see one from Nic. The subject line reads, "Congrats!" There is a link in the body. I click on it and I'm transported to a pair of Gucci booties. It makes me smile, but I think it's just her way of coping with the fact that her wing woman is pregnant and won't be able to drag her off some drunk guy's arm at Pravda at three a.m. with "an emergency." The cute e-mail was way too immediate. She's hyperventilating at her desk for sure. The other new e-mail is for a press event happening tonight. There's an open vodka bar. Perfect, huh?

After lunch (I made myself eat a salad with chickpeas and a slice of whole wheat bread even though I feel like my nerves might permanently quash my appetite) I e-mail my girlfriends from North Jersey. They have live-in boyfriends or fiancés—one's already married (she should probably be making the baby announcement, not me). They own condos and cars and have money for tropical vacations. My friends in New York City are renters and sometimes go to work in last night's makeup. I fall somewhere in between the two. The e-mail is blunt: *So guess what? I'm pregnant.* I press Send and wonder who will get the news first, then distract myself copy editing the horoscope page with a red pen.

Later on that night, I'm propped up against my headboard waiting for A to call so we can "talk" when my phone rings. It's Katie—guess she got my e-mail. Here goes . . .

I pick up the phone. "Hello, Katie."

"It's Liss—and Katie!" they say.

I think back to high school and how we used to do double three-way calls to plan our Friday night or talk about how our boyfriends were probably cheating on us—again.

"Cop?" Katie says. My friends call me Cop, short for Coppa.

"Yes, I am pregnant," I say very calmly.

"Holy shit," they say in unison. I smirk and pull the phone from my ear. They quickly make up for it.

"Congratulations," they say over each other.

"Thanks," I say. "What'd you think of my e-mail? Typical Christine?" I say over a gurgle of laughter.

"Honestly?" Katie says. "That you were joking!"

Katie and Liss live in the same condo complex. Katie lives with her fiancé and Liss with her husband. Katie explains that she got the e-mail first, called Liss, who hadn't, so she ran up to the fourth floor from the second in her socks, and together they sat in front of Liss's computer and contemplated whether or not I was joking. And I don't blame them. I am certainly the prankster of the group and the ringleader who convinces everyone to have one more drink, dance to one more song. I'm not exactly the one who has a baby. Except now I am.

"Wasn't joking," I say.

"So what does A think?" Katie asks.

I don't know what to say to her, because at this point, I hardly know myself.

"Oh, you know. Shocked," I say, and quickly slide into another topic: the reason I bailed on our annual girls' dinner. I tell them about the ironic movie I watched while I ate popcorn for dinner. Katie bursts out laughing.

"Cop, we spent the better part of that evening drinking dirty martinis and wondering when one of us was going to get pregnant, *already*," she says. I say nothing.

"We even played that weird necklace game, when you swing a chain in front of your face and if it swings side-to-side and not front-to-back, then you're destined to have a girl . . . or is it a boy? I can't remember," she says. When we hang up I unclip my yellow gold Tiffany's heart from my neck and dangle it in front of my face. It makes a circle.

I walk into work the next day and slump into the chair next to my boss, Maria's, desk. I'm wearing dark plum tights and an A-line black shift dress. I don't look pregnant. We're good friends, so I feel like I can tell her what's going on and she won't immediately start giving my pages away and put an ad on Mediabistro.com for a new assistant. Whenever she walks in wearing a new outfit, I joke: "The Devil Wears Banana Republic" or "Did the devil buy that at Anthropologie?"

"Hi, dolly," she says. "Let's order coffee—and bagels."

"I'm pregnant," I say, my right black ballet slipper dangling from my toes.

"Okay, coffee's on me today," she says. "Decaf?"

"Ha ha," I say.

"Congratulations?" she says and opens her arms. I let myself fall into her and I stay fixed in her chest for a moment. She smells warm, like cinnamon and hot wildflowers.

"Don't fire me," I joke.

She jokes back: "Actually, I think that's illegal. You may have just bought yourself an 'I-have-food-poisoning' ticket for the next nine months."

"Ma-riiiiiiii-a!" I whine. "What am I going to do?" I ask.

"You'll be fine. Did you tell the girls? What does Lo think?" she asks.

"I e-mailed Lo. She immediately called me. Crying a little. Not because I'm making her an aunt. I think because we were supposed to go to Spain this summer," I say, pulling away from her and slumping back in the chair. "What's the maternity leave like here?" I ask, having no idea.

"It has nothing to do with here, per say. New Jersey maternity leave is actually pretty good. Six or eight weeks paid—and twelve unpaid, if you like," she says. My eyes well with tears. *Mascara, Christine. Do you want to look like a hooker at the office?* I think, willing them away.

Back at my desk I see an e-mail from A saying he's sick and going home to rest. Seconds later, a text from him, revealing he might have the flu. Maybe he caught my morning sickness. I text back telling him to "feel better" and dig into a drawer of file folders.

When James, my buddy, the creative director gets in, I pull him into the conference room. He drinks black coffee, has a killer Prada jacket, and his substantially higher paycheck allows him to buy me fifteen-dollar martinis and introduce me to important writers at book readings. We can also communicate with our eyes, so today I hardly look at him in fear he might blurt my news to the office.

As he follows me into the conference room, I realize he probably thinks I'm quitting, and since I don't report to him, he's eager for some juicy details about how I finally infiltrated my way into *Vogue*. We sit across from each other and before he can even utter "What's up" or "So?" I blurt my news out . . . and he hugs me. He doesn't look at me crooked or cup his hands over his mouth in shock. I feel his scruff on my face and smell cigarettes on his shirt. There is genuine warmth in his embrace. I almost don't reciprocate his hug because I am a bit taken aback at how instant his demonstration of congratulations is. We sit back down and I fold myself Indian-style into the chair.

"It's crazy, huh?" I say.

"Chrissy, ask yourself. Have you always imagined kids, or a kid, in your life?" he says.

It's one of those lightbulb moments. Yes, yes I did imagine kids in my life. It was the only question/answer that mattered or ever will. Despite the obvious circumstances, this is pretty stellar. I'm having a baby! There's a person growing inside of me—a whole new life. As nervous as I've been, it actually feels good to break the news to people and share my happiness. I'm sick of seeing pregnancy test commercials featuring happy women and thinking, Gee, I wish I were her—because I've come to realize *I am her*. But the thing is, I'm almost embarrassed to flaunt my happiness because I'm pretty sure the rest of the world thinks I'm a fucking idiot to be keeping my baby. I almost told a stranger I was pregnant in the Starbucks the other morning. I watched as she stuck a straw into an organic chocolate milk container and slid it across the table to her two-year-old-ish daughter, who was wearing thick, cable-knit wool tights and patent-leather Mary Janes. I imagined her name was Madeline or Olivia. She looked like a peanut in the soft armchair and her legs jutted straight out, just slightly inching over the edge. Her mom had on an important watch and she looked at it like she was late for something, but didn't care. When she saw me looking at her she smiled and said, "She's in charge!" and pointed to *Madeline . . .* or *Olivia.* I opened my mouth and placed my hand on my belly at the same time and I was about to say something like "I'm expecting," or "So this is what I have to look forward to!" But I didn't. I told her her daughter was beautiful. As I left, I watched her wipe chocolate milk from her daughter's chin with her thumb and thought, I can do that—be her.

It's becoming more physically real, too. In the quiet of the shower's cocoon, I recognize changes in my barely pregnant body. My nipples are a darker shade of brown, fuller and tender to the touch. My stomach is bloated into a thick little pouch that never dissolves. My body is shapely now and I don't look so tomboyish. There are times when I'm at work, mulling through samples for photo shoots, editing copy for my own first-grade grammatical mistakes, and I realize it's two p.m. and I haven't eaten yet. *We* haven't eaten. I panic. The other day I was scrolling through the crib section of an online store visualizing a mod nursery, in hues of lime green and chocolate. There is an overwhelming surge of happiness and terror, I can't decide, exploding in my stomach like a constant firecracker—it's like I'm on the verge of sneezing all the time.

I ride the subway home with my friend Matt, an editor from *In Touch*. I'm usually very chatty, drilling him on the latest celebrity gossip, but tonight all I want to do is sleep the whole ride home. Matt nudges his elbow into my side.

"What's up?" he says.

I look over at him, open my mouth, but nothing comes out. He starts saying something about Brangelina. His bubble jacket looks flat and too small for him. He's an overwhelmingly kind person, and if I slid my hand into his right now he would hold it until we parted at our different stops. I stuff my hands into my coat pockets. The woman across from me is knitting something orange and five boys in

T-shirts to their knees and bomber jackets are roughhousing with one another. Matt is in midsentence, talking about how someone checked in and out of rehab in one day.

"I'm pregnant, Matt," I say, staring straight ahead at the spool of orange yarn.

"What?" he says, nudging my side again.

I look over and nod at him, then take a breath.

"Are you okay?" he asks.

I think for a moment, pulling my hat from my head, dipping it into my bag.

"I'm okay," I say, smiling at him. His eyes look concerned. They are squinting in half moons now. He's waiting for me to say something, but I don't.

"You'll be okay. Everything will be okay," he says, tapping my leg with his palm. I believe him.

I meet A at the movies. It's been a long few days. The film is about the last pregnant woman in the world. People are trying to steal her baby. I laugh inappropriately through most of it. I should not be watching this movie.

We walk home and don't hold hands. Cabs flash past us. Last month A hailed a cab for a random couple. The guy's nose was oozing with blood. When he did that, I felt lucky he was my boyfriend. It was one of those nice, uncensored things he often did. I look up at him, but he doesn't catch my gaze.

"Are you cold?" A asks.

"Nah," I say, but I'm really freezing and my nose is running.

"So, have you thought more about—this?" I say, looking at my feet. I sound like a nag, but I don't care. My waist is getting thicker.

"I have. I'm not sure, Chrissy. I think we need to think things through more," he says. I see he's been thinking a lot in our absence from each other. I'm actually glad he says this. He's right. I think we need to say out loud that we are breaking up but remaining friends and figuring this out. And soon, because I imagine myself nine months pregnant, having the same conversation, getting the same delayed response. When we come to the crossing for Penn Station he tells me he's going uptown to his friend's place. I walk home alone, pregnant, at eleven p.m. up Third Ave. *This is what happens when you're not married. There are no guarantees.* All of this is starting to sink in. I feel heavy—like there are weights strapped to my ankles. Still I continue up the avenue.

5

First Sonogram

I am at my twelfth-week sonogram—alone. A had a trip to his college town in Indiana. He said he'd come with me and I imagined that seeing our "tadpole" would help put things in perspective for him, since although it's pretty obvious we're not a couple anymore, it's not so obvious that he is going to be a father. I called him a couple of times, but my voice mails and text messages went unanswered for days until he finally called me last night to say he was extending his trip and wouldn't be home in time for the sonogram. I wasn't mad. I was just disappointed. I know A is scared—I am, too—but this isn't about us. I keep thinking he just needs some time to get used to all of this, that he'll soften up a bit. Just six weeks ago he was telling me he was happy that I was pregnant. Or maybe Carlo (and my gut feeling) is right. Maybe he wants nothing to do with his baby.

Two days after A left for Indiana, I called Carlo.

"Hey, Car." My voice cracked.

"How do you feel, everything okay, what's up," he said in one breath.

I was at my desk with a pile of *Cosmo* tear sheets to thumb through—research for the sex pages.

"He hasn't returned my calls," I admitted.

"Well, Christine, you say you don't want to be with him," he says.

"I'm carrying his baby—our baby!" I say.

"Okay, well, where the hell is he?" he asked.

"In-di-ana."

"You realize this is it. Guy is gone," Carlo said.

Sitting there at my desk, I wasn't sad for myself when he said that. I was relieved. I had a weird feeling—like the balloon finally popped but I didn't startle. He just needs to realize that he can't just come over and collect his things from my bedroom. We're having a baby, and in that aspect we're "together." He's not a bad person and he's in my life forever now, so we'll have to just figure this out.

At last, the technician enters and she is wearing goofy scrubs with bubbly hearts all over them. She reaches for a tube of gel.

"This is going to feel warm and gooey," she says.

It sounded oddly pleasant compared to my last sonogram, when the technician thrust that dildo-ish probe up me. She rolls the tool over my belly and I stare wide-eyed at the screen. It is a cloudy mess of black and gray, until the tool moves lower, just above my pubic bone. I'm excited. And feeling excited, feeling this natural rush of energy with no reservations, assures me I made the right decision. I'm just about popping out of the chair when suddenly there is a tadpole on the screen. A round head too big for its body and boney little legs and arms. *Huh*, I think, *would you look at that*. My baby is bouncing up against me, back and forth, but

I can't feel her at all. She's no longer the size of a sesame seed—she's even bigger than a "big plum."

"Is she okay?" I strain my neck up, smiling at the screen, and ask the technician.

"She? You think it's a girl?" She smiles and pushes the tool into my belly and it hurts a little bit.

"Oh, yes," I admit, and think how cute the name Mia is. "I know it's early but can you tell if it's a girl?"

She smiles and says everything looks normal and that my doctor will go over the sonogram with me at my next appointment. Then she smiles slyly and says, "Trust me—you're having a boy." My stomach flip-flops. A boy? It had not really occurred to me that the baby would be a boy. What the hell am I going to do with a boy? How am I going to pull off a rendition of the *Gilmore Girls* with a boy? I ask her again and I explain that I really feel like I'm having a girl and that at my last facial the European lady said my skin looked like I was carrying a girl. When I hear myself say that out loud I feel almost as stupid as I do for not having used a condom. She tells me that I'm only twelve weeks along and the sex could definitely be determined at twenty weeks, but if she had to put money on the sex—it's a boy. A boy? She tells me to get dressed and to meet her in the hallway because she needs to take blood to test for Down syndrome. It's standard and I'm young and healthy, so Dr. Collado said I should have nothing to worry about. What I *am* worrying about is this baby *boy*.

I plop down on a stool and the nurse grabs my hand and starts rubbing my pointer finger with her gloved one, trying to make a vein pop.

She grabs a tiny gun and pops my finger with a stick. I jump, but it doesn't hurt. Next she dabs my finger one, two, three times on a tab of paper. She bandages me up and I leave. I stand outside a bank of elevators and wonder how I'm going to raise a baby—and not just any baby, a boy baby—alone. I could see being a single mom to a little girl. I'd let her wear my lipstick when she was four, for fun. We'd go on Mexican vacations and lie in the sun. I'd let her stay home from school the first time she got her period and we'd go out to lunch, then the spa. The elevator bell tings and I blink and come to. *A baby boy*, I think. I can handle this. Sure. Boys love their mommies—this is a fact. Who needs a teenage girl to fight with in sixteen years?

In the elevator I check for missed calls. None. I spread my palm over my belly and in the quiet of my head tell my baby we are going to be okay. *I love you, Baby.* I think the words two times wishing them to the core of my belly.

I am deliriously exhausted, so when I get back to the city I retire to my bed in a pair of elastic-waist pants. I've been trying to eat healthfully, so I have a big bowl of greens and cherry tomatoes and other veggies in my lap, and there is a wedge of lemon sunk at the bottom of my water. It's all very pretty and colorful and nutritious, but what I really want is a burger and a strawberry shake—and a bowl of green olives. No, the baby wants a burger, I laugh to myself. I'm a little anxious about the weight gain. The idea of voluntarily gaining weight is a little overwhelming for me, especially amid the skinny minieditors in the biz. I'll rely on salads and grilled chicken until the baby absolutely needs ice cream or lemon meringue, or strawberry shortcake. It all sounds so good and the lettuce looks so, so green. I push it to the side.

I lie alone in bed and contemplate calling A to tell him about my sonogram. *Why hasn't he called me?* I realize he's in Indiana, but *hell-o*, they have phones there. He's clearly drifting away more and more, missing key moments in his child's life. Moments he'll never get back. I don't know what it will take for him to come around and realize he is a part of this. It's impossible to live in limbo much longer. My panic revelry is suddenly sidetracked by a pang of feed-me-now hunger. The salad is wilting on my nightstand. I rise up and fix myself a big plate of scrambled eggs with broccoli and cheese. I fill a coffee mug with orange juice and grab a piece of wheat bread and the jar of peanut butter. After seeing my baby today, I imagine him curled up with his arms under his chin like in the poster from the imaging office. I shovel eggs into my mouth and ease into the pillows, pulling my comforter up to my chin.

The next morning, I swear my pants fit tighter. I'm starving for something like cereal—a box of Cinnamon Toast Crunch with whole, creamy milk and coffee—real coffee—none of that decaf crap. On my way to the bathroom, a wave of nausea almost topples me over. Now I just want soda water and my bed, but I muscle on anyway. The streets of New York City seem different today—like everyone and everything is heaving against me. The wind is mean as it whips through my hair and the taxis seem to be honking for no reason at all as I walk to the subway. I pass two carts on the way and I want coffee and maybe one of the glazed doughnuts pushed against the window. Damn, I am pregnant. Those pastries glued to the cart's window used to make me gag. As I make my way into the station, a man pushes past me and I almost lose my balance. I grab the railing with both hands and center myself before continuing down the stairs to catch the B to the A to the GWB bus terminal. The station smells like pee and gasoline and it sours my stomach almost instantly. I feel my mouth sweat with saliva as I search the station for a trash can or vacant corner.

I bite my Coach glove off and keel over, relieving myself, leaving a puddle of bile on the concrete platform. I wipe my lips, pop a piece of gum into my mouth, and join the crowd of people waiting by the tracks for the train to arrive, pretending like I didn't just puke in public and they all didn't just witness it. I feel their eyes on me and even though my belly hasn't popped, I hang my purse over the front of my red tweed coat. Maybe they're staring at my fantastic Cole Haan boots. *You can do this, Christine.* I put on my iPod and close my eyes. Madonna often cheers me up. Not today. And definitely not "Like a Virgin." The train pulls in and the crowd swarms the door. I'm standing next to a woman with a stroller. Businessmen in suits shove past her. I step on and hold the door open with half of my body, the doors trying to close as I smack them back open.

"Thank you so much," the woman says. "So much."

"Oh, no worries," I say. *This is my new sisterhood. We moms have to stick together*, I think, admiring her diaper bag. It appears to be Burberry. Who knew?

I get to the office early and no one else is in yet. As I'm checking my e-mails, my phone rings and I note the number. It's him. I let it ring a few times, readying myself for "the talk" we've been meaning to have for weeks now. *Deep breath.* I pick up and this is what happens. A tells me he can't be a dad now—timing is off—it's the best decision for *him*. His voice shakes when he says he thinks my brothers and dad will help give our child a good life. He reminds me we haven't been together that long. *Wow.* This is a seamless break, he thinks. Even though I've seen this coming, I feel incredibly duped. All along I thought this could work out—for everyone. I must have been on drugs. This is far more complicated than I ever imagined. He says good-bye. I hang up the phone and stare at the blue computer screen. Five minutes pass.

The phone rings and I startle. I can see from the caller ID that it's a publicist from Factory PR, no doubt highly caffeinated, calling about sending jeans over for tomorrow's test shoot. I could run out of my cubicle and go hide in a bathroom stall. I could fake being sick and burrow in my bed for the day, maybe the whole week. But instead I summon my most professional, slightly chipper voice: "This is Christine," I say into the phone and lower my free hand to my belly. I don't have time to freak out right now. I'm pregnant and I have a photo shoot to schedule.

Twenty minutes later I'm freaking out. My brow is clammy

when I push a piece of hair from it. This intense feeling of dizziness can't be good for the baby. I count to ten and dial Kateri's extension. When she picks up all I say is: "Emergency. Hallway. Now." I hang over the railing, staring down at a line of fake plants with dust on their leaves. I see Kateri's feet coming down the stairs, her flats with chunky gold chain links sewn on the toes, and start to cry. I'm about to tell her I'm a single mom now—about to say it out loud, admit it to someone, make it real. I press up from the railing and look over at her, and she catches me as I turn to slump back down.

"What happened?" she asks.

"It's over," I say. "For real."

"Okay, well, it's been over," she says. "Right?"

"No, it's really over. He doesn't want to be a father. He's . . . he's done," I say.

Kateri looks at me, her eyes glassing over with tears.

"How can I do this all alone?" I say, shaking my head.

Kateri wraps her arm around my waist and pulls me into her.

"It's going to be okay," she says.

"I dunno," I say, combing my fingers through my hair. "I just don't know."

"Hey," she says, looking up at me. "You're not alone."

6

Destination Maternity

I carefully tuck three dollars in change into my wallet and thank the Asian store owner, who is wearing thick gardening gloves, as he hands me a small plastic container of watermelon. Prior to getting pregnant I probably would have crumpled the change into my back pocket and discovered it like a jackpot later on in the week when I was doing laundry. Now I responsibly place every precious dollar back in my wallet. When I do so I see my checkbook and frown angrily at it—even if it is dressed in a classic Coach cover. I reviewed my account balance online yesterday, and although I'm not exactly broke, I clearly need to start considering my purchases. I saw a line for minus two hundred and ten dollars attached to a boutique in Soho: It was for one shirt. That is not okay. Now that A has made it two times clear that he's not participating, I'm a *single*-income family *(family?)* with a baby on the way. The idea of raising my baby fabulously solo is one thing, but on one income is quite another. It's kind of a disaster. Every two weeks my paycheck gets direct-deposited into my checking account. I buy clothes

I don't need. Treat friends to drinks. Eat out way too often. This has got to change. Now.

On my way back to my apartment, I pass Starbucks and suddenly a decaf vanilla latte sounds amazing. I'm just about reaching for the door when I subconsciously slap my hand away. I've only officially been on my new budget for seven minutes. I need a radical shift in priorities, though, because the more I page through the Babies "R" Us catalogue and add things up—crib: $400; 250-count of diapers: $35; bottles: $40—the more I realize how in over my head I really am. I run across the street and sit on the stoop of my apartment building and look out at Fiftieth Street.

I love New York, but, as fabulous as Manhattan is, the food, the celeb sightings, the shopping, it's also one of the most ludicrously expensive cities in the world. This means the majority of its inhabitants are forced to squeeze their entire lives into tiny shoebox apartments that anywhere else in the country would not be deemed large enough to house the family pet. I think my current bedroom is the size of the full bathroom in the house I grew up in. Let's put it this way, my dorm room was bigger. Which brings me to my closet, which is in the hallway of a three-bedroom apartment I share with two girls I met on Craigslist.com—only in New York. I guess it could be worse. My friend Sherri once lived in an apartment with a bathroom just off the kitchen (like, when you walk out of it, you are confronted with the stove), with a roommate who kept rats as pets and drew pictures of poop for fun.

I moved to this dark apartment with an old-fashioned

elevator after my old roommate announced she was moving in with her boyfriend a couple months before our lease was up. Suddenly homeless, I panicked and started trolling the "Housing Wanted" section of Craigslist.com. I responded to a lot of ads, but deemed each a dead end when I actually saw the space. One woman claimed she had a cozy room with a closet to rent in the East Village. Perfect. Well, "cozy" apparently means the size of a cubicle, and "closet" translated to a weathered wardrobe without a door. Oh, and she neglected to mention her dogs—three yappy Chihuahuas. The place smelled like pee. I also responded to an ad posted by a guy with an amazing apartment—marble kitchen countertops, real furniture (none of the usual Ikea stuff), and an outdoor space with lounge chairs. But the guy was less interested in my credit history than in my ass. He kept trying to run his fingers through his buzz cut, and an internal *Oh. My. God. Get-me-outta-here* dialogue played on repeat in my head. So, when I saw an ad posted for a female roommate in a spacious three bedroom in a part of Midtown called Turtle Bay, I sent an e-mail right away and got a speedy response. In a strange bit of foreshadowing, it turned out one of the roommates worked as an editor at *Parents* magazine, and the other designed children's clothes (seriously). Even though the exchange was just over a cold e-mail, I instantly knew I'd found my new home. I was so relieved these girls were normal that I wasn't fazed at all, not by my hallway closet, nor by the scary fire escape just outside my window, which, to me, seemed like an advertisement for a potential rapist. Suddenly I realize the quirky apartment I love to hate might well be my last one in the city. *God knows I can't afford to live in NYC with a baby*, I think.

It's only nine a.m. but the sidewalk is already thick with traffic. A woman in sweats, urgently power-walking, cuts off a grandmother pushing a basket of groceries. The more people walk past me, the more I begin to fantasize about their lives. A group of three girls, linked arm in arm, skip past in yoga pants. The two are dragging the other along. She's behind a pair of sunglasses and her hair is pulled back in a half-ponytail. Bet they were out until four a.m. but prepaid for yoga class. I've been "that girl" wobbling over the cobblestone in heels in the Meatpacking District at three a.m., hailing a cab with my girl-friends wading around me, giggling and still dancing to the muted, booming music, wafting out from a club with a big steel door. I haven't had a night out like that since I found out I was pregnant. I can't imagine sipping water with lime dis-guised as a vodka tonic while I position an oversized clutch bag over my abdomen. I feel so far away from my friends. Kateri, Nic, Lo and I have been playing phone tag—though I'm not exactly in the game. I let their calls go to voice mail on purpose. What is there to talk about? I'm pregnant. You're not. See you in nine months. I'm not depressed. I'm realistic. No one wants to tote a pregnant friend around at a nightclub. Before I met A I was luxuriating in the single life in Manhattan and loving it. I was navigating my career, taking any extra work I could get just to beef up my clip book—even a reporter gig for a no-name newsletter in Battery Park and a stylist's assistant job for the well-known national gay glossy *Passport*. There was no better feeling than heading out for a night on the town with my girls, and stumbling back home at three or four in the morning, feet aching from dancing. Waking up to a text that read: *Mimosas. Spring Street Natural. Noon.* Brunch is another highly exaggerated tradition in Manhattan—it's just eggs and booze, but nonetheless I love it, especially behind a pair of oversize sunglasses that shields my pounding, hungover head from the sun. Nothing a Bloody Mary can't fix. These days I can't even imagine going to dinner with my friends, which is crazy because Kateri and I ate out all the time.

We grabbed quick dinners and wine at our favorite café, Gitane. I saw Leonardo DiCaprio there once, drinking espresso, and a pregnant Maggie Gyllenhaal and her husband running their fingers down a menu. One night Kateri and I were sitting at the counter aglow with stubby candles in chubby glass cups when a handsome suit with a receding hairline slid onto the stool next to me. I picked up my wine and winked at Kateri. I smile and ease back on the stoop, stretching my legs out. The memory of that night comes flooding back like a pretty black-and-white photograph, the characters coming to life . . .

"You should get the couscous," I hummed in his direction.

"Oh yeah," he said, smiling down at the menu. His bottom teeth were crowded.

"It's the best," I said, and upped my glass in the air signaling the waiter for a refill.

Kateri nudged my side with her knuckles and dissolved her laughing with a big gulp of wine. We spent the next hour flirting with him and arguing that while "Paris may be magical, New York isn't just hard." Before his check arrived he brought up his wife—*wife?* And kid—*kid?* I couldn't imagine him with a doting wife on his arm or a little barefoot girl with arms and legs wrapped around his chest. I wonder if one day people will see me and be shocked that I have a toddler at home? Here's hoping my postbaby body isn't a telltale sign.

I step out of the shower and flip my head upside down, crisscrossing a towel over my damp hair. As I stare in the vanity mirror, I'm pleased my face doesn't look pregnant. I thought for sure I'd have chimpmunk cheeks by now. Whenever I gain weight it first shows up in my face, then my ass. Still, as I fold the towel over my body, I can't help but notice the thickness in my hips. I've got clothes on the mind now that I'm fifteen weeks pregnant and starting to grow out of most of my wardrobe. I push a towel around the tile floor with my foot to sop up the water, and switch the light off. As I approach my closet, I hope my yoga pants are hanging in there and not in a ball in my hamper. I hear a roommate's door open, then close, then the bathroom door close, and I suddenly loathe my closet. I'm standing here in a towel, with a thick waist starting to round at the belly button. Sometimes I don't want to be pregnant, but I *do* want my baby—all in the same thought. Wearing a belly and not a wedding ring bothers me. My life is backward. My roommates are sweet girls but I can't help but wonder if they think I'm an idiot for getting myself "knocked up." Probably. I told them over an e-mail and I'm sure a lot got lost in translation since the gist was: "Pregnant. Moving out July 1." Both sent back e-mails to the tune of congratulations and it was otherwise never discussed. That is, until the children's clothes designer roommate walked into the kitchen when I was washing my dishes. When she asked how things were going, I told her. Told her I was single now. She proceeded to tell me about a friend of hers from college, who, incidentally, went through a similar situation. She said the baby was the best thing that happened to her friend. We talked for a few more minutes but all I kept hearing was *the baby was the best thing . . . the baby was the best thing.*

As I flip through hangers of jeans, I realize I'm officially down to one pair that still fits, and that's only because the denim is mixed with elastic. Otherwise my jeans only fit when I loop a hair tie through the eye and around the button, and even then, the thighs are tight. I decide to slip into a pair of black yoga pants and an oversize, off-the-shoulder sweat-shirt. Paired with laceless Converse, I look kind of cute and not *so* pregnant, which is ironic since I'm heading to a clump of maternity stores. It's time. As tempting as it is, I can't live in pajama pants for the next five months. Kateri offered to come with me, but I prefer to go alone. If she did come it would be just one more thing that is different. We used to eat brunch on Sundays and raid Urban Outfitters afterward in search of tops for "going out." I can't deal with, um, plus-size shopping with my friends who are reed thin. Besides, I have Baby to keep me company. We're a team now.

I grab my black coat with the fur-trim hood and my ridiculously overpriced Marc Jacobs handbag and head out— only to get halfway down the stairs and realize I have to pee— again. I pee so much now I might as well not leave the bathroom. I jumped out of the shower this morning and squatted over the toilet while a puddle of soapy water collected at my feet. The urge to pee wakes me in the night and it's like nothing I've ever experienced before. If I don't hotfoot it to the bathroom, I'm peeing in my bed. I've recently thought about keeping some sort of container in my room should the need to pee be compromised by one of my roommates occupying the bathroom.

It's March and cold. I jump over the snow pushed up against curbs. I am completely disguised as just another twenty-something in the city thanks to my layering technique. As I approach Fifty-seventh Street I see the massive, one-stop store known as Destination Maternity. It houses Pea in a Pod, Mimi, Motherhood, and Edamame—a swank mommy spa that offers prenatal massage. As it gets closer and closer I think seriously about turning around and shopping online. *I cannot believe this is happening* is all I'm thinking as I surrender to the megastore. As I look up I hear the theme music to *Rocky* in my head. *We can handle this, Baby—it's just shopping.*

Upon entering Pea in a Pod (I figure I'll work my way up), I see a chipper salesgirl making a beeline for me. I cautiously slip my left hand into my pocket.

"Shopping for a gift?" she says as she weaves her fingers into one another and bounces them midchest. I decide I hate her and I kind of want to mimic her and quip "No" in all my snarky glory. I don't.

"Actually, I'm shopping for jeans—for, uh, um, me," as I run my finger down a wall of folded-up denim. I wait for her to think I'm kidding, but she doesn't. Hmm. Point noted. Random person doesn't find it particularly odd that I'm with child.

"Congratulations!" she squeals, and she takes my arm and walks me over to a rack of jeans on hangers. I kind of love her now.

"We have Sevens, True Religion, Joe's," she hums while pointing to the mosh of indigo.

Sevens?! Interesting. I have Sevens at home. They don't fit anymore, but who knew my favorite jeans came for the pregnantly challenged? The salesgirl asks me if I want her assistance and I feel bad saying no, but my biggest pet peeve is salespeople trying to up-sell me. I don't care how cute that shirt looks with those jeans. I don't want it. There's no persuading me. I'm the worst, and sometimes I leave clothes in the fitting room. I politely decline her help and she offers me orange juice or a bottle of water. *Orange juice or water?* It occurs to me that this might be the most incredible shopping experience of my life. She's probably scared to counter my

"No, thank you" with an "Are you sure?" because she realizes pregnant women are hormonal and no means *no*.

I notice a few other women perusing the store. I'm not sure why I do this, but every time I spot a bump, I look for a diamond, and bam, every pregnant woman in the store has one—most of them are pretty diesel, too. After all, we're on Madison Avenue, about a step away from Dior and Chanel. Just as I fling a second pair of jeans over my arms, I notice a handsome, clean-shaven man with wavy hair combed back scoot in with a cup from Jamba Juice. His wife (I'm assuming) wants to know why he removed the paper from the straw. He apologizes. I smirk and walk past them as she piles a bunch of tops onto his unsuspecting arms.

There's a set of couches just outside the row of fitting rooms. Two men are sitting on them, looking bored; one keeps looking at his watch. The salesgirl asks me if I am "up for that juice yet?" as she removes the jeans from my arms, sweeps a curtain open, and hangs them up for me. *Geesh, enough with the juice already. Do I look folic-acid deprived?* I decline, but thank her anyway. On her way out of the room she reminds me to "wear the belly, to forecast the perfect fit." I smile and, of course, try to look like I know what she is talking about, but I don't. What the hell is she talking about? And then I see it—a puffy little pillow with a Velcro strap. *Hmm,* I hum as I peel my jacket off and let it fall carelessly to the floor, catching my reflection in the mirror. *Hello in there. It's Mama. We're buying jeans for us now. I'll buy you some bitty jeans soon.*

I already bought the baby a onesie. I bought it on impulse

one afternoon while I was out walking. Which was a far stretch from the last thing I bought on impulse before getting pregnant: a Marc Jacobs bag. It cost a helluva lot more than the eight-buck onesie, which I talked down to six. I handed the vendor six bucks and she smiled at my stomach, still defiantly flat, and said good luck. I took the onesie out of the bag and looked at the iconic I ♥ NY image as I walked to the F train that would take me to Midtown. *We love New York, Baby*, I said, under the watchful tower of the Chrysler building in the distance. I balled the onesie up and stuck it in the back of my underwear drawer when I got home. It was my first official baby purchase and later when I was rummaging among my thongs, lacy panties, and potpourri-scented pillows I found it and it freaked me out a little. In these early days it's somehow easy to momentarily forget I am pregnant until little reminders like a baby shirt tangled in with my underwear jars me back to reality. This baby pillow is screaming reality.

I do not want to wear it. I fully intend to be the girl who barely shows with the skinny arms and face and just a basketball bump under her sweater. But when I realize I'm potentially about to spend $225 on *one* pair of jeans and this just after depriving myself of a four-dollar latte this morning, I decide I better strap it on. I center the pillow and secure the strap. I pull my sweatshirt down over it and stand there in my underwear and white ankle socks. I fold my hands on the front of my shirt and shift to the side to observe the roundness. I wonder if the pillow is too high or too low. I bet the salesgirl would love to rescue me right about now, juice in hand, but I just pull on a pair of jeans.

There is a wide, navy blue band where the button and zip-per should be. *Hmmm.* I shimmy them up over the pillow and my belly squashes under it. For some reason I don't think my real belly is going to cooperate like this pillow—this *shit* is lame. I release the straps and hear a quick scratching from the Velcro. I scoot to the side and hold the elastic band out as far as it will go. This is ridiculous. I can't spend $225 on a pair of pants. What the hell is wrong with me? I clip the jeans back on their hanger and leave them hanging on the hook on the door. *Okay, back to the budget. Time to hit up the Liz Lange section at Target,* I think as I step into my yoga pants and dance them up my legs. I hear the woman in the room next to me call out, "Does this make me look fat, hon?"

"You're pregnant and beautiful, dear," answers a hefty voice.

They sound like the perfect couple and I bet he's going to pay for her dress with his platinum AmEx and then they'll retire to their duplex on the Upper West Side, where the nursery is half-done, spotted with eggshell on one wall and mint green on the other, as they're still not sure what works best. He'll teach his son how to play baseball in Central Park. Which gets me thinking about my kid. Not only, by some cosmic miracle, do I need to financially provide for her, I'm going to have to rear her as a mom and a dad. And if the sonogram technician is correct and her is indeed a he, then I'm going to have to learn how to throw a football and pitch a tent to boot. Part of me wants to live in this tiny dressing room until everyone leaves the store. I suddenly don't feel like mother of the year. Those $225-dollar jeans are starting to look more cute and less expensive the more time I spend in here and listen to this happy husband tell his happy wife she looks "hot, pregnant." I grab my bag, jacket—and the jeans.

The salesgirl greets me at the counter. She hands me a clipboard and asks if I want to sign up for a credit card. Tempting. No, thank you. How about a copy of *Parenting* magazine? she asks, and points to one. I glance at the smiling woman on the cover, holding an adorable cherub, definitely wearing blush or Photoshopped for sure. No, thank you. She rings me up and I fork over my debit card, wondering if there's enough to cover this pair of ol' golden jeans. Hope so. She hands me my bag and tells me to come again. I'm exhausted. The purchase doesn't make me feel immediately better like it would have six months and three sizes smaller ago. I half-smile: "Can I have some juice?" I definitely need a drink.

On my way home I receive a text from Nic. It reads that if I don't meet her at Bloomies for a mani/pedi now, she's "kidnapping me and bringing me there with my hands tied up in a Pucci scarf." *What the heck*, I think. After spending $225 on jeans, another fifty isn't going to kill me. Maybe today will be like one of those "bad days" when you're dieting. So I ate a burger and ice cream cone. Tomorrow, I'll have a salad. Today was a little extreme on my debit card, tomorrow will be like a game: I wonder if I can go all day sans spending even one buck. When I walk into the salon, Nic is reading *Cosmo*. She looks up: "Hey, Mama!" I smile and climb into the pedicure chair next to her.

"Hi, Baby," she says, leaning into my belly.

"How was your day?" she asks me. "Mine was crazy. Spent most of it at the office working!"

"It just got better!" I say. "Thanks for texting."

"Any new A interaction?" she asks, and my eyes fill with tears—sad or angry ones, I'm not sure.

"No," I say, passing a bottle of nail polish, called "Soul Mate" for God's sake, through my fingers, too embarrassed to tell her that I called him the other day when I was at the New York Health and Racquet Club trying to defy the baby weight. I was on the treadmill and suddenly pushed the big red emergency stop button and steadied myself on the railings. I pulled my cell out of my back pocket and dialed A to ask him if we should have dinner downtown to talk more about this. Clearly he would have calmed down and come to his senses by then. But he told me he didn't want to be involved and that his mind was made up. I stuttered "okay" and got back on the treadmill, feeling my feet push off the slow, level plank and how it actually felt like I was heaving up a steep hill with no peak in sight. I stared out the floor-to-ceiling windows. The city was overcast and gray all over. I look over at Nic, who's digging in her purse.

"What exactly happened with you two?" she says with her nose in the bag.

"I don't know, exactly. Too fast, too soon, I think," I say. "We just wanted . . . different things."

"He monopolized all of your time, Chris. I mean, the third day you guys were dating he showed up with things to keep at your apartment. Hello—red flag!" she says. I look over, half-smiling, shrugging my shoulders at her.

"It's all my fault. I wigged out and scared him with how much day care costs and told him to find us a nice apartment and said I wanted to break up, we hardly knew each other and . . . It's just all my fault," I say, shaking my head.

"So, do we hate him?" she says, looking at me. Do we hate my baby's father? I turn the thought over in my head.

"No," I say, tears escaping me.

I'm so irresponsible. How can I be enough for my baby? How will I do this on my own? I think. Nic breaks off a piece of her vegan cookie, smiles, and hands it to me. It shouldn't be enough to make me feel better, but right now, in this very easy moment, it does. We both lean back into the chairs, the city dimming some just outside, as day turns to dusk. I survived another day, I suppose.

7

Men

I can't sleep. The heater sounds like a jackhammer. It's dark and I find the moon in the window. My bed seems bigger. A used to sleep on the side pushed up against the wall. I still sleep on *my* side—just a wrinkle under the covers. I feel exceptionally anxious about money right now. I was such a bonehead for buying those jeans—and getting my nails done. *But they do look good,* I think, admiring the subtle flecks of red in the black polish. How am I actually going to support this baby? Maybe I can write an essay about this—at two dollars a word I could make two thousand bucks, easy. Wait. Do I want to write about this? I roll over and open the drawer of my night table. I pull out a folded piece of paper—an essay by Maya Angelou, one of my favorite writers. Early last week at work I found myself with a binder of tear sheets in my lap, a pile of jeans at my feet, and a "single mom" search processing on Google. Up popped: *The Decision That Changed My Life: Keeping My Baby.* Maya Angelou wrote about getting pregnant at sixteen and hiding it from her parents. When she finally told her mother, she proclaimed: "We are going to have our baby!" Years later when Maya was married and she tried to get pregnant, she couldn't. I read the article twice, stifling the tears because I was at my desk "working."

I pull the essay up to my lips. *I can write about this. This is the happiest and scariest time in my life! How relevant*, I think. I am not the only twenty-something out there who's single and pregnant. Perhaps my story is relatable—to someone, anyone. I turn over thinking about how the Keith article in *Glamour* was so well-received—it has already been optioned by the United Kingdom and French editions. Now a producer from *20/20* wants to interview me for a segment about "making tough choices." When I got the call last week, I was wishing away morning sickness with a piece of mint gum. *20/20* wants to interview *me*—fucking now! Great timing! I e-mailed Genevieve Field, the editor of the article, to tell her that *20/20* was interested and also that I was pregnant. I sent her a onesie a couple of months ago congratulating her on her new son. Now she was wishing me well and asking who the lucky guy is. After a nonchalant e-mail explaining I was a warrior single mama in training, I asked her if she knew anyone at Babble.com—an edgy parenting website. Genevieve hasn't gotten back to me yet.

Working full-time, in-house on the start-up magazine, recently named *Cocktail*, and freelancing at my apartment late into the night is exhausting, but it's my livelihood and, I'm starting to realize more and more, our lifeline. I don't think I'll ever be able to retire. It's a scary thought and it's sabotaging any chance of falling asleep at the moment. I know I should collect child support and it should be as easy as just cashing the check every week, but it's not. He doesn't want to be a part of this, so fine, then I'll handle this on my own—that's the proud Christine talking. My mind is racing: Can I even take a full maternity leave now? How will I afford it? I hear my phone ringing. I whip my covers into the air, looking for it.

"Hello?" I say.

"How are you feeling?" my dad asks.

"Fine," I say.

"What are you up to?" he asks.

"Nothing. In bed. Tired," I say.

"Well, I just wanted to check on you. Good night, then," he says.

"Night. Love you," I say.

"Love you both," he says.

My father had his jaw removed and reconstructed with titanium and bone grafts four years ago after he was diagnosed at Sloan-Kettering with ameloblastoma. The tumor was benign but it was aggressive, increasingly deforming his face and muffling his speech. He got sick two months after Keith broke his neck. The two most important men in my life were slipping away . . . I felt like they were dying even though they weren't, really. I was being pulled from hospital to hospital—the floodwaters were fast, came without warning, and left me breathless. Everything I knew felt like a lie, and the walls were closing in on me. I decided to be a hero—it was all I knew. I feel similar now.

Tomorrow is my twenty-week sonogram and I should be asleep, but I'm wide awake thinking how I'll explain A's absence to my unassuming child. When that day will come, if maybe I'll be married or still alone in a tiny apartment—uncertain moments like these plague me. I'll be at my desk at work, or standing in line at the grocery store, or waiting for the subway, and I suddenly think: *Holy shit, I'm pregnant. I'm going to be a single mother. I'm not ready for this. How the hell did this happen. How will I pay for college?* My heart races and I have to do everything in my power to quell a full-on anxiety attack. I always talk myself down from the ledge. My baby constantly returns me to calm. Sweeter images dance in my head—a little hand wrapped around my finger, baby blankets smelling of soft powder; quiet nights in the rocking chair (that I need to buy) watching the sky explode into a mess of pink and orange until the sun is too low to see. You know, shit you see in movies. But right now, tonight, those images are not making me feel any better. I take a breath, then another one. *My baby is going to hate me when she realizes it's just me. Is Gen going to call? I need to get my teeth cleaned. I'm low on OJ. I—What was that?* I shoot up in my bed and pull the covers out, looking down at my stomach. I feel it again. A flick-flick. *Baby?* I wait for her to flick me again. She does. "I feel ya!" I say out loud, realizing I'm *not* talking to myself—I'm talking to my baby. "Do it again!" I wish for it. Her fluttering comes again at such an amazing time. I'm exhausted with anxiety. Second-guessing myself has become sort of an obsession, but then this happens, this miraculous thing. I flop down, spreading my hands over my belly, and try to sense her again. Nothing. *Good night, Baby,* I think as I turn over, tucking the Maya Angelou essay under my pillow.

The next day I hop, not-so-effortlessly, into a skinnier version of a dentist chair and wait for the technician to enter. It's April 20—my brother Brian's twenty-fourth birthday. I make a mental note to call him. I'm having a sonogram today to measure my fetus's growing anatomy and most importantly, find out once and for all whether my baby has a penis or not. As I lay back in the chair I think about the fruit manifestations my baby has gone through over the past couple of months—I've signed up on a website that sends me a weekly e-mail comparing my fetus to a piece of fruit. This week I got an e-mail telling me my baby is no longer the size of an "apple" (she's been a "sesame seed," an "apricot," a "big plum") but now, a banana. A banana? It's a weird, skinny, yellow comparison.

Skinny. Something I'm definitely not anymore. I'm really starting to show. I'm no longer going through a weird, chubby stage, as it often seemed to me those first few weeks. I iron my hands over my stomach and feel that things are starting to balance out in my abdomen as my palms curve down the hill poking from under my shirt. People on the street notice my belly and smile—at it, not me. This morning at work before I left for this appointment, Piper, an editor just two years older than me, palmed my belly and declared it "amazing." I think she also meant: "Thank God I'm not pregnant!" James and I started a little (kind of sick) joke where I call him "Baby Daddy" and he tells me I'm "glowing." Everyone isn't so articulate. My brother Brian recently told me I looked "chunk." Just "chunk," not even chunky. I don't know which is worse.

My biggest realization of my new physique came when I let my friend Sherri photograph me. We met in college at the University of the Arts and easily bonded over Olde English forties at loud parties thrown in courtyards of apartment complexes. Life was predictable then. Sleep. School. Party. Repeat.

I broke the baby news to her in a MySpace.com message. After the OMG response, she said she wanted to shoot me. She's a photographer and my friend so even when she mentioned it would be nude, I thought, *Um, why not?* When we were in school I posed for her assignments. In one I wore ripped fishnet stockings. She positioned me on the counter next to the stove's burners and just behind a block of knives. It was freeing and beautiful to pretend—jump into a world of make-believe where everyone wore red lipstick and panty hose with suggestive runs in them. My belly shoot was not make-believe. Instead, the sun filtered in through the blinds and created swirly designs all over my hard stomach. My hair, tangled in knots, fell appropriately on my chest and the reflection in the mirror was prettier than I thought it would be. I looked healthy and young. Inhibition went out the window. I sat for an hour, cradling my stomach under my hands, not once feeling afraid or anxious, just completely calm. The images are in black and white—a perfect moment suspended in time.

A nurse comes in and places a tube of gel on the tray, shaking my art-house images from my head.

"The tech will be in shortly." She smiles.

I know this hurry-up-and-wait routine. She's totally lying. I'll be here for another thirty minutes before the tech comes in. My mom wanted to come. Kateri wanted to come, but I wanted to go it alone. I've turned into a bit of a loner and, I'm not sure, but something tells me I'm subconsciously preparing for single motherhood.

I hear the nurse tell the tech, "Coppa behind curtain three is ready," so I start to tuck my tunic into my bra, revealing a nipple just as *he* walks in. He is very cute, wearing faded green baggy scrubs and old-school Nikes with an orange swoosh. Suddenly I realize my nipple is still very present and things start happening in slow motion. I should quickly cover up and say "hello," but the rush of heat spreading across my cheeks distracts me. I start to swallow air and make believe I don't know he's here.

"What's up? I'm Jake," he says, while slowly typing something and looking down at the keyboard.

Silence. I cannot believe a guy—a hot guy, at that—is doing my sonogram. This has got to be the most sensitive man on the planet; he takes pictures of fetuses all day long and squirts gel on big, round bellies. *Don't ask me about the father. Don't ask me about the father,* I think as I lay here, belly exposed. Jake gets up from the stool on wheels and reaches for the tube of gel. As I follow Jake with my eyes, feeling a mix of vulnerability and pure attraction, I realize A will in all probability never, *ever* have to endure the *Please don't ask about the child I abandoned. Please don't . . .* because no one knows about his little secret. A is tall and handsome, has a wide smile and an easy midwestern twang in his voice. No one would ever suspect he abandoned his unborn child. He looks like the poster child for "boy next door."

"You know the drill. It's going to feel warm." Jake smirks and I realize he has a chip in his front tooth and an almost invisible scar running through his left eyebrow. Adorable. *Focus, Christine. Focus—on Baby and impending single motherhood.*

He rubs the tool over my belly and says: "Big day! We're going to see everything. Do you want to know the sex?" He smiles at the screen when he says "sex." I bet he has pictures of his little patients taped to his fridge, but not in a creepy way.

"Yes, I want sex!—to *know* the sex." I did not just say that. Seriously. *Seriously,* I did. He smiles and scoots to the desk.

The screen is a wash of gray and black, until he dips a piece of paper towel into my jeans, forcing them lower, so the tool can inch south. "Just need to get a little lower," he says.

All of a sudden there is an actual baby and not a tadpole on the screen. She's curled up, then she's stretching, then she's bouncing off my uterine wall—literally popping back and forth. I am amazed how much my baby has grown in just eight weeks. "Hello," I say out loud, reaching for the screen like I could pull the baby from the murky pool. I try to feel her moving, but I can't.

"I can't feel her," I say, a little worried.

"Her?" Jake says, staring at the screen, squinting his eyes.

"Yes, well, I'm still thinking it's a girl. Is it weird I can't feel her, but she's moving?" I persist.

Jake holds the tool still on my belly and clicks the mouse several times, saving images.

"Well, she's still pretty small," he responds.

I shift my gaze from the screen to his beautiful arm. His bicep is popping and flexing with each click of the mouse. I find myself wondering what kind of underwear he's wearing. As I lay here musing and cooing over my baby—and Jake—I start to wonder if I'll ever get to date again or if I'll be observing men and playing the guess-the-brand-of-underwear game for the rest of my life. These days, everyone I know is quick to tell me I'm beautiful and smart and I'm obviously going to fall in love, get married, my husband is going to adopt my baby . . . and happily ever after we will be. It's reassuring in theory, but I just don't agree with the majority vote on my love life. Show me a guy who is going to jump headfirst into a relationship with a woman *and* a baby. My friends use the example of the singer Seal, who fell for supermodel Heidi Klum (when she was pregnant with her ex's baby) as a way of defending their argument. When I point out that I'm not a supermodel, they quickly go to the favorite backup, the actor Matt Damon, who married a single mother who was working as a bartender in Florida when they met.

I'm halfway through the appointment and Jake hasn't asked about my "husband," or "boyfriend," or the "father of the baby."

"Are you comfortable?" Jake asks.

I shift uneasily, because honestly, my back hurts and I have to pee—really pee.

"I'm great!" I lie.

"See this little cross, flexing up and down?" Jake asks while tracing his finger on the image on the screen.

"Yep." I smile and gaze at him, not the cross.

"That's your baby's heart," he says.

I stare at the screen and watch as the cross pops back and forth like two little sticks trying to make a fire. Suddenly I am very aware of my own heart and my breath and I feel like I can't catch it, but I'm not scared or anxious. I am sustaining this heart, this ever-gentle life. I feel my mouth open in amazement and when Jake asks me if I want to know the sex, I turn to him, smile, and nod yes. But I realize it doesn't even matter anymore. A tiny force is growing, moving and living inside of me. The cross is thumping up and down and the flicker of a quiet white light is the only thing I see—my baby, my whole heart. "Hello, little one," I say out loud, forgetting Jake is even in the room.

"Say hi to Mommy," Jake says, smiling at the screen.

Jake rolls the tool over my belly a couple of times and all of a sudden Baby startles and swims away. When Jake tries to catch her, she zips off again. It's like a video game. Jake adjusts the chair back and I watch as Baby slides off into a nook and settles. Soon Jake is back to freezing images, and when he zooms into one and points to a tiny nub, a little sprout of a thing, I smile.

"Can you tell?" He smiles.

"Yes." I smile, never taking my eyes off the screen. All

eyes are on the new guy in the room—my son—I'm having a son. *Hello, Baby Boy*, I think as I watch him tuck his arms under his chin.

I excuse myself to the ladies' room while Jake crunches numbers and completes the report for Dr. Collado. As I wash my hands, I am relieved I made it through the appointment without having to get into the husband/father thing. In a way, I feel like I dodged a bullet. Just last week someone at my office told me she didn't realize I was married. I'm not. It's something I'd just as soon not talk about, especially with nosy strangers, so getting through this hour-long appointment with no mention of my personal life is kind of epic.

I walk back into the room to collect my bag and jacket.

"Are we through here?" I ask.

"Except for one thing," he says, and hands me a square of paper.

It's a printout of my son's head from the sonogram. His nose looks like a tiny ski slope and his lips—his lips are, uh, full with a quirky little word bubble that Jake typed in above them, reading: "Hi, Mommy and Daddy." I could make this a nonissue. I could thank Jake for the gesture, slip the photo in the front pocket of my purse, put my jacket on, and go get a strawberry milkshake at the McDonald's drive-through I noticed on my way here. I turn to leave, then stop halfway. This is not cool. I don't want this shit in the scrapbook I fully intend to make for my son. Not once did Jake ask about the "father" so why would he assume there is one? I could be an artificially inseminated lesbian. Or what if my husband died in a horrible car crash after getting me pregnant? Or what if my boyfriend was dating a supermodel, like the Tom Brady–Bridget Moynahan–Gisele Bundchen triangle? How dare this guy, this Jake person, assume there is a "father." He's suddenly not so cute anymore.

"Actually, Jake, I'm a single mom. Can you edit this for me?" I smile and hand the photo over to him. Saying this out loud, admitting my reality to a stranger, is empowering. So what! I'm a single mom. Yeah, I am. It doesn't sound as bad as I thought it would. I'm not a criminal. I'm a pregnant woman.

His cheeks are the ones that change color this time and I feel his fingers touch mine as he scrambles to remove the image from my grip.

"Oh. My. God. I'm so sorry." His voice shakes.

"Nothing to be sorry about, Jake." I smile, upping my nose, just slightly, in the air. *Nothing at all to be sorry about,* I think as I watch Jake type: H-I M-O-M-M-Y onto the screen. He hands me my new photo and apologizes again, but he sounds muffled. *My baby has a perfect head,* is all I'm thinking as I push through the curtain.

While I wait for the elevator, my phone tings with a text message from Kateri. It reads: "Pink or blue?"

I smile. "Blue," I say out loud as I key it in.

8

Babymoon

I sit on the steps of an oval, saline pool and squint up at the afternoon sun, while my fingers comb through my hair and twirl it into a loose bun. *I can't believe I am six months pregnant on a babymoon in Palm Springs, California—all a-lone.* I can't believe the term *babymoon* is in my vocabulary. When I first boarded the plane, I asked a flight attendant if she could please help me hoist my bag into the overhead storage compartment. She pinched her lips together, looked me in the eyes, then in the belly, then in the eyes again, and said, "That isn't my job." I understand the evolution of stewardesses to flight attendants. I get that I'm not getting my pillow fluffed, but I'm pregnant and I thought the human thing to do would be to take two seconds and help me. I really want to snap back, but I also don't want to risk getting thrown off the plane, and these days it doesn't take much to be escorted to a back room in the airport.

"I got it," I hear someone say as I whirl around. A handsome man with his top button opened and tie loosened smiles and shoves my bag into the compartment.

"Thanks so much." I smile and subconsciously touch

my stomach. I love the idea of meeting someone while traveling. When I was in college I took the train home every now and then. I once met a New York City stockbroker and he bought me beer because I was only nineteen at the time. We spent the whole ride talking about New York City and Philly and debating whether Geno's or Pat's had the better cheesesteak sandwich—Geno's, or so I argued. We exchanged numbers and spent a couple of days sending each other flirty text messages, but I never did see him again. File it under missed connections.

"Do you have anything else to store?" He extends his hand to mine. I want to slip his hand into mine, if only to feel connected to another person for a moment. The last person I kissed was A. That was in February and it's July now. I'm starting to feel a little robotic. Eat. Sleep. Work. Repeat. Jake had me squirming in my seat at my ultrasound and even Joey on *Friends* is appealing these days. This can't be it. I'm pretty. I'm smart. I'm funny. I'm fucking twenty-six.

I settle into my seat and stretch out the seat belt as my good Samaritan introduces himself. "I'm Chris, by the way." And he excuses himself as he scoots into the middle seat.

"I'm sorry, let me get up," I say.

"Nonsense," he says, and buckles his belt. "I hate the middle seat." He smiles and pulls his iPod out from his briefcase. I want to say something back to keep the conversation alive but something comes over me suddenly, an uneasy feeling of dread. *What the hell am I doing? Why am I going to Palm Springs?* I think as the engines start to rev and a stale gush of airplane air kisses my forehead. As the plane speeds stead-

fastly away and up, my baby starts to kick me uncontrollably—
and we're off. Suddenly I'm caressing my belly, trying to calm
my baby down, so much so in fact, my own fear dissolves. If he
were here already, he'd be on my lap and I'd be stroking his
head and pinning a pair of plastic wings to his shirt collar.

I sleep for most of the flight and even welcome the layover
in Dallas. I can't wait to stretch my legs and buy a magazine
and a soft pretzel (maybe two) that tastes like a cinnamon bun.
I mull around the airport and take a photo of a funny rack of
cowboy hats with a sign above them that says, "Howdy."

Back on board, Chris catches my eye, and although we're
not sitting together on this flight, he comes over and says hello.

"Palm Springs?" he says.

"Yep. Taking a little vacation, before my little surprise
comes." I wait for him to look at my naked ring finger. He
doesn't.

"Nice. I have a business conference." He smiles as he wig-
gles into another middle seat two rows up.

I get up to pee six times in the course of four hours and a
middle-aged flight attendant with a few silver hairs keeps
looking me up and down. I don't care. I'm exhausted. I just
want to get to my hotel, order a huge pile of macaroni and
cheese (which I know exists because I saw it on the website's
menu section), and take a nap in a hammock. I sense the
plane descending when the pilot comes on over the speaker.

"Okay, folks, we're preparing for our final descent into
Palm Springs, California, where it's ninety-two degrees, dry,
and sunny."

I'm relieved to hear him say we are almost there because I

am suddenly very claustrophobic and clammy. As the plane thumps, lower and lower, I feel my stomach drop. My head clouds with a mix of anxiety and dizziness. *I'm going to puke*, I think as I furiously pull the pocket on the chair in front of me open. *Bag, bag, bag! No bag?* I wrestle my seat belt off and just as I come to my feet I am confronted by ol' silver hair, who tells me to "take a seat."

"I'm going to throw up." I cup my hands over my mouth.

"Ma'am, we're getting ready to land. Take your seat," she insists. But I nod no and tell her I need, need, need to use the bathroom.

She takes my arm and leads me to the narrow bathroom where I proceed to throw up pretzel into the sink. A couple of seconds in, she starts pounding on the door telling me I need to take my seat—that the plane is about to land. She's lying. We have a good half hour more in the air. I open the door and she leads me to my seat. I expect her to turn away and buckle up herself, but she doesn't.

"You're a liability," she says. She's a bitch. I wonder if she's related to the one who wouldn't help me with my bags.

I look at her blankly. I want to tell her to fuck off.

"If you are prone to get sick—carry a baggie!" she says.

Tears pass through my fingers and my nose runs until I wipe it with my hand. I hear Chris yell, "Jesus, lady," and the woman sitting next to me offers me a tissue. When silver hair disappears another flight attendant ducks down on her knees, looks up at me, and apologizes. "She's a little testy. Can I get you anything?" I catch my breath and wipe the mascara from under my eyes. I realize I'm not crying because of the flight attendant. I'm alone. I'm all alone.

I cup my hands into the water and splash my face a couple of times. *Man, it's hot,* I think as a reed-thin blonde dips in next to me. I smile, casually, into the air. Her hip bones are poking out from under the spaghetti-string ties looped on either side and her calves pop as she wades in. When she comes up from the water, she spreads her palms over her hair, swims to the side, and rests her face on her forearm.

My stomach is big, hard, high, and resting on my knees. I'm wearing a pink and white seersucker bikini. That's right, a bikini. When I was shopping for my babymoon, I contemplated buying a one-piece or a tankini from a maternity store, but as I fingered through a rack of shiny, stretchy suits, some with skirts (skirts?), I realized, what's the point? I'm obviously pregnant—there's no hiding the fact that I'm with child. And, I must say, prancing around this resort half-naked, a place where no one knows my name or situation is quite liberating. It reminds me of when I laid out topless in Mexico. I was twenty-two and fearless and in love with Keith. It was the trip before the accident.

A tall girl with a spray of freckles over her nose, in a white tank top and short, pleated skirt, hands me a fresh-squeezed lemonade and tells me John said, "I am at her beck and call," in a delicate, not hefty German accent. John is the Parker Palm Springs manager and when my belly greeted him at the desk, I felt obliged to tell him I was on a prebaby getaway— "a babymoon!" I enthused. By the time I got to my room there was a fruit basket the size of a Christmas tree waiting for me, and a welcome note from him, saying I should let him know if I need anything. "A husband," I joked to myself. "Some sex . . . and a stiff drink."

I almost didn't book this trip. I was a little hesitant about traveling alone. My married pregnant friends all went away on babymoons, and they all insisted that I go away to "relax and rejuvenate." Nice for them to say, but I can't really afford this trip. However, when a big freelance check came in, I decided to treat myself, because in a couple of months I'm going to be a mom—a single mom—and I don't foresee an opportunity to jet off to a spa for maybe eighteen years. Carlo, of course, thinks I'm "fucking crazy" for blowing money on a "stupid trip." I don't care. I work hard. I will continue to work hard until Baby graduates with a master's in something. I doubt A is depriving himself of anything, but when I think this I realize A doesn't matter. He's not involved. He can be on vacation right now, or burning his money for all I care. I can't continue comparing myself to him, because he's not the one about to become a single parent. *Okay, this trip officially marks my final splurge. Period,* I think.

So far, I think I've accumulated four onesies and a package of booties—and a very nice Gucci duffel Nic thrust into my hands a couple of weeks after I told her I was pregnant, announcing, "It's for when you deliver." She's coping with my pregnancy by spoiling me with luxurious gifts. It works. I remember thinking how in a couple of months I'd strategically pack my nightgown, socks, and brush and position the bag by my bedroom door in case my water broke, waking me suddenly.

Before I left for Palm Springs, I met Nic for dinner and she passed a big, brown box secured by a gold bow over the table. I couldn't imagine what it was—after all, she'd already outfitted me with an overnight bag that I assumed was my non-baby gift. When I opened the box and peeled back the tissue, I looked down at the fully loaded diaper bag and I had another moment when I felt like I was looking at myself from over my shoulder. For a split second I wondered what the hell I was to do with a diaper bag. Nic and I stay out until three a.m. and retire on my couch with a jar of animal crackers between us, fall asleep in our clothes, and eat brunch in last night's makeup. Why the hell was she giving me a diaper bag? Then I came to and realized how fabulous it was. Of course Carlo thinks I should eBay it for "big bucks."

Even though I should probably be using this vacation money to buy things for a makeshift nursery, I'm going to spend the next five days eating taco salads like the one I just saw the waitress bring over to a guest, getting massages that will leave me smelling like honey and lavender, and floating topless in the indoor saline pool. Kateri has been threatening me with a baby shower anyway, so I'll probably get a lot of necessities like diapers and bottles and burp cloths. (Someone actually came up with the idea for a "burp cloth" and marketed it. It's basically a washcloth.) I just hope she listens to me and doesn't force my friends to play lame guess-the-amount-of-jelly-beans-in-the-jar games. I vetoed a family shower because I refuse to be the "knocked-up" cousin at a kitschy banquet hall, while Italian aunts dressed in black shake their heads and say, "Bella girl, such a shame," because they will, in between sips of coffee and bites of liquor-soaked biscotti. "Really?" my mom whined. I told her I'd revoke her grandmother duties if she went against my wishes. She promptly started buying staple items like hooded bath towels, receiving blankets, and bibs that said "What happens at Grandma's—stays at Grandma's!" "Cute, right?" she said, looking like she was praying for me to go into labor. "Yes." I smiled and held it against my belly. It was.

I hear my phone ringing, so I wobble up and scoot over to the lounge chair draped with a big white towel the size of a bedsheet. It's Carlo.

I pick up the phone. "Hello."

"Everything okay? Got there safe?" he asks.

"Yep, I'm fine." I squint at the towering line of palm trees lacing the grounds.

"What are you doing?" he wants to know.

"Sitting by the pool, getting wasted," I say.

"Christine! You can't drink!" I can feel his face getting red through the phone.

"I'm totally kidding," I say as I lean into the lounge, reaching for a bottle of water.

"When you get back, we'll move you out of your apartment and start getting your room at home ready," he reminds me.

"I have to go," I tell him. I'm not ready for reality. I throw my phone into my bag and grab the complimentary tube of sunblock that was in the bathroom vanity. I squirt a blob on my palm and work it into my belly, then legs. It smells like basil and lavender. Carlo's right. As soon as I get back to the East Coast I need to pack up my big city life and return to Jersey. I feel like New York City kicked my ass and it's laughing at me. Meanwhile, my whole body is sweating. Everything is sweating. My baby must be overheating. I tiptoe across the patio and walk into the pool, sliding my butt down to the last step. A thin blonde is lying on her stomach reading *Cosmo* and there's a middle-aged, balding man hanging on the edge of the deep end with a pair of goggles around his neck. He's waving over a woman in a bikini with dark, flat-ironed hair. Suddenly a little person pushes through her legs. He's wearing swim trunks and his diaper is peeking out of the top.

"Carter!" she yells and runs after him.

The guy in the pool claps his hands and opens his arms and Carter runs, full steam ahead, but cautiously stops as he nears the edge. His father tries to coax him in but he remains tight-lipped and shakes his head. His mother is now standing behind him and shadowing him as he walks around the pool. As he gets closer to my end of the pool, I realize how impossibly blue his eyes are. His mother approaches the stairs where I am sitting, smiles, and says: "See what you have to look forward to?" in a sarcastic tone.

"Yes." I smile, and not to be polite, but because Carter is one of the cutest babies I've ever seen—yet. When he folds down to the ground, a soft little roll of belly spills over his bathing-suit top. He's trying his hardest to pick up a pebble.

"Hello," I say to him.

He comes to his feet and goes to touch the metal railing curving into the pool. Just before his fingers tap against it, he smiles at me and whispers, "Hot." His mother grabs his hand and I watch them walk away, until the child melts into her lap, under a big yellow and white striped umbrella. There is something very beautiful and effortless about their exchange. Her chin is resting on the top of his head and his chubby fingers are gripping the strap of her bikini top, while his pink cheek kisses her breast. I watch them for a while—the way her fingers trace his back in little, perfect circles. The sudden release of his fingers from her strap, the heavy eyes at last surrendering, the tiny supple mouth warm and dry and barely open. The easy look on her face as she combs her fingers through his hair. Then her husband grabs Carter from behind and his small, limp body hangs over his shoulder. I watch the two disappear into a cabana until I can't see them anymore.

"Hello," the thin blonde with the perfect calves says in a lovely British accent as she sits next to me.

"Oh, hello." I pat my face with water.

"Congratulations," she says, smiling at my belly.

"Thank you." I smile back at her.

"I'm Charlotte." And she extends her hand to me.

"Chrissy, nice to meet you." And I receive her hand in mine.

She asks when I am due and when I tell her September, she doesn't believe me because I look "so small." I like this woman. An older man waves to her and she waves back as a tear of water runs down her arm.

"My boyfriend—not my father." She smiles.

He definitely is older, but I never assumed he was her father. I mean, who am I to judge?

"Are you here with your husband?" she asks.

I hold up my ring finger and push it forward with my thumb. "No husband . . . or boyfriend . . . or anyone," I say in one breath.

"You're on holiday alone? How brilliant!" she enthuses.

I never thought of it like that. I mean, I spent the better part of the day feeling sorry for myself because I had no one to help me drag my bag through the airport.

"You know, it takes a very secure person to travel alone," she says.

"I guess." I smile down at the water.

"You guess! You better believe it. I love to eat out alone, or grab a glass of wine at the end of the day. I live alone, too. I've got the most adorable apartment. It's very lovely and girly and warm and it's just for me," she tells me.

We spend the rest of the afternoon wading in the shallow end, drinking tall glasses of lemonade with chubby halves of lemons at the bottom. Charlotte tells me about her job with Wilhelmina Models and how she books girls for Fashion Week and works with all the booking editors at the big magazines. I tell her I work at a magazine and she wants to know what I write. I explain that *Cocktail* is a new magazine debuting in the fall and I mostly write about sex and relationships.

"And I haven't told anyone this yet, but I was just contracted by *Glamour* magazine to pen a blog for their website," I say.

Genevieve had called me a couple of weeks ago to tell me she wanted to pitch my column idea to *Glamour*. Really? *Glamour* is interested in endorsing a pregnant single woman? I thought it was a long shot and when days turned into weeks without word from Gen, I figured it was a dead issue—until she e-mailed me the night before this trip to say the higher-ups loved the concept and that they wanted me to blog from July through November. I was delighted to receive my contract and quickly calculated the extra money I would receive each month (diapers, bottles, wipes, carseat . . .). I was also really humbled that *Glamour* was willing to take a chance and give me a platform to muse about single motherhood, an otherwise taboo topic.

"Brilliant! Oh, wait, let me guess. Is it like *Sex and the City*?"

I laugh out loud and quickly quip—"Oh, yeah, only Carrie's pregnant or 'Storked!,' the name of my blog, in the city."

"What do you mean? How so?" she asks.

"I'm going to be writing about the last couple of months of my pregnancy and first couple of months as a mom—a single mom," I tell her.

"That's amazing! You have your very own column?" She leans into me.

"Actually, it's a blog," I explain.

"Same thing!" she enthuses.

Charlotte tells me how lucky I am to be pregnant and she even tells me about her recent divorce as we hang on the side of the pool and push ice around in our cups with straws.

"So do you know the sex?" she wants to know.

"I'm having a boy. A son." I smile and feel my palm spread over my stomach.

"And what are you going to name him?" she asks.

"I think Jack. After my mother, Jacklyn." I look up into the sun and squint.

"You don't mind me asking, but, the father?" She looks curious, a little concerned—not judgmental.

I bounce my fingers up and down in the quotations sign and hear myself say, "Not ready to be a father."

"Did you love him?" she asks.

I want to lie and say yes. I don't want to tell her we were only together for a couple of months before I got pregnant. Telling the truth makes me feel bad. Every time I talk about him or the situation I feel like everyone just wants to slap me and say, "Should have had an abortion."

"I don't know. I think I might have. We were serious in that we weren't seeing other people, but it was also very new, and exciting, and fast . . . and . . . and . . ." I feel my eyes well up with tears and I know I'm crying, but my face is wet from being in the pool and a little pink from the sun so Charlotte can't tell.

"My good friend is a single mum. She has a young boy. Her life is brilliant," she says, and I think she realizes I'm choked up. So we wade for a while longer and watch as the sky turns into a mess of pink and purple and yellow, until the clouds are lined with an iridescent glimmer that is the sunset, and I keep hearing her say over and over in that pretty British accent: *Her life is brilliant. . . . Her life is brilliant.*

When we step out from the pool, eruptions of goose bumps

spread across our bodies. We exchange e-mail addresses and say we'll keep in touch. As I collect my things, I watch Charlotte's boyfriend rub his hands on her arms, warming them. Back in my room, I slip into a robe and page through the menu, deciding what to feed Baby for dinner. I pick up the phone and dial room service, as soft light from the setting sun spots the rug.

"Room service," the operator answers.

"I'd like to place an order, please," I say.

"Will you be dining alone this evening?" the operator asks.

I smile, take a deep breath, and hear myself say, "Yes, yes, I'll be dining alone tonight." I sit there all alone and think about how Charlotte says it takes a secure person to travel alone, dine alone. . . . She's right. But really I'm not alone. Nor will I ever be again—for the rest of my life.

I eat a never-ending dish of lobster mac 'n' cheese and watch some lame movie On Demand starring Jennifer Garner. Apparently her fiancé croaked right before the wedding. Afterward I meander around the resort, dragging my feet through sand trails, crouching down to the hot, bubbling spring fountains, letting the water erupt through my fingers, washing my hands. I stare up at the sky that's blooming into a big purple and orange explosion, wondering if I'll see another so pretty. On my way back to my room I pass a couple. She's pregnant. He's cupping her belly. I push my door closed with my back and feel myself starting to reach for a breath.

A couple of hours ago I was feeling so empowered, but now I'm walking around my room counting my panic attack away, reminding myself I am completely in control of this situation. I have a job, a place to live, money saved. *But your baby doesn't have a father,* I think, running my fingers through my hair. *Doesn't have a father!* If I weren't pregnant, this is when I'd chew a Xanax and just go to bed, but I certainly can't induce a minicoma now. It's bad enough I'm still taking the antidepressant that I've been on for four years, ever since I started having random panic attacks in college. Then when Keith got hurt, anxiety turned to depression, a heaviness so intimidating I could go days without food, not even feeling the slightest pang of hunger. My doctor assured me the drug is a Class C so the benefits may outweigh the risk. I told him maybe I should just stop, cold turkey, but then he told me about all the nasty side effects of doing that. It scared me—I just about broke into a panic attack right there in his office. So I lowered the dosage and I take it every other day now. I didn't take it today, though. I sit down on the edge of the bed, but quickly stand up, feeling urgent or like I forgot to do something. Now my palms are tingling and I feel light-headed. I pick up the phone and order a glass, one glass, of red wine. It's good for blood circulation. In France it's recommended to pregnant women for its high iron content. I'm freaking out, all alone. That's a good enough reason. When it arrives I sit on the patio overlooking the pool that's lit up in moonlight. I have a sweatshirt over my shoulders and my legs are stretched out on a little wicker stool. I sip the wine for over an hour, rolling it around on my tongue as the warm desert air pulls through my hair. I leave three quarters of it in the glass. I'm starting to realize exactly what is happening here. It's like I've been so busy perfecting my brave face, freelancing for extra money, and distracting myself with designer goods, I haven't exactly slowed down and swallowed this. Six months later, three months to go, I realize I need to pull it together. A blog for a national magazine and a thousand-dollar bag that holds diapers doesn't make the mom. I need to be strong on the inside, too. I take a deep breath and rise up to my feet, letting the tranquil moonlight wash over me, and it feels sacred, like it's making me better, absorbing the fear—at least for tonight.

The next day a bridal party takes over the resort. The bride is thin, wearing a skimpy black bikini and a floppy straw hat. She is drunk off multiple mojitos. I watch her hang on her fiancé with ease in the pool as I prop myself up on the lounge with a rolled-up towel. She's blowing mint leaves out of her mouth and splashing them away to the other side of the pool where a woman is swimming topless.

"How much do you love me?" the bride asks her fiancé. He rolls his eyes and looks over at some young guys, probably his groomsmen. "How much did you drink, hon?" he asks, looking at the guys. And they laugh and high-five one another like their friend scored the prom queen.

"Come on," she says, biting at his ear. "Say it . . . say it and I'll . . ." and she whispers something into his ear. *Hmm. Give you a blow job? Sign the prenup?* I laugh to myself.

"Saaaaaaaaay it," she says, wrapping her arms and legs around him.

"To the moon," he says. *To the moon.*

9

Exile

I kick past a sheet of bubble wrap and flop onto my bed. The floor is cluttered with open brown boxes and there is a big, black trash bag deflated in the corner. The dresser drawers are empty and the books that lined the window-sill are in a pile on my desk. It's about a thousand degrees in my apartment now. July is sultry and aggressive. *Note to self: Plan second pregnancy so you're pregnant in the winter. Side note: Have husband present.*

"Garbage?" Kateri holds up a brush thick with a wad of hair.

"Yeah—no," and I whip it out of her hand and start to pull my hair from it.

I run my hand over the mattress and collect the fitted sheet in a ball and stare down at the epic rectangle where A slept with me. I'm not bringing this into my new life. It's bad feng shui no matter how I position it in my room.

"Do you want this mattress?" I ask Kateri.

"You don't need it?" she says.

"Nah, there's a brand-new mattress on my bed. In my pink bedroom. In the house I grew up in," I lie. There is a twenty-four-year-old mattress on my bed. Nanny bought me my "big girl" bed and entire bedroom set when I was two.

"Sure. I'll take it. Mattresses are like eight hundred bucks!" she cheers. *Damn, maybe I should eBay that*, I think, but Kateri is already staring longingly at her free bed.

"Thanks for helping me pack up," I say.

"No problem, friend," she says.

"I'm so exhausted. I swear I could fall asleep right here in this heat and mess," I say.

"You're seven and a half months pregnant—it's okay to be tired! Besides, I told you I would pack up your stuff without you. Go lay on the couch and watch MTV," she says.

"No. I need to do this," I say as I search my room for the old Christine. She's all packed up, ready for new adventures.

My digital alarm clock pops to seven. I feel the tick-tick-tick of the evening and feel my hands slipping from the big minute hand I am so desperately clinging to. In a few minutes Carlo will be here to load my life into his Jeep.

I watch as Kateri collects pink-tinted bottles of perfume, wrapping them in tissue and dropping them gently into a box. She folds tiny camisoles that I can't believe ever fit me into perfect squares and lines my shoes against the wall, wondering how many boxes it's going to take to pack them all away as she counts in twos. *I just got here*, I think, as I trash a stack of magazines. Believe me, the irony is not lost on me. Here I ran away from New Jersey to escape being a caretaker and nurturer only to return in the ultimate role of caretaker/nuturer: mother. I rummage through my desk drawer, finding a picture of Kateri and me in London. The wind must have picked up the second the person took the picture because our faces are covered with wisps of hair but you can still tell we're laughing, wildly. I pull the picture up to my lips, not meaning to kiss it, but I do. I continue sifting through the drawer: movie stubs from last year, matchbooks from Pravda, clips with my byline I haven't set in my book yet, a napkin with someone's phone number on it, a Metro-Card, the train schedule for NYC to Jersey. I continue plowing through the drawer, collecting loose change in my palm, when I see a small piece of paper folded in half. *What's this?* I think, dropping the change into a mug on my desk. When I open it I realize it's an extra copy from my first sonogram. One is tacked in Kateri's cubicle and the other is in a frame, now wrapped in tissue in a box somewhere. I squint my eyes at the tadpole sleeping, gently, in the little pool. I take a deep breath, looking out the window, realizing the sky isn't light anymore. I ease onto the bed and fall back, letting my hair fall around me. I'm tired. I don't want to pack. Moving to Jersey seems like an impossible idea. It's more impossible than being pregnant. I feel like I'm about to pull my life over the GWB in a little red wagon while someone plays the bagpipes from Port Authority. I'm probably making this more dramatic than it has to be. Still.

There is a knock at the front door. I push myself up off the bed with my palms and arch my back. Carlo comes sweeping in with more boxes.

"Ready? All packed?" he says as he whisks past me. No, I'm not ready. I'm not ready to leave this place. I'm not done here. I feel like I'm not being allowed to read the rest of a story, or like I'm leaving New York City blindfolded and being brought to New Jersey against my will. I should write my own ransom note.

My closet is full of hanging clothes that don't fit me anymore. When Carlo walks past it, he wants to know why I haven't packed it yet. I'm seven months pregnant. I'm tired. It's hot. I want a cheeseburger. I slide a wad of clothes between my hands and lift them from the bar. I press them against Carlo's chest and tell him to just lay them across his backseat.

"Christine!" he barks.

"What?" I calmly say, while strategically palming my belly with one hand and pushing a wisp of hair from my brow with the other.

"You're ridiculous, Christine. Your mother is ridiculous," Carlo crouches down and says to my belly, then rolls his eyes at me.

"Be right back!" he says as he turns and leaves with the clothes.

Back in my room, Kateri drops a pair of running sneakers into a box. There are grass stains along the rubber soles and one of the laces is frayed. They're A's. I forgot they were under my bed.

"Those are garbage," I say, and it sounds so poetic.

"Really?" she says, not sure why I'm throwing out a perfectly good pair of sneakers. She thinks they're mine. I have big feet.

"They're A's," I say as I sift through my middle desk drawer, ridding it of A's toiletries and *Economist* magazines and one silk tie. I hope it was expensive. Kateri hurls his sneakers into the black trash bag.

"I know you don't want to hear this, but him bowing out now is better," she says.

"My kid doesn't have a father!" I say. "I really screwed up!"

"Yeah. But if he can leave like this now—decide over the phone he didn't want to be a father. The *phone*, Christine. Declare his emancipation from *our* unborn little boy—then, trust me, he could do the same thing when Jack is like four. All of a sudden 'Daddy' disappears. Get it?" she says.

I like when Kateri refers to Jack as "our little boy." My girlfriends talk to my belly often, introducing themselves as aunt this and that. Telling my growing son about adventures in Central Park and lazy afternoons at the Met, convincing me it's "totally fine" to bring him to a bar in the afternoon in Manhattan because that's what parents do in the city.

"Think of all the Bugaboos we've squeezed past at Spring Natural on a Sunday morning," Kateri says.

"Good point," I say. *I suppose the famed Balthazar wouldn't have such badass high chairs if they didn't accommodate tiny people in diapers*, I think as I tape up the last box and slide it into the living room with my foot. Carlo is sweating profusely and has already made twelve trips up and down.

I give the apartment a once-over before I officially exit. There's a half-full jar of olive oil in the cupboard. I hand it to Kateri and tell her to take it or toss it. The door closes behind me, my keys left behind on the kitchen counter. Even if I wanted to get back in I couldn't. It's over. Carlo and I drive over the GWB, back to Jersey. In the corner of my eye

I can see the glimmer of the skyline, but I refuse to look at it. I stare, steadfast, at the rushing lights of speeding cars heading west on Route 80. My hand finds my stomach. *Here we go, Jack. Just trust me*, I think. The radio is on but it sounds like white noise.

"You okay?" Carlo wants to know.

"Yeah. Fine," I say. I have to be. There is no turning back now. Jack is coming in two months. My apartment is empty, the contents sandwiched in this truck. I flip the visor down and comb my fingers through my hair, securing it in a low ponytail. We're at exit 64 and suddenly the skyline is fading in the mirror. I stare at it until it dips below the horizon like it was never there at all. Like the past two years of my life have been a dream I could forget.

10

Bump Watch

Two days later I'm back in New York City, running my fingers through a sea of kelly green grass spotted with sunlight. It dawns on me that I really do only live twenty-five minutes outside of the city. Maybe this won't be as bad as I think. In a couple of months, I'll slip Jack into one of those hippie baby slings, we'll pay the toll, and we'll meet the girls for coffee. Or maybe I'll win the lottery before he arrives and I'll bid on a new Avalon property in the East Village. I should start playing the lottery, I suppose.

The sun is warm on my face as I fall back on the blanket. I can almost feel my nose popping with freckles. The Great Lawn in Central Park is dotted with all sorts of people: a group of girls with chunky gold jewelry and too-small bikini tops—their breasts spilling out of the cups; a guy with tan skin and fuzzy, short hair flicking the strings of his guitar; and a little boy chasing his shadow around. His hand opens and closes as he tries to pick it up as if he wants to put it his pocket. He bends down to the lawn to examine the cutout light and his nose almost touches the grass. His mom and two other women, one with a Pucci scarf knotted around her head, are laughing as they tip plastic cups filled with what looks like sangria to their lips.

"I got you olives," Lo says. I roll over on my side and push myself up. I think I grew in the ten minutes I've been lying here.

"You're awesome," I say as I peel the plastic lid back and poke around for a big, green, meaty one. I think I've consumed over three hundred green olives during my pregnancy.

"Cheese. Bread. Fruit," Kateri says as she sets little containers from Zabar's out.

"And wine," she says, planting two bottles onto the blanket. "Hope no one catches us." She laughs as she pops a cork. "Imagine if we get arrested? Ah, the headlines. Pregnant *Glamour* blogger boozing in the park!"

I hold the damp, rosy cork to my nose, ashamed to tell them I drank some in Palm Springs after wigging out.

"Stop. Red is fine. European pregos drink red all the time," she says. Lo must have read that French study, too. *Exactly*, I think.

"Okay. Today I'm French, visiting friends in New York, and my hot painter husband is in Vienna restoring—something," I say.

"Yay!" Kateri cheers and hands me like a sip of red wine. I laugh as it rolls around on my tongue. It's warm and sweet, then bitter. It's delicious. I want more. I extend my cup to Kateri.

"Just a splash more," she says, topping my cup off, winking at me.

Ashley, Stef, and Claire show up bearing brownies and iced tea.

"Hey, preggers," Ashley says as she bends down to give me a kiss.

"Cuuuuuuuuuuuuuuuu-te shorts," I say admiring her cut-offs.

"Urban Outfitters. Vintage Levi's," she says, and I look down at my size large Jersey dress with an elastic waist.

After lunch we lie around in a tight circle. Kateri's head is resting on my legs and my head is barely touching Lo's feet.

"I can't believe he's going to be here soon," Stef says as she crosses her arms behind her head.

"I'm so excited to see him," I say.

"For real. This time next year he'll be sitting in the middle of our little circle," Lo says as she pops a green grape into her mouth.

"I know. In little denim shorts and a backward baseball cap," Kateri says.

"Did you decide on a middle name yet?" Claire asks.

"Domenic. After my dad's father," I say.

"As in 'JD'?" Claire asks.

"I guess," I say, craning my head up and squinting at her.

"This kid is going to be badass," she says, looking at Lo.

"Obviously," Lo says. "Look at who his mother—and aunts—are."

"Can we give him a faux-hawk like Gwen Stefani's little boy?" Kateri asks.

"I love Kingston. Yes!" I agree.

"I feel like we are on final bump watch," Kateri says to the girls.

"I know, I know!" they say in unison.

I have good friends. The excitement they candidly show is what I feel all the time. Only it's coated with fear and rarely surfaces for anyone to see. But I know Jack feels it and hears me when we're alone in the dark counting stars, trying to fall asleep. I close my eyes and listen to them argue about who the "coolest" aunt is and where to find a bite-size leather motorcycle jacket. My kid is never getting on a motorized bike. He can have a trike, then a Big Wheel, then a ten-speed—then a car.

The next morning I'm back in hell. I mean home. I keep thinking I'm just home for the weekend. Then it occurs to me I weigh 150-something pounds, I've outgrown my $225-dollar maternity jeans, and there is a suitcase on my bedroom floor. I smell coffee. And eggs. My father and mother are fighting over the whereabouts of Max's leash. My mother says it's hanging on the doorknob. My father says he's looking at the doorknob and it's not. Their hot-and-cold relationship and ability to make the dinner table a war zone was another one of the reasons for my exodus to Manhattan. My parents are very weird creatures, living separate lives under the same roof. I wonder how people get stuck like they have. The leash is in the laundry room. I noticed it when I went

down to switch a load last night. Max was sitting on a pile of
dirty bath towels, chewing on a damp washcloth. When I
flipped the light on, he looked at me like I was bothering
him. That dog has issues. Seeing him in there and Brian's
epic hamper with his underwear spilling out nearly brought
me to my knees. *What the hell am I doing in Jersey?* is all
that crossed my mind as I shoved my pajamas into the dryer.
Gone are the days of making eyes at the cute hipster waiting
for his jeans to dry while he reads romantic poetry and
chews on a straw. *Have time for a beer while these clothes
dry? Sure.* I slammed the dryer door so hard, Max startled
and ran out like his tail was on fire.

I turn over and look at the clock—it's just eight a.m. on a
Saturday. I feel like I'm in a dream, walking around in someone else's life. Max just pooped by the door. My father is
yelling for a "plastic bag . . . and disinfectant. Now!" I cannot
believe I am here. I pinch my eyelids shut, take a deep
breath, then open them. Still here.

Also, I'm huge. Sometimes it feels like there is an elephant sitting on my chest or like I have to sneeze but can't.
I try not to, but lately I've been wondering what A's life is
like now. In a recent post on my blog someone made a comment that he absolutely does not think about us. The commenter went on to suggest that I'd be surprised by the
selectivity of memory. That Jack and I are stored somewhere
deep in the darkest part of his brain, and if and when we surface, we're quickly pushed to the side by something as mind-
less as a billboard for orange soda. I don't buy it. Part of me
thinks A is along for the ride—reading my blog daily—which

is pretty pathetic since the only thing keeping him from his son is his own stupidity. I haven't spoken to him in five months, but confess to uncovering that his MySpace.com account is canceled and a recent Google search revealed nothing new, just a sparkly, bright-eyed photo of him from a race years ago. Looking at his photo I was bombarded by too many emotions to deal with, so I slapped my laptop shut and slid it under the covers. I wonder what he thinks when he Googles me? First, Glamour.com comes up and then a lovely link to a media blog touting me as a knocked-up girl with a bad case of TMI followed by about two hundred comments proclaiming how stupid and ugly I am. I shouldn't care, but I'm hormonal, reading things like this makes me enraged, and I call the blogger who wrote about me being a fucking c-word over an instant message to Matt. After that first attack, I called my editor, Gen, and told her I didn't think I could blog—ever again. She told me to grow a thicker skin. I wrote a blog post the following day and thought about all the baby clothes (that I need to wash in Dreft—whatever that is) the first two paychecks bought.

Sometimes when I hit Publish I break out in a sweat wondering why I felt the need to tell the Internet I once went skinny-dipping in a hot tub with friends and strangers and three—make that four—bottles of champagne when I was twenty-four and single. I try not to obsess too much and instead focus on how cool it is that I managed to score a contract with a huge women's mag, pregnant and single. It makes me feel stylish and independent and completely in control. I'm pregnant and single—and I write for *Glamour*.

People seem to like me. Gawker.com thinks I'm "cute" and "smart," and HuffingtonPost.com thinks my story is worth serializing—like I'll have time to ever write a book—ever. There is something very fulfilling about reading comments from women telling me they're on my side, advising me to buy this toy and pack this type of "granny" underwear in my overnight bag. These women have located me on MySpace.com and introduced themselves to me. They direct me to photos of their own children and tell me Storked! and coffee is their morning ritual. As I lay here in bed I wonder what I should blog about this coming Monday: heartburn? My Gucci diaper bag? Bridget Moynahan . . . ?

My father taps on my door and peeks his head in. It's too late to pretend I'm sleeping and the fact that my big belly looks mountainous under my comforter means there's no quick-turn move that will soften the fact that I am wide awake.

"Want an egg-white omelet?" he wants to know.

"No thanks," I say while racing my hand under the comforter looking for the clicker. I need some mind-numbing television about a sixteen-year-old who gets a Mercedes for her birthday after she calls her mom a "twit" and has a shit fit because the party planner can't produce an elephant for the grand entrance of her party, to shut out the fact that I live here. In Wayne. Pregnant.

"I made some regular eggs with ham and mozzarella already and I have some fresh mango," he says while smiling and shaking his head up and down, trying to coax a "yes" out of me.

"No," I say, and turn on the TV. He turns to leave and

says he's going to scramble some egg whites and spinach because maybe I'll be hungry later. He also says something about feeding his grandson and how I'm "stubborn."

I'm nearly eight months pregnant and Jack has taken up refuge between my ribs on the right side. There's a knee or shoulder or fist of knuckles bulging out and my stomach looks misshapen. I can see him moving now. My stomach literally waves and pops with Baby and it's pretty incredible—so much, in fact, I can't come up with a better word to describe it than *miraculous*. If I press on him, sometimes he kicks back. I do it often and tell him we're still okay and that we always will be. In heavenly moments he flexes when I say that. He's extremely responsive and clearly a genius.

The clock is threatening ten a.m. and I'm in the midst of an *America's Next Top Model* marathon. Someone will continue on to be America's. Next. Top. Model. There is a new pressure on my tailbone and dull twinges of stinging in my southern region. Jack weighs around four pounds and I'm at a point in my pregnancy where I feel like he could crawl out of me at any moment. I wish he would, since I can't wait to meet him and retire into a long twenty-week maternity leave during which my sweet little cherub will nap on my chest while I sit by the window and watch the leaves turn colors.

The following Monday I'm sitting in Dr. Collado's office reading a parenting magazine, wondering if World War III is commencing on my blog. Probably. The waiting room is warm with hormonal women. Despite a sign that says seating is reserved for patients, a man in jeans and work boots is sitting next to his wife, palming her belly. A woman more pregnant than me is leaning up against the wall. I want to call the guy an "ass" and tell him to "move—now" but I don't. I look down at a little foot sheathed in a crocheted bootie. The canopy of the car seat is completely covering the rest of the baby. A rush of adrenaline spreads inside of me.

My legs are dangling from the exam table when Dr. Collado walks in with a little black book so that we can schedule my C-section at this appointment. I can't believe it's July already. It feels like I was disguising my bump with my bag and climbing over snowy curbs in New York City just yesterday. I'm in the final stretch now. I don't even remember that shaking girl with a positive pee stick in her hand.

"About your section," Dr. Collado says, pushing her glasses onto the crown of her head.

"Can we do it now?" I joke.

"These last weeks are itchy, huh?" she says.

"Absolutely," I say, thinking about excusing myself to go to the bathroom to pee again even though I did just before I came in.

"We're going to get the baby about ten days before your actual due date," she says, looking at the calendar.

Wait. Ten days before? As in August? No. This can't be happening, I think as I try to quell the anxiety riding up my stomach to my heart. I hate August. People break their necks in August.

"What about September first?" I say. "It's almost ten days."

"Sep-tem-ber first," Dr. Collado says, looking at the calendar. "Falls on a Saturday."

"I can do a Saturday," I say.

She laughs.

"I only do sections on Tuesdays and Thursdays, so looks like August thirtieth," she says.

August thirtieth. I turn it over in my head. I don't have a choice. I have to love August now. Plan birthday parties with balloons. Eat cake. Smile.

"Oh, wait—I'm on vacation that entire week," she says.

I skip back a week. The twenty-third, the day of the accident, is the Thursday prior to the thirtieth. *I'm going to give birth on the day Keith was injured. This is really happening.*

"Except I don't want to deliver you on the twenty-third—that's a little too early for my liking," she says.

I stare at her blankly, waiting for her to tell me she's going to cancel her vacation to deliver my son. She doesn't.

"Dr. Keanchong can do it on the thirtieth," she says, jotting something down in the little square book.

Dr. Keanchong examined me a couple of times over the years. She's warm and always smiles at me when she sees me in the office waiting by the desk to make an appointment. She's great and completely capable, but it's not what I was expecting. It seems every time I get a grasp of reality, something smacks me in the forehead like "Ping! Not so fast!" I bet my water breaks—today.

"Can you explain this whole 'spinal' thing to me?" I ask

as I lay back and Dr. Collado measures my belly with a thin yellow tape measure. My olive green dress with stretchy straps and a double ruffle at the hemline is pushed up to my chest and I'm trying to remember what underwear I have on.

"Well, I'm going to schedule you to have a consultation with an anesthesiologist, but taking your back into consideration, I'm not sure if a spinal is the way to go," she says.

"Is there another?" I ask, craning my face up at her.

"We can put you under," she says.

"I'm going to miss everything?" I ask while she moves her hands over my belly.

"We'll bring you around as soon as it's over," she says.

I do not want to be "brought around," especially in inauspicious August, or at all, for that matter. I accepted the fact that I'll have to be sliced open—that pushing eight pounds of baby out of me and quite possibly enduring back labor isn't an option for someone whose spine is stretched out and held up by two titanium rods, set in place with bolts and screws and other things that belong in a toolbox. I've seen the scary X-rays—I wouldn't want to be liable for trying to stick a spinal in my back, either. My spine is difficult and crowded, and when it rains, it's angry. But still, I feel like I've been preparing for the show for months now, really working on myself, and now it's like an understudy is going to slip in for the curtain call. I push my dress down over my belly. The thing is, I can't deny that my back is the way it is. I can't even do a somersault, which makes Dr. Collado wonder how I'll crouch over the table so my spine reveals itself.

One day at the beach when I was thirteen, my mom noticed

my hips were uneven. I was wearing a bright pink and orange bikini with a padded bra top. I was going through a semi-anorexic phase and my hip bones were severe enough to display an unevenness that even made strangers cock their heads. A couple of weeks later, I was sitting on a plank of wood while a specialist of some sort papier-mâchéd my chest—literally slapped strips of material against my torso, which was outfitted in a nude fitted-stocking thing, crafting a mold that would be replicated into a brace. I kept thinking: *Why me? This is going to be a big waste of money for my parents,* considering insurance barely paid for the Velcro straps that held the contraption together, and *I'm so not wearing this brace*—and I didn't. As soon as I got to school I took it off and threw it in the coat closet with the accordion-screen door. Eighth grade was hard enough—especially since my breasts hadn't arrived yet and my other friends had not only transformed into gazelles overnight, one even had a real live boyfriend and scored an open-mouth kiss, tongue and all.

A year later I was a freshman in high school, going through a really bad brown lip-liner phase and my hips and shoulders were more crooked, but my doctor thought a growth spurt might grow me out of it. At my next checkup I tried to shift my weight to my left side because I seriously thought I could fake out my doctor, who always had lunch in his mustache. I didn't and he recommended surgery. Surgery? "A complete spinal fusion," he said while he traced his finger in an S down my back.

My parents dragged me around the tri-state area in search of the best possible doctor to literally straighten me out. They asked question after question, and the more inquisitive they became about "the disorder"—a severe case of scoliosis—the more removed I became. I felt extremely cheated, because no matter what million-dollar-an-hour doctor signed on, the surgery meant being nine hours under, two weeks in the hospital, and three months at home, recovering and home-schooling. The threat of coming out of the operation paralyzed was real. We ended up with Dr. Roye, chief orthopedic surgeon at the Children's Hospital at New York–Presbyterian. He was warm and had kind, sleepy eyes, but I still didn't want him to saw me open—gut me like an upside-down fish. He is the best, so I was wait-listed for a year, which meant my surgery would happen just in time to miss all the Sweet Sixteen parties and the annual dance competition at my high school. I kept that chip on my shoulder pretty much right up until the surgery date: January 29, 1997. The night before I ate a pint of strawberry ice cream and fielded good luck calls. I woke up the next morning feeling like I could throw up but had nothing in me to release. The drive over the GWB that morning was long and the skyline was glistening with streaks of morning sun, making me squint.

I remember lying there in the OR, ready to be put under, staring up at the impossibly bright, white lights, hearing clanking and smelling something clean like Listerine. A woman in green scrubs made a joke. "Bet you'd rather be in midtown at Bloomingdale's?" Fuck you, lady. I saw my parents from the corner of my eye. My mom was sitting with her legs crossed and had pale pink Reebok sneakers on. My father's hair was whiter than usual. The nurse approached me and her gloved hand was soft and smooth. "We're going to get started, sweetheart," and she reached for my arm, which already had an IV line set in place. My parents told me I'd be alright and that they loved me. I didn't even look over at them. I stared up at the bright, white light and let a single tear slip from my eye. I tasted a tinge of salt on my lips and everything faded to black.

I shake my memory and follow Dr. Collado to another room with an ultrasound machine because she wants to double-check the baby's position. As I lay back on the table, I swallow the news of possibly missing my son's arrival. It's a conundrum I can't dissect. *I'm going to miss his first cry? The nurse isn't going to tote him over to my head and let me see him?*

"Would you look at that?" Dr. Collado says. I turn over and see Jack yawning, then sticking his tongue out. *Wow,* I think.

"Oh my gosh! Look, he's sucking his thumb," Dr. Collado says. I stare at Jack sucking his thumb, curled up inside of me. He's content in his underwater world, hardly moving at all, just drifting in the gentle ease of my womb. I feel like I'm in the middle of one of those really good dreams, the kind when you wake up and try to fall back to sleep right away, returning yourself to that state of unconscious bliss where no one can disturb you or the feeling pulsing through your body, warming your heart.

"So we're all set then?" Dr. Collado says. "The thirtieth? Dr. Keanchong?"

I barely hear her.

"Sure," I say, smiling at the screen.

11

Knocked Down

Lo and Kateri take me to see *Knocked Up* today. I sit in between them with an extra-large tub of popcorn in my lap. We all touch fingers as we reach into the bucket. It reminds me of being on a date—that seems so long ago, so out of my reach. A and I went to the movies a lot. I search the theater, spotting couples left and right. I feel like the three of us are the only ones not on dates, that I'm on a spinning plate, seeing the theater bloom with new couples at every angle. The lights dim and I ease into my seat, stretching my legs out. Twenty minutes into the movie I feel so lame for relating to the main character—especially since this is a mainstream comedy. These days my life is more like a brilliant Greek tragedy. When the *Grey's Anatomy* girl, Alison, cries hysterically at her transvaginal ultrasound that determines she is, in fact, pregnant, I start to tear up and pull my hoodie into my chest like a bear. Everyone else in the theater is laughing as her chubby one-night-stand freaks out in the corner of the office. I remember staring at the screen eight months ago, waiting for it to wash up into something I could understand. That tiny flickering heartbeat was like a bolt of lightning through me. I want to yell out to the screen and tell her everything is going to be okay. Soon she'll feel little soda bubbles in her belly and think it's just gas, but it will be the baby kicking for the first time, and then those bubbles will turn into sudden jabs and that her belly will move without warning. I realize I'm really talking to myself, reminding myself how lucky I am to be experiencing this. I catch Kateri and Lo looking at me when Alison is giving birth, but I don't look over. It's scenes like these that make me excited about a C-section. No wonder so many women are petrified to give birth. Alison's vagina looks like it's going to explode or deliver a ripe watermelon baby. On our way out of the theater two guys look at me, then look at my belly, then look at each other again, then up at me again. They have sincerity in their eyes and totally think I'm pushing this baby out, sans drugs, like Alison just did.

"Thank God you're 'too posh to push,' Chris," Lo jokes.

"Amen for designer births!" I cheer.

"For real," Kateri says, and the three of us, linked arm-in-arm-in-arm, emerge out into the East Village, which is lined with bars with big, outstretched doors. People our age are drinking and flirting and laughing. We go for Tasti D-Lite.

A couple of days later I'm sitting in an empty waiting room at Hackensack University Medical Center waiting for someone to say my name wrong. (Everyone assumes Coppa is pronounced like "Copacabana.")

"Coppa," the nurse says from the doorway.

Copacabana, music and passion were always the fashion at the Copa . . . they fell in love, I sing to myself as I hoist myself up and follow her into a small room. I eye the exam table, which looks like a mountainous adventure to climb.

"Just take a seat here," the nurse says, smiling and pointing to a salmon-colored vinyl chair.

Dr. Collado has sent me to meet with Dr. Somebody today to talk about anesthesia during my C-section. Sometimes I fantasize about going into labor in my car, alone, and pushing Jack out like a hiccup. Other times the mere thought of my water breaking and of enduring the slightest twinge of a contraction is enough to exhaust me and put me to bed by seven p.m.

"Hello, Christine, I'm Dr. Osman." A tan, tall man enters and extends his hand to me.

"Hi," I say, reaching for him. I feel like a knocked-up fifteen-year-old suddenly. The doctor has a thick gold band on his finger. Jack is punching around inside of me. The helpless guppies that used to chase one another in my uterus have turned into an angry, claustrophobic octopus with no room to stretch. Dr. Osman's jaw is popping back and forth, his teeth sanding each other while he reads my chart.

"Fused from T-1 to L-1, I see," he says. "How's getting through airport security?" He chuckles.

It's the age-old joke. Will Christine's back set off the alarms like a ticking bomb or concealed gun would? No. But people can't help but ask. My father actually brings up the redundant question every time I fly. He convinced himself after

9-11 that I would, without a doubt, need some sort of official note to board a plane.

"I only created one international incident so far," I joke.

Dr. Osman snorts when he laughs.

"Here's the thing: I've given spinals to patients with hardware before, but it really is a case-by-case," he says.

"Okay?" I ask. "Did you see my X-rays? I had them messengered from Columbia Pres."

"I didn't look at them yet, and visual aside, I'm more concerned with whether the anesthesia will fully take, seeing that your entire spine is disrupted by hardware," he says.

"Okay?" Again, I answer him in a question.

"How can I explain this. Okay, say someone breaks their neck. They're a quadriplegic"—and he continues talking, but I'm not hearing him anymore. I'm thinking about Keith now and how my small hand fit in his big one and the nickname he gave me, "Paw." I tell myself to stop it, right now.

"The reason quadriplegics can't move is because the signal from the brain gets blocked by the damage in their necks and spines. You see?" he says.

"Sort of," I lie. I could write a full report on a broken neck and its effect on the body in ten minutes if I had to. He doesn't know that.

"Well, we'll just see how things pan out that morning," he says.

"Isn't that the purpose of me being here now?" I say. "To make a plan?" It comes out really bitchy. It sounds like I'm in a rush and I just asked a disinterested salesgirl at Express if she could bring me a size four—now.

"Quite true, yes, but you see, I don't know who will be on call," he says, running his finger down my file. "Let's see, the thirtieth. I can't really say if that doctor will attempt a spinal," he says.

"Attempt a spinal?" I say.

"Not to worry—just a quick pinch, then you'll be numb, promise," he assures me.

"I thought you said the medicine might not take," I say.

"They'll do a pinch test." He says it like I know what he's talking about. Like my boss telling me to write an FOB (a column page in the front of a magazine), ASAP.

"Pinch test?" I ask.

"They'll clamp your skin at various points of your body and ask if you can feel it. If you feel it—pain, not to be confused with pressure—then the meds didn't take full effect," he says.

"Okay," I say with another question mark.

"And worst-case scenario, we put you under and when you wake up your husband and baby greet you, see?" he says.

I have no fight left in me to tell him I'm single. I like the way his sentence sounds, anyway, so I smile and let him think my husband is stuck in traffic or, better yet, a rich doctor like him, in surgery fixing a toddler's heart. I don't really want to be alone for this. This feeling is more immediate than ever, like wanting a drink of water when you're thirsty. I'd like a husband to rub my feet and fetch me salty things and tell me Diet Coke is on the list of things I can't have. The closer I get to the delivery, the more I realize how backward my life is. I wake suddenly almost every night, spreading my hand on the empty side of my bed, and I realize over and over again I am alone.

I drag myself into the office, even though I'm feeling weepy and now fearing that a goofy *Scrubs*-type intern is going to try to stick a needle in my spine next month after he's been up all night fucking a nurse in an on-call room. Perfect. The office is surprisingly quiet. I'm usually greeted by a sleepy James drinking a black coffee—especially when I'm coming from a doctor's appointment. My work friends have been on bump watch ever since I came in last week looking like I grew another baby overnight. You hear stories about the twin that hides behind the other baby and doesn't reveal himself until birth. That could be me on the thirtieth. Wouldn't that be perfect? The strain of this last month is starting to wear on my back. My hand is permanently fixed in the crook between my ribs and hip. Every time I see Dr. Collado, now weekly, I will her to say the words: "I think you should go on bed rest until you deliver." She usually just tells me I look pretty and asks about Nanny, which gets me thinking about meatballs, even at morning appointments while I sip decaf coffee.

I stand on my tiptoes and peek over a row of cubes. *No one here?* I think as I peek at my watch. *It's nearly eleven a.m. That's odd.* I wobble to my desk, my flip-flops smacking loudly with each step. I have a drawer of important shoes at my desk, but I won't slip into them. *Hmmm. Julian's desk is empty, too. He's never late.* I notice this as I approach my desk. My hormones have developed an odd crush on him. Piper has peeked over her desk a handful of times and reminded me that I am "totally flirting with him." Which, okay, I was, and it makes me feel seminormal. I'm still human. *Where is everyone? Is there some kind of important meeting going on?* I think as I run my finger down my planner. *Wait. I bet my surprise office shower is today. Yay! Totally. I wonder what they got me—and, yum, what flavor cake they bought. Strawberry shortcake, I hope.*

While I wait for whatever clever ruse will summon me to the conference room, I touch up my lip gloss and then open up *In Design* to cut out a beauty spread I wrote: "First Date Fixes: Keep This in Your Purse at All Times." The entire magazine is about dating and sex. I feel less than qualified to be writing about what young women should wear to "woo" their dates or how to weasel their way out of an uncomfortable "morning after" situation. Then again, Lo works at *Brides*, and she's further away from the altar than me.

James appears in my cubicle. *This is it. He's going to lead me into the conference room to talk about some big section disaster that needs revamping, then, BAM, everyone jumps up holding baby Ralph Lauren onesies. Oh, I hope someone got me that signature sterling silver Tiffany's rattle.*

"What's up, lover?" I say, reaching for his waist. "Hungover?"

"Did you hear? Are you okay?" he asks.

"Hear what?" I ask, as I cut three words and reread the subhead "Pucker Up." *That sounds cute,* I guess. *Do people say that?* I wonder for a moment. My life is such a cliché.

"Chrissy. Are you serious?" He's looking at me like someone died. *Did someone die? Fuck.*

"What?" I play along, swiveling my chair to face him. *Did*

I hear my surprise baby shower is commencing in three minutes? I think.

"It's over," he says.

"Huh?" I say. I feel slightly brain-dead, and I read that "mommy brain" is an actual affliction, but I don't think I can blame Jack since he's not here yet but rather sleeping soundly in my uterus.

"*Cocktail.* It's dead. Not launching," he says.

"O-kay James. HA HA," I say, swiveling back into my desk, expecting blue balloons to pop up from every other cubicle right about now.

"Chrissy. I'm serious," he says. His eyes are glassy. He's serious.

"What? When? Why? How? Why? Why?" I ask.

"Something about racks and pockets and Wal-Mart," he says. "I'm going to go sit down." I watch as James slumps as if he's wearing a heavy backpack and mopes to his desk as if his ankle is dragging a weight.

I've been working on this project for two years. It went through a dozen focus groups and seven titles and two offices. Four people just started—today. The new assistant I'm overseeing is fresh out of college. She's eager and constantly e-mails me asking if she can "help with anything." I'm having a baby next month and depending on my maternity leave . . . and fuck, insurance. I dash into Maria's office like I'm not pregnant. *Wow, I'm still limber.* She's sitting at her desk with mascara under her eyes.

"Seriously?" I say.

She nods her head and throws her hands in the air. Her

office still smells like fresh paint. I made her paint the walls red. I drag myself back onto the editorial floor. Everyone is standing around waiting for someone to yell "April Fool's" even though it's July. The HR lady comes bounding toward me with her hands folded into each other like she's praying. Her hair is cut in a wedge of burgundy and she matches head to toe in a flowy shirt-and-pants assemble. She's wearing an eclectic chunky necklace and looks like she just stepped out of a Chico's ad.

"What does this mean for insurance?" I say.

"You'll be fine. COBRA," she says, in her thick Russian accent.

"How much is that?" I ask.

"Family plan, I have to check, but a little over a thousand dollars a month," she says.

I'm glad she walks away, because I have no words and the words I might have are bad. COBRA? I can't afford COBRA. Aren't I getting repurposed? I've been at this company for three years. A year at *First*—two years at *Cocktail*. There are half a dozen magazines I can shuffle to. I'll be a fact-checker for Christ's sake. I can't be fired. Laid off? *Can I?* I think as I march back into Maria's office.

"Do you have a job?" I ask.

"Yes, I'm going to *Woman's World*," she says.

Phew, clearly she's taking me with her. I'm her right and left hand. I do everything from order her coffee to direct the beauty-product photo shoots. I practically hired her new assistant. Obviously, I have a job. Right? I think as I stare helplessly at her like a puppy waiting for a piece of fatty steak. She says nothing and Pandora, the fashion director, enters and slumps in a chair with a clipboard.

"Do I have a job?" I ask.

"Chrissy, I don't know," she says. "But I need to talk with Pandora now, so can you excuse us?"

Excuse you? Seriously? Pandora's getting a job? She's been here for like seven hours, I think, as I stare, befuddled at her.

"You don't know if *I* have a job?" I say. *This is bad. Very bad. I could go into labor right about now,* I think as I turn to leave. The door pops quietly closed behind me, almost patting my butt, and even though it doesn't, I feel the shove. I walk back to my desk, avoiding Maria's assistant, because I have no idea what to say to her, except maybe, "I'm happy to be a reference." I need to call my father. He'll know what I should do. There's probably some law about firing pregnant women.

"I got . . . laid off?" I say. I'm still trying to figure out if that's what actually happened. Can you get laid off from a magazine that doesn't technically exist?

"What?" he says.

"LAID. OFF," I say, and I feel my lips trembling.

"Okay. Relax. Come home," he says.

Come home? Now I'm single, pregnant, living with my parents, and unemployed? This is not happening. I am dreaming this. Julian comes over and gives me his e-mail address and wishes me well. I am not dreaming. And the cute distraction is leaving the office with his briefcase. *Take me with you,* I think, as his back gets smaller and smaller, then vanishes through the doorway.

12

Up Again

Three days go by. I've sought refuge in my bed and become obsessed with writing Storked! I wonder if I can make a living as a professional blogger. My laptop keeps freezing. It's eight years old. The thing is probably going to explode in my lap and the timing of it makes perfect sense. *What more can you do to me, God?* Clearly this is all God's fault. I guess this is what happens when you become an Easter Catholic. My mother comes in with a glass of water I didn't ask for. She's making sure I haven't had a nervous breakdown or that I'm not sitting in a pool of amniotic fluid, too paralyzed with depression to alert someone.

"Want a grilled cheese or a cheese-topper?" my mom says, as she refolds a folded blanket. Does she think an egg with cheese, my absolute favorite breakfast as a kid, is going to make me feel better? The only thing that could possibly make me feel better is a job and health benefits. And a jar of green olives. The psycho dog jumps on my bed and starts digging in my blankets like he's in the yard.

"Max! No. I don't want cheese things. I want you to get this animal away from me!" I say, turning over to the wall.

The pink wall that's speckled with tiny holes from where I pushed in tacks to hold up my New Kids on the Block posters. I know I'm being kind of mean to my mother, here, and when I hear her close my door I want to call out to her and ask her for a hug, but I don't.

Instead I turn my attention to the online career boards, which list assistant jobs I am overqualified for. I would like to apply anyway, but I'm not sure how to start my cover letter. *To Whom It May Concern: I am having a baby next month and I need a job now.* I am suddenly enraged at how A can be so absent—especially financially. Writing a check doesn't make you a father, and he can't even do that. I shouldn't have to ask him for child support. He knows his baby is about to be born. He should set this up. The checks should just start. (Hmmm, maybe they will? Doubt it.) I need to stop being so proud and just file for child support on my own. I've been officially laid off from *Cocktail* for two days and I'm about ready to apply to Wendy's if I have to. I could be like Drew Barrymore in *Home Fries*. I feel limbless, like I'm a blob in a bed with no control over anything anymore. I'm waiting for Gen at *Glamour* to call and tell me my blog is sucking and that the commenters that I love most are just two inmates, a mental patient and a fifty-five-year-old man posing as a pregnant woman. I'm so depressed. I wonder if I should see the doctor about upping my prescription all over again? *No, no,* I think. *You're fine. And breathe.*

This morning I placed a call to Chris, a semiexecutive at the company, and asked him if there were any openings at

First. I'm waiting for him to call me back. I dialed my cell from the land line three times to make sure it was working. It reminds me of when I was sixteen waiting for my then boyfriend, Danny, to call me. *Please, please, ring,* I would internalize while staring longingly at my awesome phone that lit up in hot pink when it rang.

Chris has sleeves of tattoos on his arms but wears long-sleeved, collared shirts and glasses. I kind of want to shake him and scream: "I'm pregnant. You can't just kick me out a month and a half before I'm due." My phone rings.

"This is Christine," I say in my most professional, not-pregnant voice, thinking the HR person at Condé Nast is calling to offer me a job after I sent my résumé and identified myself as the Storked! blogger in the subject line. I have a feeling she had a good laugh while she read today's post, in which I reviewed the movie *Knocked Up* and like, *so* related.

"Hi, it's Chris," he says.

"Hello there—any word?" I ask as I scoot myself up into a sitting position.

"First will take you," he says. "But you'll have to be okay with a pay cut."

This is bullshit. I just got a raise that was going to compensate for the money that is going to be deducted from my paycheck for Jack's insurance. *Crap.*

"How much?" I ask.

"Let's see." I hear him tapping on a calculator. "Seven thousand," he says.

This is bullshit.

"Okay. Great. Thanks so much. I'll take it," I say. I need insurance. I think I'd take a ten-thousand-dollar pay cut.

Chris tells me to e-mail Carol Brooks, the editor. She writes back telling me to come in the following day. I worked with her at *First* from 2004 through 2005 before I moved over to *Cocktail* at her request. She asked me to work with her on a "new, exciting project" and showed me a series of spreads that were edgy and very pink—sort of *US Weekly* meets *Cosmo*. She needed me to start immediately, and my first assignment was doing street interviews in the Hamptons and on the Jersey Shore, asking sex questions like "What position guarantees the Big O?" or "How do you say 'I love you' without words?" Over the course of the two years I worked on *Cocktail*, the editors shifted and I haven't worked with Carol in a long time. I'm nervous. She's very no-nonsense.

I've avoided the *First* office my entire pregnancy and even used the bathroom furthest from it to lessen the chances of running into anyone there. It was just one more group of people I didn't feel like going over and over and over my news with. Actually, when I told one of the junior editors there I was pregnant, her response was not "Congratulations!" or even "OMG!" It was a wrinkled-up face and "Are you getting *married*?" I should be enough birth control for every young editor with a dream in the company. I don't want to be the spokesperson for what not to do, but that's how I feel.

The next day, I'm back at *First*. It's weird, but I'm grateful. The office is bright with afternoon sun and Carol receives me with a wide smile. She has lemon meringue hair and glowy light skin. My bag is on my shoulder and I have it so it half covers the mound under my dress.

"Thank you so much for seeing me," I say, hearing my voice shake.

"Oh, sure," she says.

"I guess you can tell I really need this job," I say.

She smiles. "Christine, regardless of the fact that you're pregnant, you're young. What are you, twenty-four?" she says.

"I'm twenty-six," I say. I started when I was twenty-four. Sometimes I feel like my high school math teacher, senior year, will always view me as the sarcastic girl with acrylic nails who was bad in algebra. Could this be true now? Do I still appear like the excited editorial assistant who wore black leather heels her first day of work? She must think I'm brain-dead for getting pregnant. Carol's worked at *Glamour*, *Cosmo*, *Men's Health*–she's made a huge career for herself. She got married. *Then* procreated.

"See what I mean! Twenty-six. Christine, you have a long career ahead of you," she says.

Career. She thinks I have a long career ahead of me. It's exactly what I think, too, but I just assumed she didn't see me like that anymore because, well, I am single and pregnant.

"I know about your blog," she says.

Oh crap. Here it comes. She's going to tell me how ridiculous I am.

"What a great opportunity for you. Just be careful how much you share," she says.

Wow. This meeting is disproving every single fear that made me feel like I was going to hurl out my window while driving here.

"Thank you. I'm starting to realize I may need a censor button," I say.

"Yeah. Keep some things to yourself, that's all," she says. "So you're due next month?"

"I am," I say. I-am-due-next-month. Next month! It sounds like an impossible statement.

Carol tells me it's "kind of cool" what I'm doing and that it's actually not that uncommon.

Hearing someone else voice my internal dialogue sounds like an opera. And then she tells me I'll start next Monday. More music to my ears. I speed-walk out of the office in an attempt not to talk to anyone. As the elevator door closes, a hand with black-polished fingernails stops it. Two fashion-able editors from one of the celebrity weeklies enters. They position themselves on either side of me. They are reed thin, one in wedges, the other, yellow peep-toes. My sunglasses are on and I am staring at the wonky reflection in the metal doors before us. The image is impossible. I look like a paper doll with a belly fastened around my torso. The editor with long, choppy bangs and pouty lips is looking at me. My palms find my belly and my eyes search for my feet, which are hiding under the silhouette of my stomach. Thank God I have on my Michael Kors sandals—and a fresh red pedi-cure. The other one, in an almost see-through wife-beater and black tuxedo vest, plucks a cigarette from a box. She pops it in her mouth, barely letting her lips hold it in place.

The door opens and I wobble out, imagining the beautiful creatures I left behind are gawking at my puffy ankles and, later, having a discussion about the weird coloring over my lip and on my forehead. Everyone doesn't get "mother's mask," a funky discoloring of the skin due to high hormone levels, but I did. Of course I did.

Cruising up Route 80 I decide to stop and see Nan. She lives in a three-family yellow house in West Paterson. It's across the street from a park called Zambrano's Memorial Park in honor of her brother, John, who died at the Battle of the Bulge in World War II. It will be an incredible piece of history to tell Jack about while I push him on a swing there. I see her walking down the block, sheathed in black from head to toe. It's eighty-seven degrees out. I'm sweating in the air-conditioned car. She can't be more than ninety pounds. Her white and gray hair is collected into a loose bun that looks like a cobweb that might fall apart. She doesn't see me. She's waving at the passing cars. The cars are slowing and the people driving them are waving back at her. It's like a parade, only it's just a Thursday afternoon. A white Cadillac Escalade with chrome rims slows and a cute guy with spiky hair salutes her. *Who the hell is this guy?* People love my Nan.

I sit in my car and watch her for a moment. Her black canvas shoes are worn in the heels and toes but she refuses to throw them out. They cost three dollars at Kmart. Carlo buys them by the dozen. She often tells him to pick up some "fresh pairs—see if they have any in the back," like she's purchasing a Hermès Birkin and wants to make sure there are no fingerprints on it. Now she's looking into the West

Paterson Democratic Convention Center, which until 1985 was her family's famed Zambrano's bakery. "People lined up around the corner for the pizza pie," she's told me a million times. Her hands are cupped on the sides of her face, pressing against the glass. I wonder sometimes if she sees ghosts when she stares in there—her mother and father, hands dusty with flour, her brothers in thin, sleeveless undershirts soiled in sweat and sugar, little children making warm fingerprints on the display window, their mouths suspended in perfect circles as they stare at the overflowing metal trays of cookies dotted in rainbow sprinkles and oozing with raspberry jelly.

When my brothers and I were little we visited her there all the time. One day as I was opening the heavy glass door, Carlo came running at it, pressing it closed with his chest. My finger got jammed in the door and I screamed so loud my great-uncles flew from the back kitchen. My father plopped me on a Good Humor ice-cream box at the front of the store and checked to see if my finger was broken. Nan appeared with a powdery jelly doughnut and my tears collected on the ring of powdered sugar around my lips. Mothers, grandmothers, what have you, always know how to distract from pain. I should bring a jelly doughnut to the ped's office when Jack has his first immunizations. I'll let him suck the white sugar from my finger.

I step out of my car and she sees me waiting for the traffic to pass so I can cross.

"Chris!" she says, waving.

"Hi, Nan," I say, leaning in to kiss her. She palms my belly.

"Hello, little baby! I can't wait to meet you," she says.

"How are you feeling, Nan?" I ask as I link her arm in mine and dance her around to her door. Her feet are swollen. It looks like there are water balloons in her shoes.

"Sick—the same as usual," she says. "I'll probably be dead soon."

"Nan!" I say.

"Come inside to eat," she says.

"I'll come in for a little bit, but I'm not hungry," I say.

"Good. I'll make you a steak," she says.

The woman has been force-feeding me since all I had were gums. My brothers and I ate squashed-up meatballs when we were barely four months old.

"Light the light," Nan says as we walk into her house, which is one hundred and twenty degrees.

"Nan, let your AC run, it's too hot," I say, turning the dial to sixty.

"Oh! It runs the bill up. The electric company is a crook!" she says.

"Nan, do you watch the news? There's a heat advisory," I say.

She's got half of herself in the fridge and when she pulls out she's holding a package of steaks, two eggs, and a head of cauliflower in her hands.

"Yes. Matt Lauer is so handsome," she says. "You should do what Katie Couric does. I tell people all the time in the supermarket my granddaughter is a journalist."

"Nan, I'm hardly a journalist," I say, pulling a green vinyl chair out from under the table. My legs dangled from this same chair when I was a little girl. In the twenty-six years I've been coming here, the only update in this whole house was a new washing machine.

"I'm going to fry up this cauliflower in bread crumbs. Delicious," she says, as she chops up the puffy vegetable on a brown paper bag.

"Nan, I'm not hungry," I remind her again.

"You'll eat. It's dinnertime," she says.

It's three in the afternoon. As I watch her saw into the cauliflower I can't help but think that just last year I was unpacking grocery bags for her and shading in dots of numbers on her Lotto tickets. She would have loved to see me try on white dresses, or, even better, walk down the aisle. I'm about to make Nan a Great-Nan. I subconsciously let out a deep breath and let my face fall into my hands. As I rub my temples, eyes closed, I hear her:

"Christina, you're going to have a beautiful baby," and she lifts up my chin with her finger.

She's the only person I don't correct when she calls me Christina. It dances off her lips and sounds like it's been my name all along. But when I hear other people slip and say it, I'm quick to say: "Christine. With an 'E.'" The steaks are sizzling on the stove. The kitchen smells like butter and warm bread. It's how her clothes smell all the time.

"Stop worrying. Here, eat this," she says, placing a plate of steak and golden cauliflower in front of me.

"Here, some lettuce," she says, as she mixes iceberg with red wine vinegar, salt, and olive oil.

"Are you going to eat?" I say, cutting into the meat.

"Me? I ate," she tells me. "Besides, I'll eat later when I watch *Law & Order*. Oh, those lawyers are so handsome. The balding one is nice," she says, easing into her chair.

Her husband, my grandfather, passed away when my father was eighteen. He had a random heart attack and died suddenly on a night when my father was driving home from college for the weekend. My father told me that on the way home a perfect drop of water slipped down the windshield. It was sunny out. He says it was an angel crying. Nanny never remarried. She's been a single mom for forty-one years— a very strong woman, someone to admire, especially *now*, and she always has the last word, hence the steak I'm eating.

13

Moving Day

It's a sunny Saturday and Carlo takes me to the beach because he thinks I need to get out more. I'd just as soon eat green olives in bed, read *Vogue*, and look at clothes I can't afford and nonpregnant women who are too thin. Now that I have a job again, the heavy feeling of hopelessness has lifted. Even so, this morning, when Carlo appeared in my doorway, he asked if I was depressed. I examined myself for a moment. No, no I'm not. I told him I was eight months pregnant and it was a hundred degrees out. That I felt like the skin on my stomach had overextended itself and that it could rip and peel back at any minute. That perhaps my ankles might re-reveal themselves today, but they hadn't yet. He told me I was "being dramatic" and to put my bathing suit on because we were leaving for the beach in a half hour. So I put my bathing suit on.

Here we are at Bradley Beach. There's a baby in a puffy diaper sitting near the water's edge, examining a handful of sand. It's wet and grainy, folded over into a little soft meatball that easily slips through her fingers, causing her to cock her head. She slips a finger into her mouth and makes a sour face like she just bit into a wedge of lemon. Her tongue pushes off the roof of her mouth in an urgent thrust before she starts screaming. A woman, her mother I'm assuming, bends down and her healthy bottom, encased in an electric blue brief confronts the beach. *Is my mom ass that big, now?* I wonder as I watch her rise and run her fingers along the inside of her suit searching for an extra couple of inches to cover her tan lines. She dumps the baby into a man's lap—the father, I guess. He's sitting in a chair, low to the sand, his feet sunk in the ground. He's unassuming and receives her like someone just plopped a stray puppy into his hands. The woman throws a yellow and white striped towel over the baby and hands the man a bottle of juice. She weeds through the cooler and settles on the blanket with a square wrapped in foil. So that's how couples do this parenting thing. *Hold this. I'm going to eat my lunch now.* Meanwhile an image surfaces in my head of Jack pressed against my chest, rolled over my arm, while I spread mustard on a piece of bread and wrestle a package of yellow cheese open with two fingers.

"I hate you!" a young boy declares to his mother after she refuses to give him a dollar for an ice-cream sandwich. I'm starting to think a day at the beach was not the pick-me-up I needed.

"No you don't," she says nonchalantly, and he runs off to the water with his Boogie board. She settles on the blanket with a chubby paperback not at all fazed that her son hates her. I'm trying to remember the first time I told my parents I hated them. I hated them a lot in high school.

I have good reason to be contemplating hate. I recently confided in my new editor that I'm half-convinced Jack is going to hate me for documenting our ... adventure. Ayana wrote back saying he won't, and when he does hate me it will be for something more pressing like not letting him borrow my car. The little boy is paddling his board across the shallow sandbar and waving at his mom to *Look at me! Look what I'm doing!* Mom gives him a thumbs-up. I guess he doesn't hate her anymore. Awesome.

A line of girls around my age are baking in the sun, every so often passing a tube of lotion down the row. My belly is greasy with SPF 50 and the vertical dark line running down it looks like a faded tattoo I tried to scrub off. I am irrelevant to them and their pretty, stringy bikinis. I'm wearing a size large tankini that's tight. Carlo drops a bottle of water into my lap and plops down in a chair next to me.

"You should really sit under the umbrella," he insists.

"You should really take your T-shirt off—are you trying to get a farmer's tan?" I say. "At least roll your sleeves up."

He ignores me as I push my sunglasses over the crown of my head and squint at the hot afternoon sun.

"Okay," I say, and extend my arms in his direction.

He helps me to my feet and moves my chair under the umbrella. Looking at us we could easily be mistaken for a cookie cutout of a happy young husband and wife, expecting their first child, with small 401(k)s and a starter home with pretty, financed furniture and an unfinished basement that doubles as "the playroom." Little does anyone know that Carlo is my older brother, and he is now on the phone coordinating the delivery of his nephew's crib.

"I need to change the address of the delivery," he says.

"No. It's not going there anymore. It needs to be delivered to Twelve B Luxe Road," he says.

"B. Not as in dog. As in boy!" He mutters "idiot" under his breath.

"Yes, on August second," he confirms. "No, same time. Nine a.m."

"Noon? No. I can't do noon. I have to leave for work at eleven—as it is I'm going in late," he insists.

"Don't worry, I'll meet them there," I say, furiously waving my hands in front of his face. He pushes my hands down.

"Okay. Noon," he says and flips his phone shut.

"Don't miss work! I'll handle it," I say, squinting at him.

"Christine. The delivery guy is going to dump a huge box in the middle of your apartment. It's not like they're going to put it together and assemble the mobile. And knowing you, you'll trip over the box in the night and blame it on me," he says, bringing a peach to his mouth.

I probably would blame it on him, even though he's the last person in the world to be mad at. Carlo is doing everything. He had the oil changed in my car yesterday. His reasoning: Your car is going to break down on the highway with my nephew in it. True, and the last thing I wanted to do was show up to a smelly garage, pregnant, asking for an oil change. Carlo is very efficient and there is security in that. I hope Jack grows up to be exactly like him, too. I stare out at the roaring sea of blue, rushing to the sand, then pulling back, then returning. It's so constant and lovely, brimming with a foamy white life.

"Everything is packed, I saw," Carlo says.

"Yep. All ready for tomorrow," I say, as my eyes chase a

wobbly toddler, her meaty legs teetering across little hills of sand like she's concentrating on a tightrope.

"You're sure you want to move out?"

"Yes, for sure."

"You can live with me in Connecticut for a little bit," he says. "We'll put the crib in the loft upstairs." He nods.

"No, it's better this way."

It would probably be easier his way. I'd have someone to warm the bottle while I change a diaper in the dark at two a.m., but what would that mean for him? Would he tiptoe around his condo? Stop having friends and even women over? He's looking out at the sea but explaining how he just got "new living room furniture that has sanded, rounded edges which are safe for the baby."

"Thanks, but I'll be okay on my own," I say.

"Okay." He looks to the left, then right before burying the pit in the sand.

"Litterer!" I say in a loud whisper.

"It's biodegradable," he says.

"A seagull is going to choke on that probably," I say.

"You overanalyze way too much," he says.

I click the chair back and close my eyes, letting the warm sun and breezy, salty air blanket me. Two summers ago I was sitting on this beach with Carlo and his college buddies. We sat in a circle. I flirted with Carlo's friends, mostly the one with the sexy Argentinean accent, and drank vodka and cranberry concealed in a water bottle, claiming the Crystal Light was refreshing every time the rent-a-cops motored by on quads. We debated whose turn it was to shower first before we lugged the chairs and cooler back to the house. We ate cheeseburgers and drank beer. Then went to the club on the foot of the boardwalk that smelled like sweat and sand and alcohol, where we got neon bracelets and slurped Everclear punch out of literal fish bowls with gigantic straws. At three a.m. we caravanned in cabs to Three Brothers Pizza for slices and Cokes. I'll never forget that summer because it was the one when Carlo tried to bring me back to life, as I was still mulling over the Keith breakup in my head, feeling guilty and worthless. I remember sitting on the back porch of the summer share laughing, soda spewing from my lips, while the grill ignited in a fire ball. I was conscious of this and I stopped and quickly cleaned up. Carlo looked at me and told me it was okay to laugh and smile, that I deserved to. Burrowing my toes in the warm sand, I look over at my brother, who's studying the water like a lifeguard.

The next day I direct my brothers from the cushy, black leather couch in my new apartment. *My new apartment—ah that sounds good*, I think.

"Those boxes can go in my—I mean," and I cup my belly and smile, "our room," I say as Carlo shuffles in carrying one too many boxes labeled "Clothes."

The one-bedroom apartment I found in my hometown of Wayne is cheap and safe—and compared to what I lived in in New York City, it's a huge castle with no strangers to share the space with.

"Kitchen," I say as Brian walks in with three shopping bags from Bed Bath & Beyond.

"You're welcome!" Carlo and Brian say in unison as they leave for more boxes.

"Thank you!" I crane my body over the couch and yell. "Jack, love, you have good men in your life," I say out loud, caressing my stomach. I look around, boxes and garment bags everywhere.

I'm not the only one moving. A moved back to Indiana—permanently, according to my lawyer. Just like that he packed up his life and boarded a plane, like I never existed at all. All this time I thought he might sweep in at the last minute and be there for his son, but I guess it's clear now he's not going to. I stretch out on the couch, lying flat out, and my belly pops on the right side. *Hello!* I press in on my side. Pop! *Hello, Mommy,* I imagine Jack saying. *Don't worry, darling, by the time you get here I'll have some pictures on the walls, some things that sing and light up in your toy box . . . the bottles sterilized. We'll put the rocker right there by the window and watch the bees zip through the flowers and we'll look up at the sky and play the cloud game—you know, that cloud looks like a bunny and that one looks like a pumpkin and—*

"Who are you talking to?" Carlo thumps in with more boxes, dropping them on the floor.

"My Jack," I say.

"Oh, that's weird. I mean nice," he says, grabbing my glass of iced tea from the coffee table. He tips the glass back, catching a cube in his mouth, and passes the glass to Brian. There's a pitcher of iced tea in the fridge and twelve glasses in the cupboard. Brothers. They collapse on the couch next to me.

"You sure about this?" Carlo says.

His words are muffled by the ancient air conditioner, which juts out of the wall under a bank of windows looking out at a manicured green lawn and bushes flowering with red buds that look like roses but aren't.

"What?" I yell in exaggeration into his ear.

"This is bullshit. I told the landlord I wanted a new air conditioner before you moved in," he says, punching numbers into his phone.

"Yeah, Joe. Carlo. What's up with my sister's air conditioner?" he says and pauses.

Brian comments that the hardwood floors are "probably like twenty years old, but they look new, right?" I look over at him with a wrinkled face. He nods and smiles and tells me to look at the "nice floors."

"This place was built in the sixties. Try forty years old," I say. The panic feeling is brimming again.

"You okay?" Brian asks.

I'm not. My hands are sweaty.

"I'm fine," I say, looking at him. I'm down to three pills a week. It feels good, but at times like these, it's just a little scary.

"Tomorrow is no good. I'll be here until six p.m. Send someone over today," Carlo says. My brothers are great—having them here sends my anxiety away for now.

Twenty minutes later a man who doesn't speak English and has paint on his pants bounds through the door with a big box. That crisis averted, Carlo moves his attention to the fridge.

"All you have is iced tea, a Brita, and a bag of baby carrots," Carlo announced as he peers into the fridge.

"So! I plan to order pizza for us later. My treat, too," I say.

"Christine. You're having a baby in, what, twenty-nine days," he says.

"Yes. The thirtieth!" Saying that out loud isn't scary. It was a little scary in my boss's office the other day. Now it's thrilling. "The thirtieth! The thirtieth!" I say it again.

"Yeah, I heard you. You still need food!" he says. "You need to get it together."

"I have oatmeal in the cabinet and three takeout menus in the drawer—and pita chips." I thrust an almost empty bag in the air.

I am more than together. I moved out of my New York City apartment to my parents to my new apartment in less than two months. I am a warrior single mother and my kid hasn't even arrived yet. *Together. Geesh.* I have two jobs, for Christ's sake, and a new home.

"Oh my God. I'm going to the grocery store. Do you even have a coffee pot?" he wants to know.

"Yes—no," I admit.

Carlo stomps out and I look around the apartment. The kitchen floor is old and ugly and speckled with designs that make it look dirty even though it's clean. I need a rug in there, with gigantic yellow and red peppers on it—something cheery for sure. The walls seem whiter than they did when I first saw the place—a little too institutional white. *You have a big walk-in closet, Christine. Room for lots of—baby clothes*, I think, trying to convince myself this place is fine for now. The new air conditioner is in and barely humming.

"I'm freezing. Can you get me a hoodie out of that box?" I ask Brian and point at a taped box.

"Let's just shut the air off," he says, walking over to it. Is he crazy? It's nine hundred degrees out.

"No! Just get me a hoodie!" I say.

"Jesus! Okay," he says.

I stifle a laugh.

He rips open the box and starts rummaging through it.

"Ew. This box is all underwear," he says, kicking it to the side.

"It's clean, moron," I say with a laugh.

"You're my sister. I don't want to see your thongs," he says, throwing a gray sweatshirt at me. I pull it over my head and bring the sleeves over my hands. Brian is fidgeting with the television plug. *It's not so bad, here. It's home,* I think.

Soon enough Carlo comes pushing through the door with a couple of grocery bags.

"Brian, go get the rest of the bags," he says.

Rest of the bags? Carlo already has four in his hands. I hear him clanking cans into the cupboards and jumbling things, big apples, into the fruit bin. I walk into the kitchen to find a mosh of tuna, canned vegetables, and, *mmm,* black beans scattered on the counter. My nesting instincts kick in.

"Let me put this away," I say nicely, and tell him to go rest— the guy has been up since seven a.m. and hasn't sat down yet. But that's beside the point—Carlo doesn't know it's not okay to just throw produce, still in plastic bags, carelessly into the bins. He also doesn't know that the mere sight of mayonnaise makes me gag. My mouth fills with saliva, then air, as I shove the little yellow jar to the back of the fridge instead of appropriately next to the mustard and salad dressing and—what is this?—black olives? Carlo calls to me from the living room: "I remembered your precious olives!" He sounds so sure of himself. Only, I love green olives, not these crazy canned ones that have a metal aftertaste. I peek into the living room. He's hanging a mirror over the couch, then looking at it from across the room, then adjusting it slightly until it's perfect.

"Thanks for the olives. They're my fave!" I say.

Then, all too soon, my brothers have gone. The cable and Internet isn't hooked up yet, so it's very quiet. I walk around the space, peeking into rooms like someone might be there and I could disturb them, but, there is no one here. The lights work. I switch them on and off, on and off. The water is running. The stove lights fine. I refold a couple of blankets and adjust the hand towels in the bathroom so they are perfectly aligned. This is it, I suppose. I'm not sure what I expected—maybe to feel more settled or reassured. I don't feel like that, though. My face falls into my hands, tears passing gently through my fingers. My hand traces the wall in the hallway looking for the lightswitch for my bedroom, and when I turn the lights on I am in a foreign place. My things are in boxes. I fall into bed in my clothes, blotting my tears with my hand. I pull the hoodie up over my head and peer around the room feeling like I'm away at summer camp for the first time. A rainstorm is tumbling in. It seems as though I was sitting in my car just yesterday, nearly nine months ago, willing a snowstorm to delay this all—the news I was scared to share, the inevitable swelling under my shirt, the intense feelings of fear or joy—I couldn't decide. I can hear the rain *shhhshing* through the leaves now. It's soothing, like a wind chime.

14

Back to Work

There are sunspots on my comforter. *It can't be morning yet,* I think as I pull the sheet over my eyes. *Better get used to this. Gone are the days of sleeping in once your little roommate arrives,* I say to myself, and Jack kicks on cue. "Good morning, Jack," I say, rolling over onto my back, toward the source of light streaming in through the blinds. The rain has come and gone like I knew it would. It's my first day at my new job and I feel like calling in sick. If I call in now I'll get the managing editor's voice mail, and just a quick word and scripted cough will do. I don't feel sick, but I am anxious about sharing a cubicle with nonpregnant editors who don't know my whole story. *My God, what everyone in that office must be thinking!* I think as the alarm clock buzzes. *I don't care what they think, Jack—you and I? We're alright!* I roll over onto my side and gently push myself up. Here I am again trying to find my center.

When I was reluctantly recovering from my back surgery at sixteen, the physical therapist taught me how to get up just like this. I let him roll me over as if I were paralyzed onto a blue mat two inches off the ground, and he positioned my right arm over my chest. "Push up," he said, but I couldn't. I was weak and pinned down with anxiety, fearing the wrong move might snap something that took nine hours to set in place. He was a tubby guy and very encouraging. I think he had been a male cheerleader in college. Every time I flexed, even slightly, my spine cramped into what felt like a never-ending charley horse. "I can't, I can't" was sort of my tagline the first couple of weeks of recovery. But as the weeks passed, I realized the only person who was going to get me out of my bed was me. I was still a kid, but it was time to grow up. When I did stand up, I felt like a puppet on strings. It was an odd feeling—like someone was dancing me around with a little crisscrossed hanger. It's funny, the literal feeling of that tightness and pulling is gone now, but I can't help but feel like I'm back on those strings while a laughing puppet master pops me to the doctor's office, then the maternity clothes store, then work, now this apartment.

Sitting here in bed now, it's hard to believe my surgery was eleven years ago. I was such a young thing then, probably daydreaming about some boy, stressing over the back-to-back super Sweet Sixteens I was going to miss on account of being laid up in a hospital bed. I never would have imagined this for myself, then—single, pregnant, in a one-bedroom apartment in Jersey.

I think back on my life often these days. It's like my mind is ripping through a journal I never wrote enough in. There is absolutely no way to expect or plan for the things that will end up making our lives—the moments that will shape us most and decide exactly who we are and will become.

I tiptoe around my apartment, maybe hoping to smell food cooking or hear someone say "Good morning." The unapologetic silence returns me to reality, where I am alone and mere weeks away from giving birth. Soon there will be bottles to make and tiny fingernails to clip. There will be someone living in the crib that Carlo put together that's pushed in the "baby corner" of my room. The crib is a more powerful statement than my belly. It's Jack's bed. It belongs to him. He's coming to sleep in it soon, which reminds me to launder the small linens so I can fix up his crib like the one in the Babies "R" Us store.

The bathroom is spotless. I feel like I'm in a hotel, that this place is not really my home. My toiletries are in an aqua travel bag on the counter and the vanity is empty. I don't like how this feels. I should be in a perfect little cocoon by now, with a soft blanket over me, my feet up, resting on a pillow with a crocheted case over it. My home should feel familiar, but it does not.

I hate A at this moment. My hate for him is intense but fleeting. I hate him when my back hurts or when I want a piece of lemon meringue pie and there is no one to fetch it. I hate him when I have anxiety about money and imagine him buying another girl dinner. I should plaster signs all over Indiana with his face and the words: Don't Date Him. But then my hate for him dissolves like a dream I can't remember I had.

"Hi, Christine," says PJ, a coworker I worked with two years ago at *First*.

"Hey, PJ," I say, standing up. "Huge, huh?" I don't know why I always feel the need to declare my physique to everyone, but I do. Telling people I'm fat with baby is like saying "good morning," or "two sugars, please."

"You look great!" she says. "Excited?"

"Of course," I say, resisting the rest of the sentence: *and freaked out.*

"Well, welcome back! It's great to have you," she says and turns away. She's very thin and tall and beautiful with ink black hair. She's engaged now, too, to Ryan—a good guy—a doctor, in fact. They both met A on my twenty-sixth birthday at my cramped karaoke party at Japas in the Village. A and Ryan serenaded me with that "Bye Bye Bye" song from 98 Degrees or 'N Sync, was it? An ironic song, these days. It's funny, on my twenty-sixth birthday I introduced A to all the important people in my life. And two months later I was pregnant and we were over.

I feel out of sorts when Joanne, the editor I am working with, approaches me. She has a daughter and a husband. We've never worked together before but her spirited hippie skirt and silver rings on every other finger tell me she's cool. Her smile is wide, but she's looking at me like I should say something, even though she didn't ask me a question.

"Hello?" I say it with a question mark.

"Hi," she says, nodding her head, pausing again and looking at me like she's a little drunk with baby envy. I'm not sure what to say, so I say "Hi" again.

"Any day now, I see," she says.

"I can't wait. It's too hot to be pregnant," I say.

"Uh, I can imagine," she says, smiling at my belly.

She sets a bunch of cartoons on my desk and tells me to edit them down to selects for the back-of-book. The assignment is just what I need—not stressful. I sit in my cube, peeling through the pages of hand-drawn cartoons with cliché word bubbles, when the *Décor* editors, my cube mates, enter. *Here goes*, I think, not looking up.

"Christine!" Cathy says, coming over to me with her arms extended. I stand up and she pulls me into her chest. Trish and Breanne are looking over Cathy's shoulder, smiling bright-eyed at me. When Cathy pulls back I can't help myself.

"So you guys know right?" I say. "Obviously, I'm pregnant—and my boyfriend is not involved," I just blurt it out, giving them no time to even respond to the question.

"Of course we know you're pregnant!" Trish says. Obviously—you could balance a coffee cup on my belly while I'm standing up.

"And you'll be fine," Cathy says, walking back to her desk. "I was a single mom for a while, too, you know."

"You were?" I wonder, thinking things must have worked out, because I know she is married.

"Oh, yes—and it was great! I had my son all to myself," she says, smiling. "We laid in his little boat bed and made shadows on the wall before he went to sleep every night. Very good days are ahead for you, Christine. Trust me."

"She's right! You should have seen my Ava this morning

calling her big sister 'Sista' and running at her with her lips puckered up," says Trish.

"No, I know. All that stuff sounds fabulous. I'm just, just scared I'm never going to meet anyone. Ever," I say. I think this is the first time I have admitted this out loud. I think I was thinking this and didn't mean to say it.

"My friend felt the same way. She was a single mom and she's married now!" says Trish.

"Ahem, I'm married, too!" says Cathy.

I sit down and turn back to my computer. I have an e-mail from Kerry, my soul sister in California. She found me on-line and wrote me a beautiful letter when she read my essay about my relationship with Keith in *Glamour*. She said she went through the exact same thing with her boyfriend and that my words were really soothing and reassuring. It was the first time I felt like a "real" writer. I had made a difference in someone's life. I put something out into the universe and someone I never would have met otherwise embraced it. These days I'm the one thanking her. She's a single mom— such an odd coincidence. First we share quadriplegic boyfriends in common, now absent ones. Kerry sends me cyber pick-me-ups whenever I need them. Just the other night I e-mailed her asking if she ever felt "freaked out, because I think I might be going crazy." She responded with a story about how she and her daughter, Callia, walk hand in hand to Baskin-Robbins every night after dinner. That was enough.

After work Kateri, Matt, and I meet our friend Jaz for dinner. Jaz lives in LA, and the last time I saw her was during the scandalous skinny-dipping incident that took place in the hot tub in the famed Hollywood Hills. She was next to me, pouring champagne down the mouth of someone whose name I can't remember.

Jaz is tipping back a beer and her bare left foot is resting on a chair when we approach her. A four-way hug ensues. The beer looks so cold and so good. I subconsciously lick my lips. Once seated we open our menus and I find myself edging over mine looking across at Jaz, then Kateri, then Jaz again. I'm worried about missing moments like this. Like my life is going in a different direction and my friends will carry on without me at dinners just like this one. I look at our grown-up purses slouched on the floor and Jaz's BlackBerry and I can't help but remember the three of us, linked arm in arm, gallivanting down Walnut Street, making friends with strangers, who would invite us into exclusive smoking clubs that smelled like cloves and order us drinks that came in short, chubby goblets. All the classes spent communicating with our eyes, and evenings at the Irish pub where the bartender knew our names and beers. I don't even recognize those girls anymore, but what I'd give to trade places right now, just for an hour. I miss those easy days—kicking through leaves in Rittenhouse Park, sitting on my stoop watching people gawk at the dildos in the sex shop window next door, indulging in afternoon naps. I never should have left that place. That was my first mistake. Thinking this way makes me feel bad, because as much as I don't want to be pregnant, I really want my baby. I'm trying to dissect this reasoning a little bit each day but it's too hard. It's like the pregnancy was unintended but the baby is not.

"Coppa. COP-PA. Cop!" Jaz says and I finally come to.

"Ordering?" Jaz says, pointing to the waitress. I straighten up in my chair, pretending like I was examining the menu this whole time.

"I'll have one, no, two, veggie rolls, an order of edamame, a seaweed salad, and a water with lemon," I say and hand my menu to the waitress. "Oh, and the chicken teriyaki."

"Hungry?" Jaz jokes, then she taps my belly with her pointer finger and announces, "That's weird!" Kateri and Matt looked at me hold their breath, but I burst out laughing. It is weird. I'm pregnant.

"It is," I admit. "It's awesome, too. Especially when he stretches inside of me. I feel him poking every which way."

"You don't talk to *him* at all anymore?" Jaz wants to know as she pours soy sauce into a tiny bowl. I'm staring at a baby with a mess of red hair spilled on top of her head.

"No," I say while waving to the baby with my pointer finger, then say, "Wait, who? The baby? Jack? We talk all the time." I'm still looking at the baby.

"No. What's-his-name. Darren? Dave? He'll regret it," she says. The baby has perfect fingernails and is flirting with her mother by sucking on her bottom lip and turning her face to the side, then surrendering to a big, pink, gummy smile. I turn back to Jaz.

"Huh?" I say.

"Never mind." She smiles.

The food arrives. The edamame is warm, salty, and buttery and I suck back bean after bean while mixing a bowl of soy sauce and wasabi. Jaz is drilling Matt on the latest celebrity gossip and Kateri is rubbing her chopsticks together. It's dinner as usual and I can't help but think that despite how different things are, they seem unflinchingly the same. Every other word out of our mouths is "Stop," which translates to "Wow," or "Get out of here." Though I admit, I am the only one looking over Matt's shoulder admiring that baby's chubby feet and the way her brother pets her head as if she were a dog. No father in sight, either, but I bet he's just stuck on Wall Street closing a deal. Mom does not look overwhelmed, even when her toddler attempts to stuff two pieces of sushi into his mouth.

"Whoa," I reach for my stomach and squirm a bit.

"What the hell?" Jaz throws her chopsticks down and air hugs me, almost embracing me, but it's like she's scared to because she might push a button and out would pop Jack. I laugh and push the wasabi and soy away from my plate.

"Nothing. Jack is kick, kick, kicking me. He probably tastes the wasabi!" I say.

"No way!" Jaz blurts out now, almost touching my stomach, but really just warming her hands to it like it's a small campfire.

"Seriously. Jack has taste buds. He can inhale and exhale, too," I say.

"It's like you have an alien in your stomach," Jaz searches Matt and Kateri's face for approval, but they just laugh and shake their heads no.

She's a little right. Sometimes I feel like I could spontaneously morph into that scene in *Spaceballs* where Barf and Lone Starr are in the diner and that creature unassumingly rips through that guy's stomach. The baby has fallen asleep and her mom has covered her—all of her—with two linen napkins. How lovely. My friends want to go to the wine bar around the corner. I'm tired and my bed is far away in Jersey. I go anyway. We settle into a little table by a bank of open windows. Matt has gone home to work. I sit with the girls and they order glasses of peach sangria. It's loud. People are laughing and passing plates of appetizers around. Jaz is telling us a story about how her boss had her chauffeur Jude Law home one night. "He had a zit. And is really short," she informs us while plucking fruit from her glass with a toothpick. My eyes search the room for something familiar, but everything seems as though I'm watching it happen from backstage.

"I'm going to go, girls," I say, pushing my untouched glass of lemon water to the middle of the table.

"No," Jaz says.

"I wish I could stay but I'm just exhausted. It's lame, I know, but look at me. I don't fucking belong here anymore," I say.

"You do. Both of you do," Kateri says.

"No," I say, pushing myself up from the bench.

"We'll walk you," Jaz says, and they both stand up.

"No. No. Stay. Enjoy!" I say.

"Uh, no, it's late. We're walking you," Kateri says.

"I need to go alone," I say, giving them a look we have all used on one another too many times to count, one that means "enough."

"Text us when you're home," Kateri says.

"I will," I say and step over the windowsill onto Kenmare Street.

The laughter and chatter all around me seem louder than they really are and in slow motion. I should whirl around and start crying, throw my hands up to the purple sky, yell "Why?" Really make this a movie moment. I don't, but I imagine myself doing it the whole way to my car.

I turn on all the lights in my apartment when I get home because I am certain there is a murderer waiting to kill me in my lovely, extremely safe town of Wayne. Something about living all alone, though, surely does make every creak and ting sound like Freddy Krueger clawing his way through the screen. I punch through the shower curtain and swing the closet door open. No one. Not even a murderer. I can't sleep so I work on a freelance writing assignment. I've accumulated so much work over the past couple of months. Tonight I am sifting through a batch of e-mails from women who are explaining in great detail "How I like to be kissed." One says she likes it when a guy "nibbles my bottom lip," and another says she can "do without tongue." I hold my hand up to my mouth and think seriously about kissing it, like a twelve-year-old practicing. My phone chimes. A text from Kateri reading simply "Okay?" I forgot to text them. I forget a lot lately. I make lunch and then leave it in the fridge. My cell phone stays behind on my night table. The AC runs all day while I'm at work. I'm distracted. I have Baby, my baby, on the brain.

15

Party Time

B*itches decorated,* is all I'm thinking as I walk into Sunday brunch that is actually a baby shower in disguise. I should have known Kateri was going to do this even though I asked her not to make a fuss. I've been calling her "Charlotte" my entire pregnancy because she reminds me of the *Sex and the City* episode where Miranda says she'll only have a shower if fried chicken is being served. I should have demanded green olive centerpieces.

Spring Street Natural in Soho is crowded as usual. People stare at me as I make my way to the four tables pushed together, center restaurant, each chair looped with a string attached to a blue, then white, then blue balloon. The strangers following me with their eyes are smiling at me, like, *Aw, the mommy-to-be is here.*

"Surprise!" my girlfriends say in a loud whisper. More people look over at us. We're in the midst of a traditional, civilized New York City brunch. Guys are wearing Lacoste polo shirts with the collars popped up and women have on designer sandals with designer bags hung over their chairs. My table is dotted with candy bars that say "Welcome Jack"—every letter colored in with bubbly dots.

There is a mound of presents at the end of the table—one odd one in a brown box that looks recycled, the sides held together with duct tape. Classy. I love my friends. The make-shift gift makes me smile. It's plopped next to professionally wrapped boxes in cheery yellow paper, garnished with plas-tic rattles and big old-fashioned lollipops. I smile because I identify with that brown box, which maybe doesn't fit in with all the other glossy, perfect presents but is full of character and heart nonetheless.

"Hi, girls. Thank you," I say.

They all look so proud and accomplished. They should be. They were the annoying girls on the packed subway with an overwhelming, uncontained bouquet of balloons. Kateri stands up and pulls the chair next to her out for me.

"I love you," she says, wrapping her arms around me, pin-ning my arms to my sides.

"Love you, too," I say and I pull back from her and look into her eyes, saying nothing, but so much, that my eyes fill with tears. Kateri has lifted me up my entire pregnancy. I often feel like she piggy-backed me to this very day, and all my days.

"And I love you, little man," she says, cupping my belly.

"O-kay, enough of that," I say, rolling my eyes, pushing a tear to the corner.

"Mascara everywhere?" I say, opening my eyes to Kateri.

"You look gorgeous," she says.

The waitress comes over with a tray of champagne flutes brimming with orange juice and champagne.

"This is just juice," she says, handing me a glass, smiling at my belly. "Congratulations!"

"Thank you," I say, pulling my seat in to the table.

I lean in and look around the table. Lo is running her finger down the menu and Claire, in a pretty blue halter dress, is snapping candids. Her hair is swept off her neck in an impromptu French twist. She looks up and smiles at me. We get along famously and have the kind of conversations that leave me feeling relieved, even when I wasn't anxious. I continue down the table smiling at Ashley, then Stef. Nic is absent today. My wing woman is in Italy being glamorous. Speaking Italian to Gucci executives, dressing models, buying the fall collection she'll stock America with, eating at Nobu, then jetting off to Greece on holiday. She's fancy and busy and in demand, but she's also called me every day since she's been away to check on her "nephew." My phone lights up in all zeros, and when I answer she doesn't sound far away.

The food arrives and I push my salad around hoping no one notices I'm not exactly eating. On my way into the city, I stopped at a strip mall in Jersey to buy batteries for my camera. That's when I smelled pizza—at eleven a.m. The baby made me do it—eat two slices before a massive brunch I knew would be topped off with an expensive cake. I had yogurt and granola for breakfast and decaf tea with lemon, but these days when Jack is hungry, we eat. I sat in my car with the little paper box propped on the steering wheel and folded a slice into my mouth—until I realized I was going to be late for brunch. I tossed the crust in the box, the box on the passenger-side floor, and cruised over the GWB. *Ah, there it is again*, I thought as the hazy skyline revealed itself. *We're back. Scene of the crime—I mean conception.*

"Time for games or presents?" Kateri announces.

"Games?" I ask and Lo catches her laugh in her hands like a sneeze.

"I told her not to," says Lo, holding her hands up like she's innocent.

"Games," Kateri confirms and starts passing out tiny newborn diapers. They look like napkins folded over. *I can't believe I am in charge of something that is going to fit in this*, I think as I examine the cottony soft puff that's stamped with Pooh bears and honeypots.

"These are so cute and *wittle*," I say holding a diaper up. A prompt "Aw" ensues.

"Okay. Open. Taste," Kateri says.

"Taste?" *What the fuck?* I think—then I open the diaper. "Ew."

"It's melted candy bars," Kateri says, and everyone just stares blankly at her like she said the most impossible thing ever, like "Aliens are coming to dinner tonight."

"What? I saw it on *The Girls Next Door*!" she insists. "Those ladies know what's up!"

"They also share an eighty-year-old and wear underwear to parties," a voice from the opposite end of the table declares. Everyone roars with laughter.

"Girls! Focus! Whoever guesses the right candy in their diaper gets a gift certificate to Starbucks." My overworked, underpaid friends peel back their diapers and gnaw at the brown goop like Manolos are at stake. Free coffee is free coffee, though. Stef is the first to guess right. "Baby Ruth," she exclaims. "Baby Ruth!"

As my friends pass presents down the table, my eyes light up and I feel like it's my birthday. One by one the pretty, ornate boxes shuffle down, and I peel through tissue paper that reveals bite-size T-shirts with studded skulls and booties small enough to glove just a finger. Then a bag that says: "Kitson."

"Tanika! You're awesome! What is it?" I ask, looking down at my college pal, who flew in from LA to be with me today.

"Just open!" she says, leaning over the table.

I whip tissue paper onto the floor and pull a tiny outfit from the bag. The shirt has a tattoo decal on it that says: "Mom Forever." I dance the matching pants across the table.

"It's perfect! I *love* it!" I say.

"Knew you would!" Tanika says, tipping her glass at me.

Seeing her here in New York City and not just as a blinking screen name on my computer means so much. When I told her I was pregnant, she congratulated me—didn't even utter "Oh my God." A few days later there was an expectant mother card in my mailbox, which I happily slapped onto my fridge when I moved into my apartment. Now she's here.

At last the ugly brown cardboard box is heaved down to me. Up close there is a label that reads: "JD's Badass Baby Kit."

"His badass baby kit?" I say, laughing. "Amazing."

Kateri and I pull at the box until it falls open. It's like a never-ending treasure chest: Onesies in my favorite color, black, that read "Cruising for chicks" and "New York City boy," lullaby renditions by Coldplay and Nirvana, a mommy guide to NYC, a rubber duck with a nose ring! And what's this—a jacket? A big jacket, surely for a four- or five-year-old. I whip it open and hold it up. I think it might fit me—sans belly. I look at Lo and Claire, wondering if this is for me.

"His first motorcycle jacket," says Lo.

"It's badass," continues Claire.

My kid is never riding a motorized bike, but he can wear this jacket. It's fabulous.

"There's more in there," says Lo, so I run my hand along the bottom of the box, finding what feels like airplane bottles. *Airplane liquor bottles?* I pull out a couple of bottles of Jack Daniels. *Jack Daniels?*

"JD for JD!" Claire says.

"Rub it on his gums when he's teething," Lo says. "Read it on the Internet. Not sure if it's legit."

My friends think of everything.

The next day my mother comes over to help me make up Jack's crib. His linens smell like baby shampoo. I think I want to take a bath in Dreft detergent. There should not be a science to making up a baby's crib. This morning as I ripped at the mattress with my fingers, trying to hoist it up to tuck the sheet under, it occurred to me I needed help. I don't want to ask for help. When it's three a.m. and Jack pees through his diaper, I will need to figure things out on my own—or let him sleep in his bouncy chair. But today it's not three a.m. and I'm too pregnant. I'm going to have to learn how to ask for help.

"Hold this side up. I'm going to slide the sheet over," I say.

"I think we should take the mattress out. Lay the dust ruffle down and put the sheet on while the mattress is on the floor," my mom says.

Her idea sounds brilliant. She lifts the mattress up and wrestles it to the floor. Watching her exhausts me. I lie down.

"I'll do this. Relax," she says. I should stand up and help her. I'm the mom now, but I can't. The pillows feel like marshmallows and the afternoon sun is setting: the perfect ambience for a nap.

"I saw Phylissa at A&P the other day," my mom says.

"Oh yeah?" I say, folding the side of the comforter over me like a burrito.

"You're going on Friday night, right?" she says.

"To my 'other' baby shower?" I say.

"I didn't say that," she says, convinced she has ruined their surprise.

"I'm going," I say, watching her smooth out the chocolate-colored sheet. She pulls the mobile from the box. A little gray elephant, a monkey, an alligator, a red bird dangle from satin ribbons. The apparatus is in three pieces.

"Leave it for Carlo," I say.

"Good idea," she says. "He knows how to do—"

"Everything," I finish.

After my mother leaves I linger over the crib, situating the stuffed monkeys a hundred different ways. I drape a soft blue blanket over the railing and stand back, admiring the darling nook I have created for Jack, and promptly promise him that this is not it, but that humble beginnings are okay—that this place is home for now and it's all ours.

Friday rolls around and I'm at Katie's for baby shower number two. She buzzes me into the complex and I ride the elevator to the second floor. As I approach her door, I smell tomato sauce, then cinnamon. I notice a set of emergency stairs and imagine Katie running up them in a panic, alerting Phylissa to my "I'm having a baby" e-mail. *I can't believe it was winter when I e-mailed them,* I think as I blot my clammy forehead with the back of my hand. *It's too damn hot.* I blow a piece of hair from my brow.

"Surprise!" Katie, Phylissa, Aimee, Krista, Tracy, and Renee say.

"Surprise!" I mimic.

"It's a Boy" balloons are floating around the living room, but I'm more interested in Katie's baby niece, Kaylee. She's lying on Katie's sister-in-law, Lisa, and when I ease onto the couch next to them, Lisa asks if I want to hold her. I open my arms and receive the little one, just three months old. "Hello, sweet girl," I say, and she blinks up at me. What an extraordinary thing to be sitting here with a baby on me. "That's Jack, in there," I say, pulling Kaylee closer to me.

"You guys didn't have to do this," I say as I eye a contraption made of diapers that looks like a cake. A diaper cake! I've heard of these things. It's too pretty to ever dismantle. I think I'll display it on my coffee table.

"Yeah we did. We're your friends," Renee says.

"Can one of you get pregnant, please?" I say half serious. "Like you, Liss—you're married, you know."

"Rocco wants to—yesterday—but I want to finish my master's and get tenure first," she says.

Phylissa's life is very responsible. College. Career. Pretty proposal. Wedding. Baby. I've never had a plan. Every single day of my life since I was five years old has been a guessing game, a page unwritten. Even when I try to plan something it explodes like a firecracker, be it exciting and wonderful or defying and crippling. Seeing Phylissa's ring catch the light makes me feel like I've skipped a step, but it doesn't make me feel inadequate today, or much at all these days. It's been eight and a half months and I've moved into my own place, secured an extra income through my blog and freelancing, picked a name for my baby, haven't so much as forgotten to take my prenatal vitamin. I've started to believe in myself more and I'm allowing myself to feel scared sometimes, because it makes me feel alive and reminds me that I'm growing. Growing up.

I open some more presents. I am now recipient of a denim hamper filled with diapers and packages of bibs and more burp cloths and little cotton onesies. I have so many of these darn little things that snap in the crouch. I can't imagine finding a use for them all in the time they will actually fit

Jack. I peel back some wrapping paper dotted with foot-
prints. A baby gym, I read. Apparently it unfolds into something that looks like the uneven bars. Baby lies under it and
plays with the birds that dangle from it. To think I spent five
bucks each on little pig and frog hand puppets. I open another gift—a set of walkie-talkie things. I probably won't be
needing this since Jack's crib is in my room, but we can certainly use it to play secret agent or whatever little boys play
in a few years.

The following Thursday my mother tells me to come over for
dinner when I get off work because she made homemade
mac 'n' cheese—and because I've "been hibernating." I have,
and mostly on account of being too tired to function after
working all day, then blogging at night. I am again too exhausted, so I go home to my empty apartment and collapse
on my bed, contemplating crafting up a salad, or ordering a
mushroom pizza, when I feel something like a sharp men-
strual cramp. *There it is again*, I think as I massage the stinging in my side. Five minutes later I feel it again—a jolt
popping in my pelvis then slowly dissolving. *Are these contractions?* I think, reaching for my pregnancy book. As I
stretch for it another ting pierces me. I call the doctor and
she tells me to go to the hospital. *Really? But I didn't even
pack my bag or sterilize the bottles yet*, I think as another
wave of cramping suspends me. I call my father, who arrives

at my apartment three and a half minutes later with a beam-ing smile.

"Is the baby coming?" he asks. "Tonight?"

"I don't know. The cramps stopped. Maybe it was indi-gestion?" I say.

He walks me to the car with his arm linked in mine and I settle in. *Could this be it? I am three and a half weeks away from my C-section!* I feel myself start to panic. This can't be it. I'm not ready. The sun is low and the sky has erupted into a mess of purple and pink, the clouds etched in thin, glim-mering lines. *The sky always looks like heaven this time of day,* I think as we cruise down Route 80. Over the clearing I find New York City in the sky. It seems far away and is over-shadowed by the iridescent light all around me. Maybe the heavens are sending Jack to me today, after all. A monstrous cloud is streaked with white light up ahead and the rearview mirror is popping with orange and yellow. Such a lovely evening—it's distracting me. I hum a little to myself, closing my eyes, letting my head ease back against the seat. *This is it—I'm having a baby tonight.*

16

Baby Blanket

When my father and I arrive at Hackensack University Medical Center we go directly to the maternity floor, like we're on the list at Marquee in New York City. There is no waiting or questions. I tell the person at the front desk, stone-faced, that I am having contractions, *I think,* and she hands me a pass and wishes me well. Reminds me of other days when I would announce: "I'm covering this event for *In Touch*—I'm on the press list" (and think: *Don't give me shit. Check Coppa off your little list and let me in*) to the snotty doorman who thinks he sits at the right hand of God. I don't understand how a clipboard can make a person feel superior to another, but these bone-heads at the steel doors or behind the red ropes honestly think they hold all the power. I wonder if they tuck the clipboard under their pillow at night thinking it might grow a couple more inches on their man parts. Nic once explained point-blank to a woman with excellent legs at a West Village club that she was a "door person with a clipboard" when she refused to let us in. It wasn't that big of a deal, but she got so much glory out of preventing two hot girls from entering the bottle-service shrine. I chuckle out loud and my father asks, "What's so funny?" *Ah, nothing,* I think, as we step onto the elevator to go to the maternity floor. I am relieved we're not stuck in an emergency room waiting room that smells like vending machine coffee and where people are holding bloodied kitchen towels to open wounds.

When we step out of the elevator, there is a high desk and a series of closed doors. A security guard signs us in and says: "Big day?" Ew. Does he think my father is my husband? I don't answer him and take a seat on a chair attached to a pod of four. My father, as usual, starts chatting him up. They're talking about the Yankees. I stroke my stomach and start to imagine things like the scary spinal needle, the white lights in the operating room, my baby crying, when a nurse with hair that appears to be permed approaches me with a *clipboard.* Her bangs are curled over once in a puffy little roll. It reminds me of the job my mom used to do on my bangs in second grade with the pink curling iron and Paul Mitchell hairspray.

"Christine Coppa?" she says. *Copa-Cabana,* I sing to myself.

"Yes," I say, and heave myself up.

"Hello, dear. I'm Olga and I'll be your nurse this evening. Come with me," she says, holding the door for me and leading me to a curtained nook with a bed and fetal monitor. My father waits in the hallway and while I change into a gown I hear him on his cell phone telling Nanny I'm fine and not to call him again. She called him seven times on the half-hour drive to the hospital.

This gown is stiff and scratchy, stamped with scary-looking stick-figure people with squiggly smiles. Olga comes in and tells me to lie down, because she is going to hook me up to the monitor to "see what's going on." *What's going on? Uh, I'm in labor,* I think as I ease into the pillows, trying to sense a contraction or gush of something wet in my underwear. She holds a little remote-control-looking thing on my belly and slips a strap through its eye–then pulls on it and secures it to a patch of Velcro. Seconds later I'm looking at two lines, my heartbeat and Jack's–it's extraordinary. There we are, blipping away with each other like synchronized swimmers in a pool. Or like little ballerinas tiptoeing along with each other, unable to make a move without a partner–in it together. I stare so long at the flickering it starts to look fuzzy.

"Two strong hearts," Olga says, tracing her finger along the lines.

"He's okay?" I say.

"Looks great," she says, and my legs jolt out and stiffen up.

"In pain?" she says.

"A little. It's a fast zing, but it went away," I say as my legs relax again.

She pulls the sheet over me and tells me to get comfortable. The monitor is going to record the contractions, if they're contractions at all.

"I'll be back in a second with fluids. Your doctor wants me to run a line," she says. *A needle–great,* I think.

"The baby is coming tonight," my father says from the chair in the corner.

"I know. Should we, like, call people?" I ask him. My mind is racing—mostly about someone stabbing me in the spine with a needle the size of a fireplace poker.

"Let's wait a little while longer," he says.

Olga comes in with a tray and sits down on a little backless chair on wheels.

"I have really tiny veins. Can you use a butterfly, please?" I ask. I know this because when I had my spinal surgery the nurses searched for bigger needles on account of the fact that I was sixteen but in the children's ward. Finally the nurse just pricked me with a butterfly needle and joked that I have small veins which must be why I was in the children's ward. I don't know if I truly have small veins, but butterfly needles don't hurt.

"I don't have one with me," Olga says. "Don't worry—I'm a pro," and she pulls out a scary, thick needle that looks strong enough to sew canvas.

She grabs my hand and turns it over and starts rubbing my wrist. *Oh crap. She's going for the mother of all veins. This is going to suck.* I pull back and she pulls me in, telling me to "just relax" and to "think of something serene like a waterfall." Olga attempts to start the line five times, blaming it on a "rolling vein," before she actually sets it in place. Every time she sticks me it feels like she is driving a steak knife into my wrist, or a fancy ice pick. She spreads a wide, clear piece of tape over the thin tube. Taking it off will probably hurt more than the needle.

"There we go. Now let's check these so-called contractions," Olga says and tears a long sheet of paper from a small printer.

"Hmmm," she hums, running her finger down the page. "You are having some little contractions, here. But they're not all that consistent," she says.

"Is she going to have the baby tonight?" my father asks in his signature stance—his hand under his chin and his body rocking side to side.

"No, I don't think so," the nurse says, but I'm not listening, because I hear Carlo. *No, it can't be. He's in Connecticut,* I think craning my neck in the curtain's direction.

"Hello." The security guard beckons from behind the curtain. "Everyone decent?" he says.

"Yes," the nurse says, and with that Carlo whips through the curtain.

"He showed me his badge," the security guard says.

"No one answered their phone so I decided to just come," Carlo says.

"From Connecticut?" I ask, my face wrinkling up in confusion.

"Well, I mean the last time I spoke to Dad he said he was bringing you to the hospital because you were having contractions," he says. "Are you?"

"I guess. Wait, you drove from Connecticut to Jersey?" I ask. "And you're going to drive back, because you have work in the morning, right?"

"Yeah. Is Jack being born tonight?" he asks.

"No, not likely," the nurse says. Carlo searches my face

for the truth, like he did when I was in high school and he wanted to know if those condoms in the hotel room were mine. Really, they weren't. I shrug my shoulders at him, half convinced I'm totally in the beginning stages of labor and slightly panicked that my overnight bag isn't packed. I'll explain to Carlo exactly what I need before the labor takes its course and I'm whisked into the OR for an emergency C-section. Knowing Carlo, he'll shoot across town to Kmart and buy me a package of Hanes Her Way underpants and a pink toothbrush.

Carlo settles into the chair in the corner and my father goes to the cafeteria for coffee and a sandwich for Carlo since he "skipped dinner to get here." I study him. His fingers are drumming against one another and he's watching the fetal monitor. All of my fears about A not being around for Jack are starting to dissolve. I think I feel them swimming out from me, like little lightning bugs so far away the flickering of their tails is untraceable. I should have put the pieces together over the past couple of months—the way Carlo moved me from New York City, helped me look for an apartment, texted me to remember to take my prenatal vitamin, wrestled my mattress, then dresser, then couch into my new apartment, stocked the fridge, changed the locks, double-checked to see if the windows were locked, took me to the beach when all of my friends were in the Hamptons in bikinis, drinking things with umbrellas in them. Carlo drove from Connecticut tonight with the intention of returning there in a couple of hours. I hope he knows how much this has meant to me—that he made me feel less alone this entire time.

"Are you cold?" Carlo asks.

"I'm tired. And hungry," I say.

"Well, when Dad comes up you can have my sandwich and I'll go get another one," he says.

When I was sixteen and in the hospital recovering from my surgery, I was scheduled for an X-ray during one of Carlo's visits so he wheeled me down to the floor. When we got there the waiting room was dotted with outpatients—mostly Hasidic Jews with straggly beards and stiff top hats. Their wives had sullen faces and bounced impatient toddlers on their laps. One of the babies had a cast on his leg and it made me feel sad. I wanted him to be catching snowflakes on his tongue. It was January and the view from my room's window made New York City look like a frosted fairy-tale land. I thought he ought to be wearing a puffy snowsuit that would make him wobble about—not be here, sick in a hospital. There's plenty of time to be sick, not when you're a kid, though. After five minutes the pain of sitting in the wheelchair became too intense. I felt like someone had knifed me midback. The woman behind the counter told us five times we were next and when Carlo asked again she told him I needed to "just wait." By then tears were rolling down my cheeks. He told her I couldn't wait any longer, that I'd had a nine-hour surgery just days ago and perhaps she could move me to the front of the line because I needed my rest. He rallied like a politician, even lying to her, telling her I felt faint. "Look at her," and he pointed at me slumped in the chair, keeled over with both hands clenching its arms. When she said no he turned my chair to the door and she told him not to leave. But we did. He whisked me away like a super-hero, rolling me straight to my room, where I got a shot of painkillers, and then Carlo brought me some cherry Jell-O.

Olga walks in, her thick-soled rubber shoes squeaking.

"Just got off the phone with your Nana," she says.

"My Nanny?" I ask. *Dear God*, I think, pulling the sheet to just under my nose.

"Yes. Darling woman. She says your father shut his phone off and that she isn't standing for any of his funny business tonight," she says. "She called him an S-O-B."

"O-kay," I say.

"She's very excited to be a great-grandma, you know," Olga says, shaking out the IV bag.

"I know," I say.

"She told me you were going to have a beautiful baby," she says.

"Yep, that's my Nan. She's been telling me that my entire pregnancy," I say.

"Sorry to hear about your ex-boyfriend," she says. Carlo looks at me, smirking, and rolls his eyes.

"She told me he wasn't Italian and that after you have the baby you're going to meet a nice Italian boy," she says. *My God*, I think, rolling my eyes at Carlo.

"What else did she tell you?" Carlo asks, straightening up in the chair, his eyes smiling.

"That your father is stubborn and if she didn't get

through to someone she was going to take a taxi here because she has money," she says. Carlo and I exchange a glance and laugh.

"Or the bus. She said she could grab the bus in Paterson," Olga says. "I told her not to, that it might be dangerous, but then she told me she isn't scared of anyone or anything! She sounds so tough."

"She's like eighty pounds, but I wouldn't cross her," Carlo says.

"Oh, and she told me why my meatballs come out so dry. She says to soak the breadcrumbs in a little warm water. And to add some grated cheese for zing. And who's Brandy, again?" Olga asks.

"Our dead dog," Carlo says over a gurgle of laughter.

"Car-lo!" I scold him. *Aw, Brandy-baby-girl. I miss her,* I think.

My father returns with a turkey sandwich and a couple of coffees.

"Here ya go." Carlo plops the deli goodness in my lap. It has mayo on it and I don't even care. I could eat a jar of mayo I'm so hungry.

"She can't eat," Olga says and hands the sandwich to Carlo. "Not until the doctor sees her." I hate Olga now. Her hair is stupid. It's not 1990.

"Okay, let's see if you're feeling better," she says, pulling the long sheet of piled-up paper from the floor. "Yep, looks like you are!"

"The tings went away. I'm tired. Can I go home?" I ask.

"Sometimes women this far along cramp up when they're

a little dehydrated. So the fluids definitely perked you up. As for going home, unfortunately, no, the doctor needs to examine you. I paged him," she says.

"Then can I have another pillow?" I say. "If I have to be here then I'll need sleep because I have to work in the morning."

"You're not going to work tomorrow," my father says.

"I most certainly am," I say. "My boss did me a favor giving me a job. Especially when I'm leaving for a twenty-week maternity leave in a couple of weeks."

"It's pushing eleven. We won't get home until after midnight," he says.

"Why don't you leave," I say. "I'll take a taxi home."

"Like Nanny!" Carlo says, laughing, and Olga and my father join him.

A doctor knock-knocks. My father and brother leave and the doctor puts on a pair of gloves. *Great.* He looks like Adam Sandler or Ross from *Friends,* I can't decide. He's wearing a yarmulke, set in place with bobby pins, and has Nikes on that look like he just took them out of the box. Olga is going over the printouts with him and he's nodding his head then turning back to his left hand because the glove seems to be stuck on his ring.

"Okay, Christine, I'm just going to check you, so I need you to bring your knees up and open your legs," he says. I do and look at the wall. This doctor doesn't seem like a doctor anymore. He seems like a random dude about to touch me. *Ouch,* I think, resisting him.

"You're not dilated—at all. You can go home. Remember to really hydrate in this heat," he says, folding the gloves into each other and air-shooting them into a wastebasket. *That's it? Drink water? I wasted all this time to drink water.* I get dressed and meet my father and Carlo in the lounge.

"Want the rest of this sandwich?" Carlo asks.

A couple of mornings later I ease onto the closet's floor and start peeling through boxes. My shoes and bags are still caged in them, and as I look up it occurs to me all of Jack's clothes are washed and hanging from the far bar, color co-ordinated and all. His size-two sneakers that he'll probably outgrow before he wears them are lined up in a perfect little row and there are two big wicker baskets overhead on the shelf filled with receiving blankets—including a very special one. I push myself up and stand on my toes, tipping the basket forward, letting the blue and white crocheted blanket fall into my arms. It still smells like my mom's parents' house. It's a weird smell, like Swedish meatball gravy and Charlie perfume and something warm. It's the only blanket I haven't washed. I'm trying to preserve the smell. I might rub it against my pillow or something. I wish I could wring it out and collect it in a little jar I could store in my night table.

This baby blanket is one of the last my grandmother made. When I was packing up my bedroom at my parents', it fell off the shelf and I didn't know what it was. I had stuck it up there in a little roll six years ago. Before it was mine it was tucked in a basket on the floor next to the side of the couch where my grandmother used to sit with her foot on the oval coffee table, propped on a thin corduroy aqua pillow. Exactly where she died. Without warning. We'd just finished lunch. I'd had two bowls of her famous macaroni salad and I was settled on the couch with a thick copy of *Vogue* listening to "As sands through an hour glass . . . so are *The Days of Our Lives*. . . . " It was her favorite show. By the time I looked up from my magazine, she was gone. I turned my head for just a split second and when I looked back her head was arched back and her mouth was suspended open like a dentist might begin working on it. The color from her face had gone. It was the first time in my life I felt real panic. *Maybe that's when and why the attacks started.* I was nineteen. My heart was beating so fast and I felt a lump blooming in my throat. I sprung from my chair only, when I opened my mouth to scream, nothing came out. I called 911 and I yelled helplessly into the phone, holding the receiver like a microphone, hardly making any sense. My words were backward: *Dying. Grandmother. Help. Send.* I rushed to her side again and her hands felt like ice. I didn't know CPR. I flew through the front door and ran next door, through her neighbor's garden. I got mud on my socks. The ground was damp from the melting snow.

I waited for my father on the porch, picking caked mud from my socks while my mother went directly to the hospital. I had never seen anyone die, or witnessed anything so profound in my entire life. Before the ambulance came I sat by her and shook her gently, and "Grandma" all but squeaked from my throat, but it was just a body; she really did go somewhere else. It was like I was sitting next to a shell. Later when my family returned to her home, my aunt Debbie started cooking a ginormous pot of pasta with capers, because when people die you're supposed to eat and sit on overstuffed couches and look through photo albums. When I found the blankets, the blue one I am clenching now and a pink one, I wondered what I'd do with them. I tucked them under my arm and sorted through some other unfinished pieces. Perhaps there was a scarf in there I could wear in mourning and sleep in, but there wasn't—just two blankets for some unborn kids that were so far from my mind. I took them nonetheless, balled them up, and pushed them into the corner of the shelf in my closet.

I pull the blanket up to my nose, feeling the gentle fuzz on my face, and I realize I'm not scared. I was scared when my grandma died. *Now that was something to be panicking over,* I think. *Not this. . . . not the birth of a brand new baby.* It's a bit of a eureka. I fold it over into a long square, then another, tucking it into my overnight bag. Some things should remain in times of change. They should anchor us.

17

Countdown

A week after my false alarm, I drop by Lo's apartment on Ludlow Street for an impromptu rooftop gathering. I parked my car in a garage and it's probably going to cost forty bucks by the time I leave. It's amazing how every penny I spend these days turns into an internal dialogue like: *Could have bought diapers, or baby powder, or formula with that.* For now I'm actually okay in the money department. All of my freelance and blog paychecks have gone directly into my savings account. It's odd to see a number in there with three zeros. Even odder, I have developed a new sense of self-control. I was in Old Navy yesterday stocking up on onesies that boasted "40 percent off" sale tags and cliché sayings ironed on them like: "Pulled an All-Nighter" and "Mr. Right." I could see the handbags looped over silver racks in the adjacent Bloomingdale's. I made myself believe I could smell the leather, too. I left the mall with just the Old Navy bag. Okay, and a four-thousand-calorie Cinnabon. Even though I've collected a nice little pile of money to live off for the next couple of months, I have anxiety attacks over college tuition that is eighteen years away. I realize this is ridiculous. *By then I could be married with two incomes com-*

ing in. I could be an Oscar-winning screenwriter; I might win the Lotto, too, I think as I make my way down Houston Street.

Now that I've been in the burbs for a month it's jarring to be reminded how ridiculous New York City apartments are. When I walk into Lo's I enter the kitchen–living room. I am confronted by a small, narrow fridge, counter space and cabinets— then a cushy blue love seat. I follow Lo into her bedroom, which is 75 percent her bed. Her TV is propped on her dresser and there are a stack of books piled on the TV. *One thing is for sure, as much as I hate living in Jersey, I have nice-size closets and fragrant grass outside every window,* I remind myself, then quickly realize I am completely full of shit. I would much rather live in New York City, but if I have learned anything at all yet about motherhood it's being selfless. I probably could have pulled off the obscene rent payment, but not much else. So I'm trying to be okay with living in Wayne, but for the most part I feel like I could pull my hair out every time the elderly man and his wife who live next door ask where my husband is since they haven't met him yet, or when the kids who ride their scooters in the parking lot leave them strategically in my parking spot (I'm pretty sure on purpose—little fuckers. Oh, wait— I'm a mom now. Little dears, I mean), or the fact that the woman in the adjacent apartment keeps seven birds (seven!) as pets and sits outside with them every night, singing in Arabic into their cages. My other neighbor cooks with forty pounds of curry. Every day. I didn't have weird neighbors in the city. I just had neighbors that didn't know my name or care to. I am completely out of my element. I remind myself about seven times a day, especially when bird lady is at it, that I am a strong, independent woman. *A strong, independent woman—I'm a suburbanista.*

When Kateri came over to visit my new apartment, she whirled around, declaring my place was "huge" and "all mine," and considering what typical twenty-somethings live in in New York City, it's a palace. I mean, I was living with two girls, and my share *alone* was $1250.00. I think the bedroom might be bigger than a studio apartment in the East Village I once looked at—asking rent there was $1950.00 a month. I was claustrophobic just standing there.

The more I tiptoe around Wayne reacquainting myself with strip malls and bagel shops, I can't help but feel that I could bump head-on into my ghost at anytime. The dramatic high school girl in her white Mercury Mystic, the Christine running barefoot through the lawn with ice cream on her chin, even the one who loved Keith. The me who walked next to Keith in his wheelchair, maybe holding his free hand, the other one heaving away at the wheel. We used to walk to the bar across the street or movie theater because it seemed easier than breaking down his chair and shoving it in my backseat. The other day when I was loading my backseat with two cases of diapers, I ran my palm over all the nicks in the leather that were made by his chair. It's hard to reconcile these memories with how different things are now. Same place. New life.

I plop down on Lo's bed and gather a piece of comforter in my hands, hugging it. It smells like fancy perfume.

"Remember the comforters at Peace and Love?" I ask Lo, not looking up, and resting my cheek on the fistful of comforter in my hand.

Last spring we stayed at a shabby h

named Peace and Love, that cost fifte

we checked in the woman behind t'

lipstick on her two front teeth and

tray, told us there was a "little boy" stayi

our room. Apparently it cost ten bucks to sleep on a b

on the floor. We spent the entire day walking around the

artist's quarter, Montmartre, wondering what exactly she

meant by "little boy." Did she literally mean a kid? We no-

ticed a family from Spain staying in the room above us. They

had two girls with them, about five and seven. Was their son

sleeping on our floor—with his bear?

"Ew. The comforter! Yes," Lo says, laughing.

"Ew? You *loved* it," I say. "Remember?"

"I was under the influence," she reminds me.

"I can't believe we took those pills from those guys from

Denmark. We're so dumb. I really hope Jack doesn't pull

that shit when he's bumming through Europe in twenty

years," I say, realizing my kid might do drugs one day.

"He will," Lo says.

"Lo!" I scream.

The guys from Denmark were raver boys—I swear they

had glow sticks bleeding with iridescent yellow light in their

pockets at all times, and I pretended that whenever they

walked into a room punchy, erratic music started playing.

They were staying at the hostel and we met them casually at

the bar downstairs, where I was flirting with the American

bartender, Josh. After examining our rooms—a cell with

comforters that had fuzz balls on them—we decided it was

tant to remain intoxicated for most of our Paris trip, nly to block out the fact we'd rather go three days sans hower than bathe in the bathroom provided. So when the raver boys offered us little blue pills, we gamely took them. A half hour later we were dancing to tribal music, trying to catch ribbons of light from the bouncing strobes gyrating back and forth. Back at the hostel, we were confronted by a nineteen-year-old boy from England, traveling on his "gap year." "'Ello," he said, from a mattress on the floor. My first thought was *Harry Potter, is that you?* He looked so little and shy from the floor. I ran my fingers through his hair to make sure we weren't hallucinating. We weren't. I pulled my hoodie over my hair and fell on my bed with my boots still on and started drilling him. Harry was a virgin. He was "starting university" next year and he didn't drink much. Lo emerged from the bathroom, peeled her jeans off, got under the covers, and told me how much she loved me. Loved Paris. Loved Harry. Loved the stained comforter. We drank a lot of coffee the next morning in a green park and watched little Parisian children "boat stick," or push toy tugboats around an oval fountain with long wooden sticks. I think about taking Jack on a G-rated Paris trip one day.

"I'd like to take Jack boat sticking one day," I say to Lo.

"We will!" she says, kicking a weather strip tight against her door even though it's not at all drafty. It's August.

"Why is there a weather strip on the bottom of your door?" I ask, pointing to the sandbag strip.

"Mice. They're all over the effing place," she says. I smile, thinking my friends have followed suit in curse-word substitution. Moms don't swear. When I stubbed my toe the other day I screamed "Salami!" at the top of my lungs.

"I was lying in bed the other night and I saw one sniffing around in the corner. I stood on my bed and yelled at it, but it didn't scare, so I threw my slipper at the wall and it ran into my closet. I hope it's not in my shoe, sleeping," Lo said, milling through a wash basket of towels. I imagine her on her bed telling the mouse to get the "fudge" out of here and the little critter looking up at her like a cartoon character with pink ears and a wedge of yellow cheese in his paws, thinking: *What the fudge, lady?*

I spread apart the clothes hanging in Lo's closet and peer in, looking for the mouse. Nothing—unless it's hiding in her Marc Jacobs lace-up boots, and hell, if I were a mouse living in the city, I think they'd make an excellent home. Same for her black Gucci heels. When Kateri arrives we climb six flights of steep stairs in pursuit of the roof and I feel slightly empowered by this journey, like I'm climbing Mount Everest, though I'm somewhat afraid I could go into labor. A couple of weekends ago at Thompson Square Park, I quizzed the girls on what they would do if I went into labor in New York City. Lo said: "Drive you to Jersey?" I looked at her, scared, thinking she might actually be serious. That if I was sitting in a sopping-wet pair of maternity jeans she'd actually flag down a cab and demand he drive us over the bridge when there are twenty public hospitals in the city. That's when Claire looked up and said: "Take you to the nearest hospital in the city." But Claire isn't climbing the steps with me now, so I'll just cross my fingers.

"Wait, let me get behind you," Kateri says, and slides past the railing.

"Why?" I said, turning around on the steel staircase.

"You know, in case you fall. I'll break your fall," says Kateri. *In case I fall. What am I doing here? Don't worry, Jack, we're not falling. Ever.*

"Yeah, Chris, please be careful," Lo says, holding the door open for me and extending her hand to mine.

I step over a crack of open space onto the rooftop. It smells like hot tar and seems higher up than we actually are—just six or so stories. It's dusk and the sun is starting to dip in the sky, casting wonky shadows all over the black rooftop. Lo spreads a couple of beach towels down and Kateri helps me sit. Surrounded by buildings and sky, I ease back, resting my weight on my hands, when Rachel appears in the doorway.

"Damn, you climbed up here?" Rachel says, scooting over to me then removing a six-pack from her oversize purse. Rachel went to NYU with Lo, and when she goes on dates with guys she doesn't want to date again she renames them in her phone: "Tom don't answer," "Dylan made me pay for drinks," "Chris bad kisser."

"I'm tough!" I say, flexing my arms like a pregnant super-hero.

I am tough. I should be home under the covers reading the last few chapters of *What to Expect* or something, but I couldn't resist Kateri's offer to spend a lazy Sunday in the city, especially since I am due in approximately seventeen days. I've become increasingly calmer as Jack's birthday nears, when all along I thought the finality of everything would cause mad panic or a more intense emotional roller coaster. But something different has happened. I feel like I'm bathing myself in a sea of warm tranquility, like I'm floating on my back and the gentle lull of the ocean is relaxing my fears away. The August air feels like hot breath on my arms and neck. Lo and Kateri are hopscotching to an imaginary track and Rachel is leaning up against the ledge with her knees pulled up to the sky, smiling warmly at me.

"I'm so proud of you, Chris," she says. "Really, I am. This is truly magical what's happening to you."

"I know," I say, and I mean it, more than ever. Kateri and Lo return to the towels and we all lie there in a circle, our heads just touching, looking up at the stars that are starting to reveal themselves like a string of dull Christmas lights.

"Do you wonder what you'll tell Jack?" Lo asks, and I feel Kateri's hand cup mine. But it's okay. I've spent a lot of time agonizing over the past eight months about this very question. I know the day will come when I have to explain to Jack why Tommy and Billy have a daddy, and he doesn't, and I've accepted that. Sometimes I think of brilliant things to say like: "Well, your friend Mary doesn't have a dog, but we do," because I'm definitely getting Jack a golden retriever to pal around with and sleep on and take on backyard adventures. Then I realize how idiotic it is to compare people who don't have pets to those who don't have their fathers around. Then I just feel like I'm staring at a calculus equation. My brain turns to mush and every single rationale I come up with sounds like jibberish.

"Every day," I say.

"It won't be for a while, so don't stress," Lo says. I wonder if I should compile a little folder of things: photos of A and me, his parents contact info—a little passageway of sorts for Jack. I'll tuck it away for safekeeping for the day when my world will stand still and I'll have to explain what I myself don't even understand.

"The only thing I think I can say is something innocent, like he wasn't ready to be a daddy, but I was ready to be a mommy," I say. "Wait, I don't even want to say that, because that makes it about Jack. And it's *not* about Jack. It's about A. Does that make sense?"

"It does, but what will you say when Jack asks why? He's going to ask why," Lo says.

I look up at the sky like it might spell out an answer in the stars, but it doesn't.

Katie opens the door and I collapse on her couch, pulling a blanket over me.

"I'm having contractions, I think," I say.

"What? Cop!" she says, sitting beside me with her face wrinkled up. "What should I do?"

"Trim my hair?" I ask. "I can't have a baby looking like this."

I'm having Jack in two days. The thirtieth has arrived seemingly without warning. I wrote out my rent check today for September. When I penned the date in I realized the twenty-eighth was just forty-eight hours away from motherhood, so I vacuumed the carpet and Windexed the television screen, then I sat on the couch alone and admired the silence, when it hit me what happened. It was like that evening in Palm Springs all over again. I got pregnant. My boyfriend skipped town. I live in New Jersey. I cried into my hands, thinking, *I can't believe I let this happen to myself. I was successful and thriving and independent and now I'm—what—a single mom living in a one-bedroom apartment in Jersey. How will I raise this baby when I'm not even done raising myself?* I calmed myself down and walked into the bathroom to splash some cold water on my face. I tried to summon the calm that had sustained me for the last couple of weeks but it had gone like winter when you wake up to find the trees dotted with pink, and it's springtime. When I found myself in the vanity mirror I saw my hair. It was straggly and thick. *I can't have a baby looking like this*, I thought to myself. So here I am at Katie's, swallowing sharp hiccups in my pelvis and ready for a trim.

"Should I call someone? Carlo?" Katie asks.

"No," I say, reminding myself of the last time I thought I was having a baby. "Can I have some water? Two glasses. Have any lemon?"

Katie dips my head into the bathroom sink and starts working shampoo through my hair. It smells like mandarin orange. She massages my scalp with her fingers and I start to feel myself coming back to that place where joy exceeds fear. There it is. Jack is coming in two days; my heart excites. When Katie pulls me up I see our reflections in the mirror. She's combing through my hair with ease and a gentleness that transcends words.

When Keith was in rehab, I really let myself go. I looked at myself in the mirror one day and my eyebrows looked like caterpillars kissing. One night I was home, showering, before going to pick up a movie for Keith and me to watch that evening at the rehab when there was a knock at my bedroom door. It was Katie. I was rushing around my room trying to find my keys and the belt to my oversized cream sweater when Katie asked me what she could do to help me—*anything in the whole world,* she wanted to know. She's a good friend. She often came to the rehab with food for me and to trim Keith's hair. I pressed my hands on the dresser and looked at myself in the mirror. There were dark circles under my eyes. My collarbone was poking out; my hair was tied back in a messy bun. "My eyebrows," I said to her. "Could you do my eyebrows?" She put a pillow on her lap and I lay down and closed my eyes. I didn't even feel her plucking away at me. I lay there in silence hoping it would take all night. I didn't want to go back to the rehab. I was exhausted. I stayed like that in her lap for a while even when she was done with my eyebrows. I think I am going to ask her to be Jack's godmother. She's very laid-back and works hard. I think she might instill this in Jack—not to take himself too seriously, never to expect anything without rolling up his sleeves. And he'll have free haircuts for life.

Katie is finished combing through my hair and starts snipping the ends. I have a lot of hair. I hope it takes a long time to clean up because, I worry that fear will return if I find myself alone in my apartment with time to think.

"Not too much," I say. "I need my long hair. Not giving that up," I say.

"You got it. Just two inches or so," she says.

I'm never cutting my hair. It's my youth. It's something that makes me feel beautiful. The hair stays. Everything else has changed, but not this. I'm keeping this for me. I'm piling it on top of my head, revealing the nape of my neck. I'm taking it down and shaking it out in a roomful of people. I'm letting the sun catch it, highlighting little streaks of natural blond. The hair might be the one thing still sexy about me, the one thing that still shines. And it's enough for me. I read about women who chop off all their hair to cleanse themselves in times of uncertainty and change. Not me.

I love Target. It's brilliant to be able to buy pajamas and shampoo and diapers—and pita chips (which I am currently eating as we walk through the aisles)—in one place.

"Are you going to pay for those chips?" Carlo asks.

"No, I'm going to steal a three-dollar bag of chips because three dollars can really make me at this point," I say.

"Okay, Christine. What exactly do you need now?" Carlo asks.

"Underwear. Pajamas. A robe. Hospital stuff," I say.

"Well, can you hurry up and pick it out?" Carlo says, speed-walking with the cart.

"No! I told you not to come because I wanted to take my time. Target is the new happy hour for me," I say, stopping in the Home Goods section, eyeing some bookshelves. I really hope Jack takes to books and reading at a young age. I hope he'll find the escape in them, like I have through the years. Whenever I didn't want to be somewhere I tucked myself away with a book and just went somewhere else. I also want him to exercise his imagination every single day. I don't think daydreaming is a waste of time at all.

"Christine, you really can't keep going places alone now. You could seriously go into labor—underwear is this way," he says, dancing me around the bend. I break free from him and thrust the pita chips in his hand.

"I think I need this," I say, pointing to a cool ladder bookshelf.

"It's two hundred bucks!" he says.

"So. I need it. For Jack's books," I say. A woman is smiling giddily at me. I see her out of the corner of my eye, but don't acknowledge her. I can't today. There is a reason I am wearing sunglasses inside. I should have a baseball cap tipped low on my brow, too. As I lean in to read about the bookshelf features, I feel something grazing my stomach and look down to find a hand with red fingernails splayed across my belly.

"Excuse me? Hi?" I say.

"Hello. Ohhhh! I couldn't help myself! You're about to pop, huh?" she says, now patting my stomach, gently. I look at Carlo who is trying not to laugh out loud. I kind of want to fuck with her and tell her I'm not at all expecting.

"I'm due next week," I say, wiggling away from her. I don't understand why people, total strangers, think they can just walk up to you and touch your body. What's next, a random dude grabbing my ass because it's fuller than usual?

"Ohhh, lots of luck," she squeals, reaching for my belly again, but I raise my hands up to block her and walk away, saying, "Thanks!" as I turn to face Carlo.

"You're bitchy," he says, hoisting the box off the shelf and setting it vertically in the cart.

"Actually, I'm pregnant. How would you like it if a random woman rubbed your belly?" I say.

His smile widens.

"That'd be nice, actually," he says. "Come on—underwear!" As we cruise to the intimates aisle I notice a big basin filled with area rugs marked 40 percent off.

"Ohhh, I like the red one for the living room," I say, running my hand up and down the fuzzy roll.

"Christine, can we please just get this stuff later?" he says.

"Later! Later!" I scream, and two women look up from their carts. "Later I'll be in freaking labor! How can I bring Jack home without a red area rug in the living room! How?" It's a totally rational question, I think. My infant son needs this red rug. Today. I start to lift it from the basin, but Carlo pulls my hand away.

"You're ridiculous," he says, and shoves the rug in the space below the cart. I smile at him, satisfied, and an older woman strolls past us.

"Hope you're not having a girl! You'll be outnumbered!" she says to Carlo.

Her comment makes me think of . . . him. Sometimes I wonder if A and I missed out on each other—if we both overreacted and were too scared to go it together so we just ended up here in this white noise, this suspended moment.

I took him suit shopping one afternoon in New York City. The sales guy kept trying to match a tie to the shirt like he was a pro, but his slacks were wrinkled. So I led A around the store, declaring that I read too many *GQ* magazines to have him go on a job interview looking like a retarded paper doll. At the counter the clerk asked how long we'd been married, but we'd only been dating for a week.

"Here, this is nice?" Carlo says, holding up a size XL muumuu dotted with rosebuds and I come to, leaving A in the space in my head I carved out for him.

"Uh, no," I say, and start weeding through a rack of capri-style yoga pants and fitted tank tops. I throw a couple pairs of pants and tops in the cart and make my way over to the underwear wall. A commenter on my *Glamour* blog, Storked!, told me to buy "granny panties" because bikinis will irritate my C-section scar. It never occurred to me. Not only am I getting a paycheck, I'm getting advice. To think I just bought five new pairs of string bikinis from Victoria's Secret. One pair even says "Pink" on the butt. Do I think I'm going on spring break or something?

"Can you please hurry up!" Carlo says.

"Can you please go over there and find me a robe? Preferably black," I say.

He returns in two seconds with a kelly green terrycloth atrocity with bright pink daisies stamped all over it. Their centers have smiley faces on them.

"Carlo, it's not funny!" I say, ripping the robe from his hands, and he laughs.

"You're tormenting a pregnant woman, you know!" I say over a rack of gray cotton robes.

We wait on a ten-minute line and just as the salesgirl is ringing us up I realize I forgot to buy slippers. I tell Carlo and he says if I let it go he'll buy me five pairs from Dolce & Gabbana.

"I don't think D&G makes slippers." *Wait, do they?* I think, walking away from the line.

"I'll be right back," I say. "Two seconds." *I need to Google D&G slippers when I get home. Carlo might be screwed*, I think as I pluck a pair of fuzzy gray slippers from the shelf.

Back at my apartment Carlo unloads everything while I make a pitcher of iced tea. As I open the fridge I catch a glimpse of the houseplant Carlo bought me when I moved in. "A house-warming gift," he called it. I set it on the windowsill so it can catch the sun. I read online I should water it just once a week. I check it every day, poking through the leaves, lifting them up, making sure the soil is still damp, convinced I am going to kill the poor thing. But it's a happy little plant with big forest green leaves springing from the packed-in soil. It's starting to flower with something red, too. It's been alive for a good twenty days now. That's a good sign.

18

Birth Day

I hear an opera of chirping outside of my window. I lie in my bed listening to the little birds, imagining their beaks spreading wide as they perch on branches springing with green leaves that will all too soon bleed into wild hues of orange and yellow. Summer has come and gone almost. I feel as if I have been transported here from the icy day in January when I willed snow from that somber sky.

I went to bed last night knowing that Jack was coming today. I thought I might lie awake agonizing into the night over things like A, or even the whereabouts of three missing booties the dryer must have eaten, but I didn't. I tucked myself in and fell asleep to the sound of the hot wind pulling through the trees. It rocked me into a dream I can't remember. Those are the best kind. I always wake up feeling so satisfied, like I must have been in love for seven hours. My cell phone is ringing and I search for it under the blankets.

"Hi, Dad," I say.

"I wanted to make sure you're up," he says. "Good morning."

"I'm awake," I say over a yawn. I hear Carlo in the background: "Tell her I'm getting in the shower and coming over to pick her up. Does she want coffee?" My dad reminds him, "She can't eat or drink anything."

"I'll see you at the hospital," my dad says. "I have to pick up your Nanny."

"It's awfully early for her," I say. "Can't Uncle Carmen bring her this afternoon?"

"Come on, Chris. You think she's going to miss this? She's been dressed for an hour." I bet she has, even though she hates being away from her home. She especially can't stand hotels, but when I graduated from college she slept over at the Doubletree—on one condition: she slept on the covers, in her housecoat. She did enjoy the room-service croissants and coffee, though. She wrapped some up and stuffed them in her purse. Do all grandmothers hoard food?

I push myself up and walk past the empty crib, stopping and peering over the railing as if Jack might be here already. In the shower I examine my big stomach for what will be the very last time. I feel myself begin to tear up. *This really happened, huh?* I think, leaning up against the tiles. I let myself cry. There will be no more time to cry once Jack arrives. But as the tears fall from my eyes I realize they are joyful ones, not scared ones. My old life is fractured in my head like puzzle pieces that don't fit together anymore. The water runs over my face, mingling with the tears. I step out from the shower and find myself in the foggy mirror. As the steam clears I begin to see myself more clearly.

Carlo helps me into his Jeep and I hang my arm out the window, letting the wind whip through my hands.

"This is it!" Carlo says.

I don't answer him, closing my eyes and inching toward the wind, letting the air sweep across my face. It smells like warm grass. The windshield is dewy.

"Christine?" Carlo asks.

"Hmm?" I ask.

"What's wrong?" he asks. "Are you mad at me?" He's the last person I could be mad at. Look at all he's done for me over the past nine months. I would be lost without him.

"No, I just need to relax," I say, reaching for my hospital pass, pushing it back and forth through my fingers. Too bad it's not on a fancy string like a press pass—that would really be ironic. *Hi, I'm here to cover the Coppa delivery. I'm on the list.* I chuckle to myself.

The sun is starting to pop more in the sky, pushing the clouds far apart on a big backdrop of blue. As we come up on the exit for the hospital my eyes find the New York City skyline, and I see Carlo in the corner of my eye looking over at me. I feel my jaw clench a little and I make myself take a breath. I smile, gently, at the skyline, nodding *hello*, and Carlo jokes: "Should we keep on . . . into the city?" I stare straight ahead as we dip down the exit ramp and the skyline disappears.

We pull up to the valet and an attendant helps me out and wishes *us* well. Of course he does. Carlo is holding my overnight bag and his smile is beaming. It doesn't matter that the attendant misreads the situation. Well wishes are well wishes at this point.

In the hospital I show my pass to the guard and he directs us to the same bank of elevators I rode when I had my false alarm. It's not a false alarm today. I keep wondering who my anesthesiologist is and what he or she has decided for me. Will I be awake—meaning, getting a spinal—or are they putting me to sleep? Not knowing makes me anxious. We step off the elevator and are greeted by a nurse holding a clipboard. She has red hair and seems about my age.

"Hello, I'm Jack!" she says, taking my hand.

"Jack! She's naming her kid Jack," Carlo says. "I'm Carlo. The brother. Not the father." I should make him a T-shirt that says "Super Uncle—Not Dad."

"Carlo. Stop," I say, looking at him. I smile at Nurse Jack.

"Let's get this out of the way. I'm single," I say.

Nurse Jack smiles at me and quips, "Me too!"

Dr. Keanchong is waiting by a bed and I smile, feeling reassured that she already knows I'm single and that no one will be sweeping through the door at any minute wondering if he missed the big moment, like in the movies.

"Christine, big day!" she says. She leans in and kisses me. I want to fall into her chest and let her hold me for a long time. Nurse Jack sets a powder blue gown on the bed and pulls the curtain. Alone, behind it, I catch my breath. *We're okay, Jack. We're still okay.* I push my arms through the sleeves and ease into the bed, pulling the blanket up over me. My teeth are chattering, but I'm not cold. I remember the same thing happened while I waited for Jack's heartbeat to reveal itself.

"Decent?" a male voice calls from outside the curtain.

"Ye-es," my voice cracks.

"Christine, I'm Dr. Krammer," a curly-haired fellow says, extending his hand to mine. He's very animated and happy with tight brown curls piled on his head. He's like a kangaroo bouncing around in sneakers and he looks exactly (*exactly*) like Miranda's Steve from *Sex and the City*.

"Hello," I say.

"I'm your anesthesiologist," he says, running his finger down my chart. "Christine, I want you to sit up and crouch over like a scared cat."

"A scared cat?" I say. It's a silly request. I think about a cat being thrown into a bucket of cold water and his fur looking electrocuted like in cartoons.

"I need to see if your spine will pop a bit so I can navigate the needle," he says.

I feel the color leave my face. Dr. Krammer touches my shoulder.

"Don't worry. I know you're scared. It's a scary thing—a needle in your spine. I've done it a million times, even to people with back problems," he says. His eyes are sincere. I slide my legs over the bed and hunch over. I feel his hands touching me. His fingers are cold and gentle, my arms spread with goose bumps. It's a connection I haven't felt in a long time—a man touching me.

"I thought I was being put under?" I say.

"I see a note on your chart here about that, but then you'll miss everything," he says. "You don't want to miss everything."

He tells me about when his wife gave birth and how he cut the cord and how his son's hair had "goop" all over it—that it was "the most awesome experience" of his life. When he says that, it's like there are little stars in his eyes. He continues tracing his thumb down my spine. I find myself fantasizing about his life. I bet his wife cooks him fancy dinners and that his son waits by the glass door with his palms pressed against the pane for him to come home. They live in a pretty house on a grassy hill and have one of those wooden swing sets with a fort in their yard.

"Bingo," he says, and I feel him making a little circle with his finger in the middle of my spine.

"Christine, I can do this," he says. It seems too easy. Shouldn't he put on a special hat with a magnifying glass attached to it?

"Are you sure?" I say, my lips trembling.

"Yes," he says, and I feel my eyes well up with tears.

"But did you see my X-rays?"

"I did," he says.

"So you saw all the stuff in my back. I mean there's a lot of stuff back there," I say, nodding my head, remembering how when I had my consultation the doctor was worried about the medication even taking because of all the hardware and scar tissue. Now I'm less concerned about the needle, and instead I'm imagining the doctor sawing me open like in that scary movie *Touristas* where the unassuming coeds get their organs stolen from their bodies while they're awake. *Oh Christ.*

"I saw everything. How is it getting through the airport?" he says, chuckling.

"Will you do a pinch test?" I ask.

"I see you've done your homework," he says. "Yes, absolutely." I think my face just got a little whiter.

"The good news is your husband can come in with you," he says. Why doesn't he know I'm single? Isn't there a "single" box checked off in my chart? After I make Carlo a T-shirt, I need to make myself one: "Single. So What!"

"I don't have a husband. Dr. Krammer, I don't feel so good. I feel dizzy," I say, and he helps me lie down.

"Better?" he says.

"I'm thirsty. I'm really thirsty," I say. "Can I have some water?" Nurse Jack comes in with a tray. She has to start a line. I want to tell her about the butterfly needle but I'm suddenly paralyzed with fear.

"I'm sorry, Chris, you can't have any water now," she says.

"Ice?" I ask.

"No, sweetie, I'm sorry. Take a deep breath for me," she says, rubbing my hand.

"I just feel so hot. Can I have a cold compress for my head?" I say.

Carlo comes in and sits in the chair.

"Mom, Dad, and Nanny just got here," he says. "What's wrong? You look . . . nervous."

"Nanny?" I say, ignoring his question. "She really came, huh?"

"She told Dad if he didn't bring her she was taking a cab," he says. "She threatened him with the name of a cab company, too."

"But she's so sick," I say.

Nurse Jack comes in with the towel and places it on my forehead. It feels cool to my skin. I close my eyes and feel her rubbing my wrist, looking for a vein. The stick is quick. I half want to ask for a drip of antianxiety medication.

"So, how old are you?" Nurse Jack asks me.

"Twenty-six," I say.

"Me too," she says, collecting the needle and tape onto the tray. I bet she's going to happy hour when she clocks out. I hardly remember what that's like. I have a vague recollection of men in suits, smelling of day-old cologne and beer.

"I'll leave and let Mom and Dad come in," Carlo says.

I hear a baby crying. It sounds far away.

"Someone was just born," Nurse Jack says as she turns to leave.

A couple of minutes later my father pushes through the curtain. My mother follows behind him.

"Hello," they say one after the other.

"Mom, can you ask Nurse Jack to make this cold again?" I say, handing her the compress. She takes it from my hand and stands there.

"Mom, physically give it to her," I say.

"But she's busy, Chris," my mom says.

"Christ!" I say, feeling my eyes fill with tears. She gives the towel to Nurse Jack.

"Christine, you need to calm down," my father says.

"I'm fine, Dad," I say.

I'm not fine. I'm scared. I don't want to get a spinal. I don't want to get sliced open. *I just want you to be here already, Jack,* I think as my mother hands me the towel and I slide a piece of it into my mouth. I suck on it intently, watching Nurse Jack's back so that she doesn't whirl around and catch me. After my spinal surgery the nurse let me suck on a cold washcloth since I couldn't have any water yet. I chewed it like a helpless little puppy. I push the towel from my mouth and press it, softly, over my face. From under the towel I hear the squeak of wheels and when I push the towel up on my forehead I see a little cart just outside the curtain. My mother peeks over it.

"It's a new baby," she squeals in a loud whisper, and my father gets up from his chair.

"Hi there, little one," he says.

I'm too nervous to push myself up and peer into the cart. I tell my mom *I don't really care* when she says the baby has red hair like she had when she was a baby. I know it's rude and I feel bad after I say it out loud. I bet that baby has beautiful hair and I wish her a great life, but my baby is still lodged below my ribs and is about to be cut out of me. *Cut.*

"We're all set. Just a few more minutes. Since you're not going under *someone* can come in with you, you know," Dr. Krammer says.

"I guess my mom will," I say, hearing my voice shudder.

"Let's get you into some scrubs," he says to my mom, and they disappear through the curtain.

Carlo walks in with Nanny. She's dressed all in black and her hair is pinned back into a little messy knot.

"She almost got thrown out," Carlo says, smirking.

"What! Why?" I ask.

"There's a huge sign in the waiting room that says 'No Eating.' What does she do? She whips out a bag of cookies," he says, laughing and shaking his head. "She got crumbs all over the place."

"I was hungry. Hi-ya, Chris. You look beautiful. You're going to have a beautiful baby, you know," she says. "Carlo, help me kiss your sister." Carlo steadies her while she bends over the railing. I feel her soft skin on mine and when I look up at her she winks at me. She stands at my bedside for a while, holding my hand in both of hers. My father tells her to sit down two times, but she stands here, holding on to me. Carlo reappears and says he needs to take Nanny out so Brian can come in. I'm feeling overwhelmed by everyone. I keep searching the small space for Nurse Jack, hoping she'll whisk me away. Brian walks in with a fistful of cigars.

"Look what I got," he says, holding one up, under his nose. I look up at him and smile.

"You're worried about the spinal, aren't you?" he says. I don't say anything and he assures me it's not going to hurt at all because the local is going to numb everything first. He starts rambling about this nerve and that nerve. He's like a walking encyclopedia. I think he and Jack are going to have good conversations in a fishing boat one day.

My mom comes back in. She's wearing paper scrubs and booties over her shoes. She has a shower cap–looking thing on, but her hair is poking out from it. She looks a little like a clown. I look over at my father, who's sitting with his hands in his lap. They both have urgent looks on their faces. I see Nurse Jack shuffling around behind the counter, until she finally looks up at me, smiling, and walks over. I know it's time now, but I want to steal away and give myself five more minutes. I need to explain to Jack, one more time, that everything will be seamless and that even though all of the pieces aren't lined up right now, he's about to cross into the world and there isn't a more perfect way or circumstance imaginable for us to meet each other. I want Jack to know he was dreamed up and that today is written down in the sand on a quiet beach where the ocean pulls in and out like it always has and will. We were meant for each other just as is. *I carried you under my heart for nine months, Jack, and I give it to you—all of it*, I think, and with that Nurse Jack pulls my chart from the foot of the bed.

"Okay, Christine. We're ready," she says. I look over at my father and feel my eyes fill with tears. The same thing happened before my spinal surgery. I looked at him with a question mark in my eyes. He didn't have an answer for me then, but I was young enough to believe he might. This time, I know better. *Let's do this, Jack*, I think.

"You can say good-bye to your dad now and your mom can come in after you have the spi—you're ready," she says. I smile at her for stifling the word *spinal*.

My father kisses my cheek, then the top of my head.

"You'll be fine, Christine," he says, and a few tears escape me.

"She'll be great," Nurse Jack says.

"Is there a wheelchair? Or does this bed just get pushed in?" I say to Nurse Jack, wiping the tears from my face.

"The OR is right down the hall, so we'll just walk. I'll help you," she says, resting her hand on my shoulder. I look up at her, nodding and swallowing, when she extends her hand to mine. I look down at my stomach. The past nine months play on fast-forward in my head. I see myself standing in the middle of a whirlwind: watching myself blink at the pregnancy test, hanging up the phone after A called to say good-bye, stepping into maternity jeans, lying in the grass in Central Park with the girls, at work in the elevator with the skinny editors, driving over the GWB in Carlo's Jeep, up alone in my new apartment transcribing interview tape, until all of the thoughts just sort of stop. I place my hand in Nurse Jack's: "Okay, I'm ready."

She helps me sit up in bed and steadies me when I come to my feet. We walk down a long, wide hallway lined with curtained cubicles. Up ahead, there are two thick doors with metal handles. Nurses in white smack a big red button; the doors slowly open, revealing white light, then close again. I stop for a minute and take a breath.

"Are you okay?" Nurse Jack asks.

I turn and look back and for a moment I make myself believe I see Christine, I see myself, and she's just standing there watching me walk steadfastly into the future. She's a young thing, with waves of brown hair all around her face and big, unassuming eyes. It's like I'm looking through a screen. I want to call out to her, at least say, "I'll be seeing ya" or something, but I don't, because when I look closer she's smiling at me. *We did good, Christine*, I think as I turn to leave her. . . .

Nurse Jack smacks the big red button and when the doors slowly open I squint at the bright white lights overhead. She leads me to a thin table and as we walk to it I see surgical tools, one next to the other in a pretty, little uniform line on a tray, and quickly turn away. Nurse Jack helps me scoot up onto the table and Dr. Krammer appears before me.

"How are you feeling, Christine?" he asks, resting his palms on my knees. I half smile and swallow.

"You're going to be fine, Christine," he says, and walks around the table. I feel fingers grazing my neck and startle.

"That's me, Christine," says Nurse Jack. "I'm just untying the gown."

Dr. Keanchong comes in with a mask over her mouth.

"Hi, Christine," she says, and takes my shoulders in her hands.

I feel a cool sheet of plastic spread over my back and a quick brush of something wet and drippy.

"That's me, Christine," Dr. Krammer says. "I'm sterilizing your back. You're okay," he says.

I feel myself excite. My teeth begin to chatter and my eyes fill with tears.

"You're okay, Christine," Dr. Keanchong says.

"Christine, I need you to do the scared cat move," says Dr. Krammer. I feel his hands on my back. *This is it, this is it,* I think as my heart races. Dr. Keanchong pulls my shoulders forward.

"You're okay, Christine," she says again.

"Just a quick pinch and a slow sting," Dr. Krammer says. I start to cry, then suck in a breath. Nurse Jack is holding my head, rubbing my temples. There is a sharp pinch, like a bee sting, then it burns, fading slowly. . . .

"That's it Christine, you're okay," Nurse Jack says.

"Tell me when you put the needle in," I say, shuddering.

"I'm in," Dr. Krammer says, and Nurse Jack and Dr. Keanchong ease me down without warning. I feel like everyone is suddenly racing around me.

"The needle?" I say.

"It's all done, Christine," Dr. Keanchong says and I feel my legs flush with heat, then a fast rush of pins and needles. I lay back staring up at the bright white lights as Nurse Jack pushes my gown up and opens my legs.

"I feel you, I can feel you," I say.

"We'll give it some time, Christine, don't worry," Dr. Krammer says.

Nurse Jack appears over my head and opens a small screen in front of my face shielding my view. *This is it.* My eyes search left, then right. I feel something tugging on my side, it's like a rubber clamp squeezing my skin.

"Chris, do you feel that?" Dr. Krammer asks. I close my eyes, sensing it again.

"I just feel something warm and soft squeezing my side," I say.

"And here, do you feel that?" he asks.

"I don't know," I say.

"Christine, pull your legs up for me?" he says.

I will them up with all of my might. "Okay," I say.

"They're up?" Dr. Krammer asks.

"I don't know, I guess." I hear things clanking into a metal dish. I sense something dripping down my stomach, but then it fades away.

"She's ready," I hear Dr. Krammer say. "Bring in Mom."

"Christine, I'm going to start now. You're okay," I hear Dr. Keanchong say.

My mother comes in and stoops down next to me. From my perception it's like she's sitting on a tree trunk. I feel her brush her hand on my forehead.

"You're okay, Chris," my mom says. Everyone keeps telling me I'm okay. The lights seem brighter. I look to the left of me, then feel like something is tiptoeing across my pelvis or like I'm being unzipped.

"I feel that. I feel something," I say.

"You're okay, Christine," I hear Dr. Keanchong say. I hear a clank again.

"You're going to feel some pressure, Christine," Dr. Keanchong says. All of a sudden I feel like there is something sitting on my chest. I reach for a breath. I try to make noise, but I can't.

"I see the head," Dr. Keanchong says.

"The baby is out, Christine," Dr. Keanchong says. I hear Nurse Jack, "Aw." Then I hear my Jack. He sounds like a little bird doll that someone wound up, until he roars with "*Eh-Eh-Eh-Ehhhh-Whahhhhh!*"

"The baby is here," my mother says, and I feel a single tear fall from my eye until I taste it on my lips.

"He's peeing on me!" Nurse Jack says and the room erupts into laughter.

"Christine, look to the left, Nurse Jack is going to show you your baby," Dr. Keanchong says.

It's like I'm underwater looking through a pair of goggles. I can see him. He's naked and pink and wet and his arms are pulled up with his fists under his chin. There is bright white light all around him. He looks like an angel baby—a heavenly little creature.

I see things happening around me. Dr. Krammer is at my side telling me I "did good," then sticking my line with something. My vein flushes with cold. My mother is standing up, craning her body away from me.

"The baby, where is Jack?" I say to my mom.

"They're cleaning him up," she says. Then I see Nurse Jack come closer. She's holding a white bundle that she passes to my mother. She sets him next to me and I turn my face to his.

"Jack Domenic," I say in a loud whisper. His face is pink and there are a few stray black hairs peeking through his white cap. I pull it off to find a damp mess of dark hair. My mother presses his cheek against my lips.

"Jack Domenic," I say again, looking at him. "Hello, my baby. I've been waiting for you," I say. And then, just like that, his eyes open and search for my voice. Then they squint to the left and blink twice. He looks at me like he has something to tell me but is too tired, he'll tell me later. His lips are full and pursed together. They open, just slightly, then close again. I brush my hand on his cheek and his eyes bat down. I study his face and memorize it instantly. Such supple skin, little folds by his eyelids, a spray of ink-black lashes.

"I love you, Jack," I whisper, taking a deep breath, squinting in the light all around me. "I love you," I say again and watch as the nurse whisks Jack away. My head rolls center and I stare up at the lights. My mother has gone to the nursery and I'm alone again, but a mother now. *I'm a mother.*

19

Owl Eyes

I've been moved to recovery, where I'm in and out, tip-toeing back and forth from a dream to reality, where phones are ringing and people in rubber shoes are speeding around. My eyes are closed but my hands are slowly examining my belly. It's flat, like someone took a pin to it. I lay here thinking how I did it, it's over, yet just beginning. Jack is far away from me on an entirely different floor, and it's barbaric. I knew this would happen, though—I'd go to recovery and he'd go to the nursery, where my family would point at him through a glass window. He must be wondering where I am and where he is—a strange new world with soft blankets and little plastic basins to lie in, with wild, white lights everywhere and people poking and prodding at him. I was with him for all of three minutes, I think, and I have his face completely memorized, especially the way his eyes smiled at me, opening just enough for us to fall in love with each other.

"Christine?" I hear a voice. My dad's. "Chris-tine." I hear it again and open my eyes. His face is hovering over me. He smells like coffee.

"Did you see Jack?" I say, tasting the dryness in my mouth.

"Yes. I said, 'Hello, Mr. President,' " my dad says.

"What?" I say, trying to push myself up with my legs. *My legs. I can't move my legs.* It feels like they are underwater, attached to two big balls and chains.

"I just have a feeling he's going to be president one day," my dad says, smiling.

"He's a half hour old, Dad," I say. "Let's not start with the expectations. He's probably learning about sugar water right about now."

"He's a beautiful baby," my Dad says. "Strong, too."

"Did you see his lips? It's like someone painted them on," I say.

Nurse Jack comes in with a bag of something.

"He peed on me!" she says.

"Making his mark in this world," I joke.

"It's crazy how much he looks like your brother Carlo," she says.

And so it starts. Since A is absent everyone is going to tell me how much Jack looks like "a Coppa." Jack has A's nose. It's like a miniature version of the one on A's face. Jack has my mouth and lips and I think maybe my eyes, but A and I both have brown eyes. The little folds of skin around them are A's. It's not that alarming that Jack looks like him. They share DNA—and A is really good-looking, so it's not a bad thing.

"When do I see him again?" I ask Nurse Jack.

"Not until we move you to your room," she says.

"When is that?" I ask.

"About an hour," she says. *An hour? That seems like a long time. Would you pluck a puppy from his mother's nipple and stick him in a closet for an hour?* I think.

"Just rest, Christine, you just had major surgery," my Dad says.

"I did?" I say. "I don't feel like I did."

"You did," Nurse Jack says. "This drip is progesterone. It's going to help your"—and she lowers her voice—"uterus contract," she says. I wonder if she thinks I'm embarrassed because my dad is in the room. Pretty sure he knows I'm not a virgin now. I remember reading about the progesterone drip on the Internet a couple of weeks ago on the couch with a blanket over my legs. I can't believe I am here. A mother—in charge of another person for the rest of my life. My legs are starting to feel pins and needles and I'm able to wiggle my toes. Carlo appears, popping through the curtain.

"He. Looks. Exactly. Like. Me," he says with a beaming smile, a cigar tucked behind his ear. He looks so happy. I let him think he's right.

"What is he doing up there?" I ask him, again trying to crane my body up.

"Oh, he's a genius. He's, get this, sucking his thumb!" he says.

"Aw. He started doing that when he was five months old. I saw it on the sonogram machine," I say.

"Nan keeps knocking on the window, telling the nurse to feed him because 'he's starving,' " Carlo says. "You should see the nurses up there behind the window. They're point-ing and waving at Nan! The nurses told me how cute my grandmother was. I was like, what about my nephew—you know, the brand new baby!"

"Oh, we have to call *Glamour*! My readers need an update!" I imagine a bunch of women I don't know, clicking the refresh button on their computers, biting at their nails. The regulars like LORIKNOWS and PAMELASC might even burst through this curtain, here.

"Okay, when we get to your room," Carlo says.

"Nope! Now!" I say.

Carlo dials, but I quickly tell him to hang up.

"Carlo. You're calling *Glamour*. Condé Nast. So don't be . . . goofy," I say.

"Christine, I carry a gun. Do you think I'm intimidated by fashion editors?" he says.

"Just be cool," I say. "Like, don't tell her I was freaking out before the spinal."

He dials again and as it rings he practices saying "Hello."

"Hell-o," he says, looking at me.

"Hey there!" he says.

"Carlo!" I say.

"Yes, hello, Ayana?" he says. "Carlo Coppa, here. Christine's brother."

I hear him tell my editor, Ayana, that Jack looks exactly like him, then that he is seven pounds and twenty-one inches. That he's healthy and strong. Finally that I am doing well, too. Carlo hangs up the phone and pushes through the curtain.

"Where ya going?" I ask.

"To hang out with my godson," he says. I hear Nurse Jack

say "Congratulations" to him and then Carlo yell back, "Thanks!"

There are kind men in Jack's life. It's one of the things that kept me afloat through my pregnancy. I'm so grateful for people like Carlo and Brian. They're so youthful and full of energy. Energy for throwing balls and pitching tents and fishing. I get teary-eyed thinking about what I would do these days if I didn't have brothers, even though I spent my whole life wishing for an older sister to envy and a younger one to teach things. If they were here now they'd be hysterical women, pawing at my son, then setting me up on Match.com before my stitches dissolved.

I feel a little bad for A. It must be the drugs. It has to be, but I can't help but think how he missed such an extraordinary moment. Our baby is here. I heard Jack screech like a yawning baby bird reaching for a breath, and saw him all pink and flushed. Jack opened his eyes to my voice, and I could cry for A. There was a time in our relationship when were walking around on the Upper East Side and I stopped to pet a golden retriever a young couple had walking with them on a red leash. The guy was holding onto a stroller with a baby, just a week old, in it. Her skin was still a little translucent. I peered into the stroller and looked up at the couple, telling them how lucky they were: "A baby and a golden!" I exclaimed, and A agreed with me, effortlessly. I remember thinking he was extraordinary right then. We walked away holding hands and I watched the couple push the stroller across the avenue to the park, the dog leading the way. It was a beautiful day. The park looked on fire because the leaves had changed overnight in bursts of orange and yellow. It's amazing how such feelings for A can never be predicted. *I suppose I should hate him more than ever today, but I don't,* I think, wiping a tear from my cheek.

"The father?" a tubby Asian nurse whispers, leaning over my bed in my room. She smells like mayo.

"What?" I say, looking over her, seeing Carlo push the little cart in with Jack.

"Give him to me," I say to Carlo, while the nurse fiddles with my IV line.

"I can't believe the father is not here," she says, *tsk*ing under her breath.

Carlo is holding Jack now. I can barely see his face because he's swaddled tight, like a burrito.

"He's really not coming at all?" the nurse says. I switch my eyes from Jack to the nurse. My smile dissolves into a placid line. I look up at the nurse and in my calmest voice I say: "No. The father is not involved." Then I stare at her until she backs away.

"Carlo, give him to me," I say, almost licking my lips.

Carlo places him in my arms. This is the first time I am holding my son. In the OR he was lying next to me while I blubbered all over him. I hear my mother in the background say something about supporting his neck, but it's like there is a mitten over her mouth. Everything around me seems to stop and fade away to gray. Jack is wide awake, blinking at me. I've never seen eyes like this before in my life—they're like baby owl eyes, so big and inquisitive. I place his cheek next to mine and whisper just so he can hear me: *I'll love you forever, Jack Domenic.* I hold him out in the length of my forearm and unravel the swaddling in search of his hands. Someone is telling me not to, because he's "good and warm," but all I hear is noise. Before I even reach for Jack's hand, it wraps around my finger; his eyes are fixed on mine. My mother comes over with a two-ounce bottle and I caress the nipple against his soft, pouty lips and watch as they receive it gently. His cheeks balloon, softly, in and out as he drinks. Now his hands are pressed on mine as I hold the bottle to his mouth.

"Smile," Carlo says, holding the camera to us.

"Smile, sweet Jack," I say as I pull the bottle from his mouth and prop him in my hand. I tap his back gently and a timid little burp blows from his mouth. Once again, his mouth opens, then sucks at the air, opens, then sucks at the air again, like he's kissing an angel I can't see.

"How did you know to burp him like that?" Carlo asks. "The nurse in the nursery showed us all how and said most people prop the baby on their shoulder and do it." I'm not sure what made me burp him like that. It was instant, like tying my shoelaces, blindfolded.

"There, there, sweet Jack," I say, tipping the bottle into his mouth. My father, my mother, Carlo, Brian, and Nanny are huddled around my bed, staring at us, all of their mouths hung, just a bit, open, in a silent *Aw*. Nan comes closer to me, resting her hands on my bed, then running her finger over Jack's hand that's cupped over mine.

"I love his hands," Nan says. "What beautiful little hands. I can hold him soon?" she asks.

My father pushes a chair over to my bed and helps Nan ease into it. There is formula collected on the sides of Jack's lips and his eyes are heavy now. I'm not ready to give him up, but Nan looks so joyful and eager, her arms extended like she's receiving a blessing from above. My father takes Jack from me and sets him in Nan's arms. In the wake of youth and age, they sit together, Jack's hand secured tightly around Nan's thumb.

"I'm great-Nanny," she says. "I love you, beautiful baby. See, Chris, I told you you were going to have a beautiful baby. That's right!" she says.

"August thirtieth, Jack," Carlo says, leaning over him. "Your birthday, you know?"

I almost forgot it was August. I never thought something so wonderful could happen in a month like this one. This time four years ago, I was in a hospital a lot like this one. I was sitting by Keith's bedside, helpless and afraid. I admitted to Nic once that a part of me died on the day he was hurt. I think I've been carrying that death around all these years, sort of mourning for myself. It's ironic how August has returned me to a hospital. But this time, the sun is filtering in through the windows, lighting up the room. The people around me are smiling and laughing. I look down at Jack and see him kissing at the air again; his little lips sucking at nothing. There is so much light and promise all around him.

"May I have him now?" I say, holding my hands out.

I bring him to my face and feel his warm breath on mine. August is a beautiful month. The month I came alive again.

Kateri comes tiptoeing through the door, her mouth suspended in a huge open circle. She's wearing a long maxidress with a braided halter-top and strappy flat sandals. She's got the meaty September issue of *Vogue* tucked under her arm. She continues tiptoeing over to me, like she might wake Jack, but he's wide awake playing our new game: staring. So far he's winning. I looked away for a second to reach for a tissue and when I looked back down at him he was staring up at me with his little owl eyes, like two teacup saucers, with an expression to the tune of: *I'm beating you at our staring contest*. Kateri hangs over me with her palm resting on my shoulder, completely silent.

"Jack, this is Aunt Kateri," I say. "She's been counting down to your birthday."

I raise my arms, offering Jack to Kateri. She reaches for him, then steps cautiously away.

"My hands! I need to wash my hands," she says, and rushes over to the sink, smacking the antibacterial soap a dozen times. I should have told her to wash up first, I think. I look down at Jack and my mouth turns crooked, my eyebrows raise a bit, like I'm owning up to my first mistake as his mom, but he doesn't care. He's still deep into the staring game, looking up at me, full of wonder, every so often making a tiny sound like a yawning kitten. Kateri walks over to me rubbing her hands like she's about to dive into a double fudge brownie with no spoon.

"He's so delicious, I know," I say extending him to Kateri.

"Hello, Jack," she says, looking down at him, walking away from me. "I'm Auntie Kateri. I've been waiting for you," she says, dancing side to side, then in little circles.

"This is dancing, Jack. I'm going to teach you salsa one day, and to speak Spanish, and how to navigate on the subway without having to ask strangers like your mama," she says, winking at me.

"That was one time, Jack, and I was trying to get home from *Brooklyn,*" I say.

Kateri is baby-dance-stepping around, humming away, then stopping to whisper secrets into his ear, likely a sign of how she'll spoil him, take him for a tattoo when I won't, buy him his first set of drums, which I'll curse her for while I'm writing at my desk, yelling "Five more minutes, then bedtime" to Jack. She'll do all the good things aunts do.

When Kateri leaves, at around nine, I send Jack to the nursery to sleep because I want to sleep. I'm exhausted. My room's been like a revolving door today. When Phylissa and her mom left, Renee and Krista entered. As soon as flowers from my cousins arrived, another set from *Glamour* appeared on my night table—it's an extreme bunch, like a tiny tree of blooms. I never saw a bouquet so big. My room smells like a garden of lavender in the summer heat. The card is from the editor-in-chief, Cindi Leive, and my blog fans. It's a little intimidating. The nurses kept asking me who they were from while they pushed their noses into them. Carlo responded every time: "*Glamour* magazine." Every nurse squealed, admitting it was her favorite magazine. One sat down on my bed and asked seriously if working for a magazine was like *The Devil Wears Prada* movie. I chuckled, since the reality is that I blog from my one-bedroom apartment in Jersey and I'm about to stretch out into a long maternity leave from the *First* office. Still I played along: "It's more like *How to Lose a Guy in Ten Days* meets *Sex and the City*, with a dash of *America's Next Top Model*." The nurse said "wow" and I asked her if her life is like *Grey's Anatomy* and if Dr. McDreamy can check my stitches. She laughed and I said, "Hooray for Hollywood, right?"

I stare over at the flowers wondering when I became the poster child for single mothers—a mother at all. My room is quiet and I notice there is a blanket and pillow dressed in a white case on the couch. *I suppose it's for my husband*, I think, feeling for my call button. I need medicine now. I feel like someone stuck a hook in my stomach and dragged me along by it. My night nurse, Deena, comes in with a syringe.

"In pain?" she says.

"Yes," I say.

"Jack's in the nursery, I see," she says. "Good call. You need your rest."

I fall asleep only to wake up an hour later, attacked by a jubilant force of adrenaline. I force my eyes shut but I can't seem to fall back to sleep. I feel high, a little like I did that night in Paris with Lo. I read about the chemical reaction that happens when you give birth, but I never thought it would make me want to dance on a table. I push my call button. I have a burning desire to see Jack right now, even if he's sleeping.

"Yes," a voice says.

"Can I have my baby?" I say it with an uncertainty in my voice, like she might say no. A minute later my nurse is pushing him in in the little cart.

"Perfect timing," she says. "He needs to eat." She sets Jack in my arms and his little owl eyes stare up at me all over again. He's so beautiful I could burst into tears. I do. His skin is less pink now and I'm just noticing his eyebrows, little, light sprays of arches. "Eh." He makes a little bird noise.

"Are you hungry, my love?" I say over a sob, catching the nipple in one of his air kisses. He sucks and sucks, not taking his eyes off me the entire time. The room is dim, lit only by a small desk lamp. It's just Jack and me now and the feeling is familiar. I think back to quiet nights in my bedroom, with my stomach under the sheets, telling him stories about the subway trains and Paris at midnight, feeling him squirm around inside of me, and now he's here, drifting to sleep, the bottle pushing out from his mouth. I keep him on my chest for a while, smelling his head, a soft mix of baby powder and something warm like bread, and rubbing his back with my fingers. When I see it approaching two a.m. I call the nurse and she wants to take him to the nursery, but I keep him with me. She sets his cart right up against my bed and helps me turn to face it. Every so often I sit my finger under his nostrils, neurotically checking his breathing. I fall asleep looking at him, feeling like the luckiest woman alive, but I startle an hour or so later from a ting of pain pulling in my pelvis.

When I open my eyes to find the call button to summon more medicine, I find Jack, swaddled on his side as I left him, but wide awake now, staring at me, his lips just slightly open. I wonder how long he's been watching me sleep. I lie on my side and pull my hands up under my chin.

"Hello," I say, and he blinks at me once. I feel my eyes well with tears as he just keeps on staring at me, as if he's waiting for me to say something or explain it all to him in one sentence. I reach over the side of the cart and stroke his cheek with the back of my hand. "I promise I'll be enough, Jack," I say. "I'll love you double." Tears are streaming down my cheeks and I can taste them on my lips. We lay here looking at each other, me gently rocking his cart, forgetting the pain that woke me, humming Jack back to sleep, watching his eyes close, then open to see if I'm still there. *I'm here, Jack. I'll always be here,* I think, humming in the quiet of the room.

20

Homecoming

My father helps me into the backseat and I shudder as I fold up, feeling a burning sting as if someone set fire to a little rope in my lower abdomen. I take a deep breath and shift myself to the middle of the backseat. My mother is standing outside of the car, rocking Jack, gently pointing out clouds, and my father is packing the trunk with my bags and flowers and dozens of gifts for Jack—including one epic blue bear the size of a six-year-old I wanted to forget "by accident." It was a thoughtful gift from my father to Jack, but when he walked into my room with it I wasn't thinking how adorable it was, I was thinking about where the hell I would put it. It's not like I have a playroom for such things. Am I supposed to just flop it mid-living room—or somewhere more appropriate, like behind the shower curtain? I see my father in the corner of my eye with the bear under his arm. Maybe he can strap it to the roof and it will blow away.

When my nurse came into my room this morning and said I was being discharged, I wanted to stage some sort of breakdown and see if it would buy me another few days. HUMC is like a hotel. You press buttons and staff sweep in with fresh salads and little bottles of shampoo and conditioner—and my baby. I can't believe my five days are up. I want to stay on this "babycation" where people constantly ask me how I'm feeling, where I can lie for countless hours staring, full of hope, at my son—then give him to the nursery when I want to sleep and shower. But they are returning me now to my apartment, where things are still in boxes.

My mother sets Jack in the car seat next to me. He's sleeping and looks like a Professor Frog because his top lip is fixed over his bottom one and he has one finger to his chin as if he's thinking about something really complicated and brilliant. His chest is moving up and down and he is completely unfazed as I fumble with the straps, twisting them more than they already were. I decide I hate car seats. This bucket contraption is bulky and awkward and there's not enough slack in the straps, but I don't know how to manage more. I look around, realizing Carlo is already at my apartment waiting for us, but this is something he could figure out blindfolded. After hearing the buckle click-click, we're off, and as the car goes past the hospital it occurs to me that I am on my way home with my baby—the hospital let me leave, completely and without question. They patted me on the shoulder and thrust a black vinyl bag full of diapers and formula into my arms. As I stare down at Jack, I wonder if he will like the place I am taking him—my crazy world of singlehood where I call cereal "dinner" and my friends "aunts." Where I can walk around naked because no one is ever around and where my worrying is uncontrollable. Worry. I hadn't factored my worrying in. This morning I asked the discharging doctor, seriously, if I was showing signs of postpartum depression. He looked at me like I *was* crazy. I'm so nervous because I think based on my history of anxiety and depression that I actually might be more susceptible to it. But then the doctor asked me how I felt and I said, "Great!" but wondered if he thought I should start taking my medicine every day again just to be safe. Then he reminded me I feel "great!"

However, as we cruise down the highway I begin to examine whether I am even fit enough to be a mother, and then I feel as if I could burst into an anxiety attack right here. I talk myself out of it. I am staring at the backs of my parents' heads. They brought me home on Christmas Eve, 1980, and it was snowing uncontrollably. My father forgot to bring my mother's boots, or even sneakers, to the hospital and so he helped her shuffle through the snow in a pair of terry-cloth slippers. I can see him leading her through the white powder, snow collecting in her hair. They are so bizarre.

As we pull into my complex, I see a couple of blue balloons swaying in the warm breeze, attached to the railing. Carlo is in the window and comes bursting through the door.

"I think we should walk in the front door," Carlo says.

"What?" I say, pulling on my father's arm, squinting at the stinging in my pelvis. I think it's easier to stay hunched over like this. Every time I straighten up the stinging returns. I might never sit down again.

"Well, this here is the back door, so I think we should walk around through the grass and go in the front door—the 'right' way," Carlo says. My brother is so superstitious. One year my father forgot to sweep the old year out at midnight (literally sweep air out the front door) on New Year's Eve and Carlo launched into a panic, driving a mop through the screen door the next day.

"We're going in the back door," I say to Carlo, as my father places Jack in my arms—his eyes squinting up at the blue sky. I wonder what he makes of it, this massive blue sea stamped with airy pillows of white. Carlo holds the door open and I step inside, peering around the small space. I take a deep breath: "Welcome home, Jack," I say, walking him into the living room, where Nan is dozing in the rocker by the window, with an afghan pulled over her legs. Carlo has set a changing table up in the hallway by the bathroom. The shelves are stocked with a basket of diapers, a few containers of wipes, and a big pink bottle of lotion with a pump spout. There is a picture of an airplane hanging over it with the words: "Soar!" ballooning from it. When I left, the changing table was in four pieces in a box. Carlo is smiling fondly at the structure as if he built a car from scratch. I set Jack down on the cushy mattress and pick back his onesie. His legs are pink and they jut out, suddenly, like I'm bothering him.

"Just a diaper change, little one," I say, peeling back the tape. Carlo hands me a diaper, but it's too late. A fountain of pee shoots over the changing table all over my shirt in a perfect, arched little rainbow. I feel confused, like I don't know what's going on and everything is happening in slow motion. The logical response to cover him with a diaper or wipe, or even my hand, doesn't register. Carlo tries to catch the pee in his hands, while roaring with laughter. My mother, father, and Brian come running over. The space is crowded. Carlo is standing over Jack with a puddle of pee in his hands. I feel like all the walls are closing in on me. I look down at Jack and his owl eyes stare back up at me with an urgent look. He's wondering why everyone is staring down at him, laughing. "You peed all over, honey, don't look at me," I say, taping his diaper shut.

Carlo takes Jack from the changing table and holds him up in front of his face. When I see them side by side like that, they do kind of resemble each other—especially in the cheeks and eyes. Carlo tells Jack they'll have to go over this "peeing thing." I go into my bedroom, closing the door behind me so I can change my shirt, which is damp with pee. I can hear my brothers fighting over who is going to coach Jack's little league team, while Nan declares that Jack is starving—again. My father calls from the kitchen telling everyone to come eat. I think he forgot we're in a one-bedroom apartment. He called so loud, I think the Indian family next door might come over with plates and forks.

"This is lasagna, Jack," Carlo says, pointing to the tray.

I take one look at the saucy, red, layered casserole and completely lose interest. I have no appetite whatsoever. I'm even thinking twice about the green olives set in a little porcelain dish on the table. Jack is making bird noises again anyway, so I ask my mother to make a bottle as I take him from Carlo. I ease into the couch with Jack and quiet his chirping with my pinky finger. He sucks at it hard before pushing it from his mouth and looking up at me like I'm a crazy person for thinking I could trick him. He starts kissing the air in between bird noises. It's the cutest thing I've ever seen. I might not feed him until he really starts screaming.

My mother is spending the night because I am exhausted and just had major surgery. I wonder how long I can use the "surgery" excuse to get people to do things for me. I want to abuse my prescription and shut all the lights in my apartment off, but Jack is awake, staring at me again and sucking on my pinky, which when he is not hungry is his favorite thing in the world to do. We're sitting by the window rocking, watching the sky turn colors. I can't believe how dark it is already, but then I realize it's the cusp of fall. I search the trees outside the picture window for the first signs of autumn, but they're all still green.

"Those are leaves, Jack, and soon outside is going to look like a wildfire because everything is going to turn orange and yellow and collide into a big mess," I say. Jack just stares up at me, content as ever. I could reach into the sky and pull the moon straight in through the window and it wouldn't matter.

My mother comes in with a bottle that Jack sucks back until he looks drunk. I bounce him a little in my arms and he falls straight away into a dream. I sit here in the rocker, tipping it back and forth with my foot, watching him. I have him semiswaddled in the blue and white blanket my grandmother made, but not completely. I'm a claustrophobic person myself and I know there's all this science that says swaddling a baby tightly makes him feel like he's in the womb, but I think it makes him feel like he's in a straightjacket, so I give him just enough slack to wiggle his arms out if he likes.

"Why don't we put him in the co-sleeper so you can lie down, too?" my mother says. I raise Jack up to my mom and follow her into the bedroom. My mom lays Jack down gently into the little bed and I tuck the blanket tight all around him, remembering that I read a newborn should never be left with loose blankets in the crib because he could suffocate in them. It was a damning thing to read; so was reading about crazy women who drown their babies, because the thought gets implanted in your mind, and if you're like me you start obsessing, asking yourself: *Wait—do I feel like that? Do I?*

Jack is lying comfortably on his back, with his night cap pulled down to his brows. My mother turns the light off and I stand over him watching him sleep, thinking how I can't wait to fall asleep myself. It's been a long day and I ache all over. Just then I see him stir. I tip my body over the little bed and start to gently retuck him in. His eyes open suddenly and I see two perfect little saucers in the darkness. "*Fla-whah-eh-whah.*" He starts crying. His face is wrinkled up. He looks incredibly pissed off. I pat his tummy. "There-there, you had your bottle. It's nighttime now," I say. "Shh, shh." I try to soothe him. My mother comes into my room, grinning.

"He's awake," she says.

"He is," I say, scooping him up, feeling a dampness in my palm. *What's this now?* I think unraveling the blanket.

"He's wet. I think he peed," I tell my mother. She pops the light on and we peer down at the little square mattress, soaked with a small oval. *He peed,* I think, looking down at him as he blissfully sucks on my pinky and stares up at me in a Look-what-I-did expression.

"We really need to get this pee thing under control, Jack," I say, walking over to the changing table. When I peel his onesie back, his diaper appears to be intact. *How'd he wet his bed?* I wonder.

"Are you a magician, Jack?" I ask him, cupping my hand over him, fully prepared for a surprise shower. He's looking up at me with his owl eyes, thinking seriously about what a magician is.

"A magician pulls a rabbit out of his hat, Jack," I say, taping his diaper shut. "You don't have a rabbit under your hat, do you?" I lift him and press his warm cheek against mine. *Let's try this again,* I think, walking into the kitchen to fetch a pacifier.

"How about a pacifier, Jack?" I say to him. "Want to try this?"

Back in my room my mom is changing the sheet on the co-sleeper mattress, so I lay Jack down in his "big boy" crib. It swallows him up completely. He looks like a little pea in the middle of a dance floor. I twist his mobile and the birds and monkey and alligator start circling around. Jack is sucking intently on his pacifier with his hands, curled in fists, pulled up to his chin. He's entranced by the plush animals overhead and is looking at them warily, probably thinking they are his new roommates straight from Craigslist.

"Want to put him back in the co-sleeper?" my mom asks, but I tiptoe away from the crib, switching the light off.

"Let's let him sleep in here for now," I whisper, and gently ease into bed. My mother goes out into the living room to resume balling up tiny socks. I lie in bed, staring up at the ceiling listening to the gentle jingle of the mobile. *I can do this*, I think to myself, letting my eyes close. "Twinkle-twinkle" is fading a bit, starting to wind down, and everything around me is quiet and still. I turn my face over on the pillow and feel myself start to drift off.

"*Fla-whah-ghah!*" Jack screams. My mother comes in and leans over the crib.

"Let me get him," she says. "You rest." It sounds like a beautiful plan, but Jack is crying and he needs his mom now. My mother helps me sit up and a burning cramp flashes in my stomach. I breathe through it and take baby steps over to his crib. I reach over and scoop him up, feeling a dampness on his bottom. *What's this now?* I think.

"Mom, lights," I say. The room lights up and I peer over the crib. I look down, finding a perfect, wet oval, center-mattress, and look at my mom, then at the mattress, then at Jack again. He's quiet, staring at me with his owl eyes, his lips pursed together. I feel incompetent. Do I not know how to diaper him? I look down at him, annoyed. "Why did you do that?" I ask him. He looks at me seriously like he has a secret and I burst out laughing. "I guess you are a magician, little one," I say, walking over to the changing table again, thinking how my old bedtime routine was so simple: Wash face. Brush teeth. Wake up the next day. I look down at Jack, who is sucking away at his thumb, his fingers splayed over his nose, and think how bizarre my life just got in the past hour. Jack is in charge now. I might double-diaper him.

21

Birth Control

Jack is one week old today. I'm rocking him in the chair by the window, humming "Happy Birthday" to him. I think his eyes got bigger overnight. They're so extraordinary, popping with new flecks of gray and maybe blue. "Your eyes are meant to see a lot of great things, Jack," I say over a yawn. He woke me like clockwork every two hours last night and I startled every time, for a quick second, confused by the sound. *What is that?* I thought, rubbing my eyes. *A squirrel?* My mother appeared in my doorway, from the couch, with a bottle, taking him from me to change his diaper then setting him back in my arms so I could feed him. At four a.m. I recommended she feed him in the living room because Jack needed a change of atmosphere. I think I slipped into a coma thereafter, because when I woke up it was ten a.m. and my father was dancing Jack around the living room, back on his "president" kick.

"Babies are really slippery when you take them out of the tub, Christine," my mother calls out from the bathroom. "You have to be really careful."

"Jack, your grandmother thinks I don't know how to bathe you. She's cuckoo," I whisper into his ear.

Up until now, I've just swiped his tiny body with a baby wipe—it's not like the kid is working up a sweat staring at me, sucking on his bottle, pooping and sleeping. I often find myself getting excited over one of his big, wide yawns because it's something less routine. I told him he was boring yesterday and then he farted as if to say, "Oh no I'm not!"

"Everything is set up," my mother says, walking into the living room, smiling down at Jack. I offer him to her and push myself up, noticing just a dull twinge running along my scar. I am recovering at record speed, and compared to what I went through when I had my spinal fusion, this C-section is like a tooth cavity. I kept reading these horrible accounts online from women who described their C-section recoveries like "knives in their stomach" for almost two months. I have to say, seven days later all that I feel is a quick stinging when I sit down and stand up and a weird tightness that never goes away. However, the pain has done something tremendous for me. It's helping me heal inside out, because I think there's been pain here all along, these past nine months in some form or another, but it's only now starting to reveal itself. Every day the pain from the surgery softens a bit—fades away—and I will it to take my anxieties with it. I envision them leaving me, so all that is left is the scar—a scar that covers an incredible wound I've managed to heal and one that will never go away, thereby reminding me of my strength.

When I walk into the kitchen, my mother places Jack into my hands and I dip him into the warm, soapy water, setting his body on the netted seat. He immediately pees in a perfect arch, all over the drain board that is full of plates and mugs. I look down at him, smiling gently.

"Jack, love of my life, it's not okay to pee on plates," I say. "We'll let it slide this time."

His mouth is set in a tiny open circle the size of a Cheerio. He's looking at me like he could burst out saying: *Lady, you popped me in the kitchen sink—and I can't pee on the plates?* Jack's twisted into a semi S and his arms are pulled up and glued to the sides of his chest. He looks like he's surrendering to something, though I think he borderline likes the water, because his eyes look dreamy like he's nostalgic for the aqua world he used to live in. My mother is clanking the pee dishes into the dishwasher. I drip a fist of soapy warm water on his belly and he squirms and starts crying. His bottom lip curls tightly, almost touching his chin, and his face changes colors from pink and happy to red and completely pissed off. *This isn't a hot tub, honey,* I think as I "Shh, shh, shh" him.

"No, no," I say, speed-washing his body with a cotton washcloth the size of a sheet of toilet paper. "We love baths!" Jack's eating tears—and bubbles now. My mother is standing next to me with a big yellow towel draped over her arms ready to receive him. I scoop him up and set him in my mother's arms, pulling the duck hood over his head. "Babies are really slippery after they've had a bath," I tell my mom. She rolls her eyes at me and disappears into the bedroom with him.

I wipe my brow, getting a spot of bubbles on my forehead, then lean up against the sink, letting my hands dip in the warm, soapy water, and it feels familiar. This time last year I was getting mani/pedis while sipping iced coffee. *Vogue* was splayed open on my knees. In this moment I feel as if someone plucked me from the city and dropped me, without warning, into this shoebox kitchen with an ugly linoleum floor. *Deep breath, Christine,* I tell myself, as I unplug the sink, watching the water whirl into a spinning cyclone, completely out of control, unable to resist the force below. I walk to my bedroom, passing the hallway mirror, and peer into it, seeing myself for what seems the first time since I brought Jack home. I look the way I feel: completely drained, like the power could run out at any minute. I have to write my blog for tomorrow, but I feel like my creative juices were removed along with the placenta. I also feel a little punchy, like I could bust out laughing at someone's funeral. I suppose I could write about that. My readers are like a horde of cheek-pinching grandmothers. I could pen a paragraph on the color of "JD's" (his alias on Storked! and something I never ever call him) poop and they'd still check in tomorrow—especially since I haven't posted a photo yet. Screen names I've never seen before are suddenly requesting photos of the baby. *My baby.* I have more readers than I thought—it's a little overwhelming. Is this how celebrities feel when they leave their homes with billowy baby blankets over their infants' heads? I often wonder if A reads my blog and I can't imagine that he doesn't, but up until now it has just been a daily paragraph examining my hormones and my love for green olives. It's time to start writing about motherhood and *our* son. It makes me sad to think that is all A is going to get. Just a daily paragraph.

Jack is lying on the bed and my mother is dangling a duck on a string over his head. I brush my hand across his cheek and feel him inching for my pinky finger. My mother hands me a bottle of baby lotion and collects the towel into a ball, leaving the room, saying she's going to smoke a cigarette outside.

"You really need to quit," I say. "Yesterday."

After she smokes I pretty much make her take a bath in the sink, a lot like the one Jack just took. I'm hoping she'll get sick of my new rule and just stop with the cancer sticks. I squeeze a dot of lotion into my palm. It smells like lavender and powder and milk and I want to eat it. Jack falls asleep as I massage it into his skin. I look down at him, thinking: *You've got the life, kid. May it always be this good.* He startles when I slip a pair of black pants on him, but doesn't cry, just sort of looks at me, like: *Oh, it's you again.* I prop him up and rest his back in my hand, pulling the black T-shirt over his head and then gently over his face. His pacifier gets stuck midshirt and he has a four-second meltdown.

"You're such a baby, Baby," I say, popping it into his mouth.

I lay him flat on his back and watch the pacifier dance up and down on his mouth. He's staring wide-eyed at the ceiling and when I lie down beside him I smile at the sun streaks sprayed across it, remembering how I read that in the first couple of weeks babies really respond to light and shadows. He's completely entranced, like he's watching a puppet show made of sunbeam people. My mother comes back in with a waft of spearmint toothpaste and cherry-almond body lotion—and cigarettes, rolling her eyes at me.

"Christine, why did you put that on him?" she says.

"Because I can," I say.

"He looks like a little devil baby now," she says. "Ugh, those black clothes."

But I love his outfit. I bought it at H&M in Manhattan on a particularly bad day. After months of not hearing from A, my swollen belly prompted me to call him. I was curious about his involvement and if he perhaps had had any revelations. I wondered if he had set some money aside, but when I dialed him I found that his number had been disconnected. I remember feeling this weird mix of anger and satisfaction—satisfaction because I was due in about three months and had gotten so far without him, anyway. I set out from my apartment on Fiftieth Street with no destination in mind at all, and just welcomed the sun on my back. Before long I had trucked twenty blocks, stopping when I saw some cute A-line skirts in the window. When I went to pay for them, I noticed an entire section of baby clothes and immediately perked up. I remember discovering the black outfit in one of those big basins and feeling like I'd just uncovered a pair of size nine Manolos at a crowded sample sale. I stare down at Jack, slipping a pair of red socks on him, designed like sneakers, and I admire my strategically styled baby. Then it occurs to me it's two in the afternoon and I'm in pajama pants and a maternity shirt that smells like sour milk.

Jack is lying on his back in the crib, examining his fingers like he's never seen them before. I keep shifting behind the dresser so he doesn't see me naked. I'm ridiculous. As I walk into my closet, I peer over the crib and see him opening and closing his fingers with an amazed look on his face, like he didn't know they did that. I run my fingers through a rack of clothes in my closet, confused. I don't fit in maternity clothes—or regular clothes. I try to pull a pair of size four jeans on but they get stuck midthigh. My ass and my thighs are still full, but I realized in the shower the other night, I don't even have one stretch mark. I stepped out and studied myself in the mirror, thinking I might have missed one squiggly, faded line, but I didn't. I can't wait until Dr. Keanchong clears me to exercise—a few thousand crunches later, I could surely tighten up my stomach, which is looking like a little droopy puddle and feels like a half-full water balloon. I decide on a billowy black dress that was a staple during my pregnancy, only I cinch it at the waist with a thick braided belt. I step out from the closet to find Jack sleeping with his hands splashed across his mouth as if he fell asleep startled. There is a knock at the back door. Jack's eyes pop open, but then slowly close, returning him to his dream. I open the door to find my father with four grocery bags—two brimming with *more* formula.

"Dad, I don't need any of this stuff," I say. "I have enough."

"Christine. Formula is like soap. Even if you don't use it today—you will use it," he says. "Where's Jack?" He bounds through the door, the crinkling bags surely waking my son up.

"Sleeping," I say, closing the door behind him. My father drops the bags in the center of the kitchen floor and walks into my bedroom with his shoes smacking on the hardwood floors.

"Dad!" I loudly whisper. "Puh-lease take your shoes off!" I've become a bit of a germ-o-phobe since bringing Jack home. I have a pump of antibacterial gel in every single room of my apartment—so that's a whopping five, total.

"Sorry," he says, stepping out of his shoes, then handing them to me.

When I walk into my room, my father is literally waking Jack up—patting his tummy, saying, "Hello."

"Dad," I loudly whisper.

"It's fine. Go to your doctor's appointment," he says.

It's the first time I am leaving Jack since he's been born. I am anxious. I should be gone for about an hour. I sat down this morning to write out instructions, but as I was putting pen to paper, it occurred to me that all anyone had to do was give Jack one bottle at two p.m. and change his diaper if need be. I wrote it down, anyway. I also took the emergency numbers list (Jack's ped, the police and fire departments) off the fridge and set it next to the instructions on the counter. I brush my lips against Jack's forehead. He's swaddled in my father's arms, still seamlessly asleep. They settle on the couch together and my father asks me for another blanket for Jack.

"He's fine," I say. "He's got on a footed thing and he's already wrapped in a blanket."

"It's drafty in here," he says. I take a deep breath and fetch a blanket from the closet, opening it over Jack.

The nurse who looks like Ugly Betty calls my name and I follow her into a small room.

"How's it going?" she says, smiling, and I remember how

scared I was when I waited for her to confirm the test and how sad I would be now if she read it any other way.

"Good," I say, unclipping my sandals and stepping on the scale. "He's an angel baby." And he really is. Jack is incredibly satisfied and content and only cries when he wants to eat. I feel incredibly lucky. I told Kateri on the phone last night that Jack knows it's just me so he behaves himself. He probably feels sorry for me, I told her. Of course she told me I was insane and that Jack is perfect all on his own without any motivation from anyone. She's probably right.

"You lost twenty pounds," the nurse says.

"What," I say, squinting at the scale. "But I haven't done anything but sit on the couch and hold my seven-pound baby." I say. "I ate pizza last night! Three slices!"

"Well, you lost a lot of water—and a seven-pound baby," she says. *I only have seven pounds to lose and I'll be back in my jeans. Awesome.*

Dr. Keanchong comes in and pulls the tape strips off my scar, then pats it with a cotton swab of alcohol.

"Perfect," she says, tossing the little ball into the garbage, then helping me sit up. She takes a seat in a backless chair and scoots closer to me reviewing my chart.

"How have you been feeling?" she says. "Anxious? Sad? Anything to be concerned with?" I think for a minute. I'm down to just one pill every Sunday morning and the things I've been feeling are normal, right? I think I keep waiting to have a nervous breakdown—which I'm never going to have. It's like I can't believe I actually survived being pregnant for nine months and continue to. I'm a lot stronger than I think or let on.

"I'm tired and settling into my new life," I say. "But nothing I can't handle."

She shifts in her chair and peels through my chart.

"Good. Have you thought about birth control?" she asks, looking up at me. I stare blankly at her, while my mouth inches open.

"What?" I exclaim, thinking this must be a joke or some sort of trick question. Why would *I* need BC? I'm a single mom. BC is for people who have sex and want to avoid pregnancy. I clearly missed the memo before.

"The pill or IUD?" she asks.

"For what?" I say it out loud, not meaning to. Then it hits me: I'm a twenty-six-year-old woman and I might possibly never have sex again. I feel myself tear up because I can't imagine a guy ever wanting to date me: I have a child. I can't just meet for drinks on a whim, or spend the night and wake up to drink big mugs of coffee in bed while sifting through the paper.

"I don't think that is in my near future," I say.

"Well, maybe not tomorrow," she says. "But, you're young and beautiful, so someday. . . ." *Young and beautiful and . . . ah, it's a broken record.*

"I don't need any birth control," I say, easing off the exam table.

While I wait to make my next appointment, one of the nurses who took care of me religiously during the past nine months approaches me.

"So, the father?" she says. "Did he ever show up?"

"Nope," I say.

22

Past

Nic is coming over tonight to watch *20/20* with me. Tonight they air the episode about Keith and me. It's going to be weird to watch this interview that I taped when I was thirteen weeks pregnant. I wore all black to disguise the fact that I was with child, even though I was hardly showing. It looked like I was going through a painful "chubby" phase, like maybe I ate Big Macs three days in a row for lunch. Elizabeth Vargas told me my life was about to change. "Good change!" she said, when we concluded the interview. But she could have told me my hair was purple because I kept thinking, *Holy shit, I'm going to be on* 20/20 and *Holy shit, her ring had to be five carats.* Carlo, as usual, escorted me to the interview because he was certain they were going to "exploit me" and ask me all sorts of horrible questions that would make me stutter and admit on national television that I was a very bad person for breaking up with a quadriplegic. I tried to explain I wasn't going on *Jerry Springer*, but he took the train in from Connecticut anyway. He had this very proud look on his face when we walked into ABC studios, like his sister was really important—and not at all single and pregnant.

Afterward we ate expensive steaks at Smith and Wollensky and Carlo called A every name in the book. He sounded like the teacher in *The Peanuts:* "Wa-Wa-Wa." When I got up to use the restroom a businessman with a smart suit on asked if he could buy me a drink. He had a Texan twang in his voice and seemed as though he didn't need another drink. I couldn't even answer him, it was all just too bizarre. Here I was eating a piece of meat I could hardly afford, after rehashing one of the most defining moments of my life for a national television show, while being suddenly single, pregnant—and now some random guy was hitting on me. I felt as if I had been dreaming this all along—that I'd wake up and wipe the sweat from my brow, take a huge breath. Back at the table Carlo made me eat half the creamed spinach he had ordered because it was "loaded with calcium, probably." It was just a very strange evening.

I'm so nervous about seeing *20/20* that it doesn't even occur to me that Nic is meeting Jack for the very first time. I set Jack in his ridiculously overpriced Bugaboo stroller and zip up his sweatshirt, pulling the hood over his head. He looks like a little worm—exactly like his Gloworm, in fact. The hood framing his face makes his eyes look bigger and wider than ever, just like the toy. We stroll up the block to wait for Nic at the bus stop; the whole time I prep Jack not to be too alarmed if she tickles him saying "Gucci Gucci goo" and not "Coo-chi coo-chi coo." Part of me thinks she may be on her way to a strip of casinos in Atlantic City, because she called me four times to check what number bus to take. The last time I told her to re-member her passport or she wouldn't be able to cross back into Manhattan.

The bus pulls up and a pile of people with briefcases and commuter sneakers spills from it. Then Nic delicately steps off in a pair of Prada ballet flats, a fitted black pencil skirt, and crisp white blouse. She looks completely unassuming as she darts her head left, then right. Her raincoat is flopped over her forearm, a big Gucci bucket purse is on her shoulder and a silver leather duffel bag with a gift bag and bright orange tissue paper poking out is clenched in her hand. She doesn't see us standing by the big tree. Jack's stroller is extended back and he's staring up at the marvelous, tangled leaves strung on twisty branches, with the lavender dusk sky splashed behind them. I kneel down and look up myself. I hope Jack will always admire such simple things, and know there are treasures like this everywhere—that it's okay to slow down and look for them—that it's important, actually. I lean over, resting my hands on the grass, watching as Nic furiously searches for her cell phone, then takes a half-step back, squinting up at the street sign.

"*Aunt* Nic!" I yell out to her.

"Thank. God," she says, popping her BlackBerry into her bag.

Seriously, praise the Lord she made it to Jersey unscathed and even sans running shoes.

"OhMyGodChris! Are you like twelve pounds?" she says, strutting down the sidewalk as if it were a catwalk. Her face is flawless. Her eyes are popping with the slightest line of blue eyeliner and her lips look as though she just reapplied her Chanel glossimer. She also smells like something really expensive. I, on the other hand, am in charcoal leggings, three-dollar bubblegum-pink flip-flops from Old Navy, and an oversized hoodie with a hand-cut collar. I might have Chapstick on and I didn't shower today. Oh, and to top it off, since my hormones are all over the place, I could seriously use a lip wax about now.

"Did you or did you not just have a baby?" she asks.

Nic was at Burning Man in Nevada when Jack was born. It was hard to picture her there, bartering food for a shower, riding around on a bicycle in the dry heat, sleeping outdoors.

"Let me see him. *OhMyGodChris*. He looks just like you," she says, leaning over the stroller. "Just!"

"*Hi-eee*, Jack, I'm Aunt Nic," she says, extending her freshly manicured finger to him. "I gave your mom a blazer by Tom Ford from his discontinued children's line for you. It should fit when you're about three." She pauses, studies him closer. "Maybe four," she says, then goes directly into her next thought. "Chris, are you aware your son can be a model? Can we strategize him as the next face of . . . some kids' clothing line?" I burst out laughing—how I've missed Nic's gem ideas. Pre-baby, they were more to the tune of: "Can we talk about how the guy in the blue suit at the bar is falling in love with you tonight?"

She pops up from the grass and opens her arms, still flanked by her bags, and we hug, the bags whacking me in the back.

"Can we talk about New Jersey transit for a minute?" she says.

"O-kay," I say, pushing the stroller to my apartment.

"I kept asking people about the Garden Apartment stop

and they kept telling me the bus stops at some mall first. It was really taxing. I kept thinking I was going to be stranded at a Forever 21 store."

"God forbid!" I say.

Once inside Nic drops her bags and peers into the stroller.

"So, can I hold him?" she says.

"Of course," I say, leaving her with him for a minute while I bring her bags into the bedroom.

"How do I get him out of this?" she says.

"It just unclips," I say from the bedroom.

When I return, Jack is still strapped in and Nic is popping her pointer finger up and down, calling it "Mr. Inchworm."

"What happened?" I ask, unhooking the seat belt.

"It looks complicated. There's like three straps in there," she says. This is the girl who can stock every Gucci store in America and solve scary "buyer" equations without a calculator.

"These chest ones clip together and they clip into the crotch one, and this clip tightens him in," I say, but she's just staring at me blankly.

"Jack, your stroller is like a rocket ship!" she says to him.

"Actually it's the Mercedes-Benz of strollers if you want to get 'tech,'" I say. "Carlo was really concerned about my mental health when he saw what stroller I registered for. All the same, he bought it," I say.

"Okay, for the record, Carlo is A-MAZING. Don't we know anyone at ABC? I think we need to finagle him as the next Bachelor," she says.

"For realz," I say, hoisting Jack up from the stroller. His knees pull up to his chest.

"O-kay. Gimme-gimme!" she says, rubbing her hands together.

"Support his neck, okay?" I say, placing him in her arms.

"Got it," she says, receiving him, rubbing her nose against his.

"This is an Eskimo kiss, Jack," she says. She stands still with him in the hallway, staring down at him.

"You can walk with him, you know," I say, leading her to the couch.

"I know," she says. "You know what? Hate me for saying this, but he does look a little like A."

"Thank you!" I say, popping my hands out. "I know. Everyone says he's 'all Coppa,' all the time. It's annoying."

"I mean, his eyes are like a direct transplant from your face, and his cheekbones, too," she says.

"I guess," I say, smiling down at Jack, unzipping his hoodie.

"But, Chris, he is all you. All the good parts."

"Thanks Nic," I say, placing my hand on her shoulder.

"Oh! Open the pressie," she directs, so I retrieve the gift bag from my bedroom. As I walk out I tear pieces of orange tissue paper from the bag, letting them drop carelessly on the floor. I pull out a kelly green onesie that says simply: "Brooklyn."

"Loves!" I say, kissing her cheek. *Love to move there,* I think.

"Great! I think Jack just crapped," she says. "So here," and she extends him over to me. Jack is looking at me with urgent eyes, saying: "Please don't leave me alone with this one."

They just teased the segment. Keith was working out on some sort of apparatus. I guess they shot some B-roll of him. They wanted to shoot B-roll of me, too, but I looked like I had a basketball under my shirt at the time, so I passed.

"Do you remember when the three of us went to Philly?" Nic says.

Back in 2005—a full year after the breakup—my college hosted a screening of *Murderball*. Keith got interviewed on my college's radio station. We all stayed in the same hotel room. I helped him with things I hadn't in years and slept next to him. I think I fell a little back in love with him, or at least the idea of it. He needed me all over again. It felt good.

"That was a fun trip!" I say, paging through *In Touch*.

"That was the most awkward trip of my life! What trip were you on?" she asks.

"Was it?" I say, squinting at nothing.

"Yeah! You were like on the verge of tears the entire trip!" she says.

"Oh, yeah," I say. But at least the trip reacquainted me with Jack. "You know he just had another baby with his lesbian friends."

"He's hot," she says. "You guys went out a couple of times, huh?"

"Yeah," I say, and I vaguely remember meeting him at this dim bar on Mott Street, where a fat, wrinkly bulldog wobbled around the table legs. I drank way too much sake, which he described as "exquisite wine," then lured him into my apartment. He didn't kiss with his tongue, but he had the most amazing lips.

"Ah, another one that got away!" I say.

The show is almost over and my segment has still not aired. The current one is about a woman who was raped, got pregnant, and kept the baby. That sounds impossible. I thought I had a "tough call to make," in deciding to end my relationship with Keith. This poor woman says she sees her rapist's face when she looks at her son. *Holy shit!* I feel so ir-relevant. I don't know if I want to call this woman a martyr or my hero. At last, my segment is on. I look fat. The light-ing is harsh. My hair is tousseled all wrong.

"Aw, look at you," Nic says.

"Look at 'Tubby,' you mean," I say.

"You were pregs, Chris! Or Storked! Are we still calling you 'Storked!'?" she says. You need to rename your blog "'Mother of the Year!'"

"Right!" I say rolling my eyes.

Keith is on now. He looks healthy and bright. He's wear-ing one of those overpriced T-shirts with rhinestones all over it. Elizabeth is asking him questions about me. His mouth is moving, but I can hardly digest any of this. I am transported back to that place where I sat beside him, my hand in his, afraid to stay and more afraid to go. I come to, catching him tell Elizabeth he "hated" me when I broke up with him.

"I can't watch this," I say to Nic, getting up to check on Jack.

"Chris, but he *also* told the reporter you were there for him twenty-four–seven," Nic calls to me.

"Now they're in his house. He's making Taylor ham," she says. "Getting ketchup!"

I don't care. Jack is swaddled in a loose bundle and his left hand is peeking out, barely touching his lips.

"Life holds a lot of surprises, Jack," I whisper into his crib. "Hold on tight, little guy."

I slump on my bed with my past wafting in from the living room and my present, future, and forever sleeping in my bedroom. I comb my fingers through my hair. Life is ironic.

The next morning my mother comes over to sit with Jack so I can drive Nic to the GWB bus stop and, in part, get away for an hour. I swear to God, my mother has a perma-smile on her face when she is around Jack. She plays a fun/scary game with him where she stands in front of the mirror in the hallway and tells him the "little boy in the mirror is your friend and he has a grandma just like you."

"Pumpkin pie," she says, taking Jack from Nic, not asking if she can. My mother has given Jack an odd nickname. I can't help but picture my mom bouncing a steaming pie, fragrant with cinnamon, wrapped in a red and white checkered blanket, when she calls him that.

"His bottle is in the fridge and he can have it in a half hour," I say, and Jack starts the windup cry: "*Eh, ehh, blahehh!*" I link my arm in Nic's and leave the apartment. It's very gray out and misting. The air is thick and warm. It's like we're pushing through a sauna. As we approach the city, the skyline is barely visible, like I'm looking at it through a sheer silver scarf. Nic is talking about her boyfriend, but my mind is somewhere else. I keep thinking how I am returning Nic now. She came to visit and now she is going back where she came from—where I used to come from. She's going to have lunch with her boyfriend, then see a show at the Brooklyn Museum.

"We'll prob just order in and rent a movie after, since it's so grrrr-oss out," she says. I pull up to the staircase where the little white buses line up, transporting people to Manhattan for a buck. She steps out of the car, opening a big pink umbrella in the sky, like a balloon. Popped against the gray sky it almost looks unbelievable, like an illusion not happening at all.

"Thanks for everything, Chris!" she says. "Ah! This fricken rain!" she barks, running off, flanked by her bags. Part of me wants to run after her, screaming, *Take me with you*, leaving the door wide open and the headlights on, highlighting the rain. But the other part misses Jack, incredibly, and it's only been a half hour. It's a very strange seesaw. I wonder when it will level out.

Something very odd has happened. I woke up one day and my newborn was suddenly eight weeks and four days old.

I'm on the couch leaning over Jack, trying to teach him how to stick his tongue out at me. I pop my tongue in and out of my mouth and he moves his lips around like he's sucking on a hard candy. He's the cutest thing I've ever seen, propped gently in this weird half-moon pillow thing called a Boppy. He's starting to communicate with me. When I say "Hi" or clap my hands, he moves his legs like he's riding an imaginary bicycle. Sometimes he pops his arms up and down, in and out, Jazzercising, then unintentionally whacking himself in the eye and stone cold staring at me like I did something wrong. Seconds later, he's resuming at warp speed, opening his mouth into a little spout, almost resting his chin on his chest, like he's trying to see his belly button. He looks extremely proud of his sporadic, not at all consistent movements.

Since it's the weekend, Carlo is home from Connecticut. He's been home every single weekend since Jack arrived, with "something to do," but really nothing at all. I'm sitting at my desk working on a blog post for Monday when I hear the lock twist. He attempts to burst through the door, but gets caught by the chain lock.

"Hello?" he says.

"Hello!" I say, not getting up.

"Why is the chain lock on?"

"Because sometimes I walk around in my underwear and you have a key."

"Are you in your underwear now?" he asks.

"No," I say, getting up from my chair.

I open the door and Carlo walks in with a plush stuffed

monkey. My brother has not entered my apartment empty-handed yet. I have toy trucks still in boxes, clothes with tags on them, two cases of diapers in the linen closet. *You're a lucky baby, Jack,* I think, watching Carlo kneel down to him.

"Hey, hey, Mr. Turkey Head!" he says to Jack, walking past me. "Turkey head" is Carlo's pet name for Jack. It's a little bizarre. When I asked him why he insists on calling my gorgeous baby a barnyard animal, he had no logical answer. Every time he says "Turkey head," I picture a lunatic running around with a raw Thanksgiving bird on his head, his hands flailing in the air.

He goes to lift Jack from the chair and the whole chair rises up with him.

"He's belted in," I say, easing the chair onto the floor.

"It's not like he's going anywhere," he says.

"I know, but sometimes when he Jazzercises I think he could tumble out."

"Jazzercise?" he says, looking at Jack, pathetically, like it's not macho enough.

I wonder if Jack thinks Carlo is his father. Everyone seems to think he is my husband. Carlo is the most prominent male figure in Jack's life. He even changes poo diapers. I study them from the kitchen table. Carlo is dangling his watch in front of Jack's face, explaining that it tells time. Jack is staring at the shiny object like it's the best thing since a bottle. Carlo wants a wife of his own and a kid to play ball with. He wants it now, but won't admit it. "I have many women" is his standard answer when I ask him why he is single. Sometimes he's a wiseass and says: "Why am *I* single?

You have a kid." I rest my fist on my chin and lean in over the table, watching them. *They were made for each other.*

"He's starving!" Nanny says from the couch. Jack is lying on her lap, cooing, with his fingers latched on to her thumb. He just sucked back a four-ounce bottle. I stick my head out from the kitchen. She's squinting at his empty bottle. It's one of those short, chubby ones. "This bottle is too small," she says with a grunt. "You're starving, huh?" Jack kicks his legs out. Back in the kitchen I return to a bowl of white vinegar and try to remember how long I am supposed to submerge the pacifiers to degerm them. I throw a bunch in and they float to the top. *Well, that defeats the purpose,* I think. I shove my hand into the Tupperware and force the multicolored binkies down. *Crap. Are my hands dirty?*

"Chris," Nan calls from the living room. I grab a dish towel and wipe my hands, which smell sour now. The pacifiers pop to the top of the bowl.

"Yeah, Nan," I say, walking over to her.

"Maybe we can let him gum something. A cookie! He's starving, you know," she says.

"Nan, he's barely two and a half months old," I say. "He can't 'gum' a cookie."

"You're crazy! We used to put egg in the bottle when your father was a baby, to fill him up good," she says.

"Nan, he's not hungry," I say, stroking his head.

"Don't you have a little tea biscuit you can soak and give him?" she asks.

"No. Nan, he's fine," I say over a gurgle of laughter.

"When you come to Nanny's house I'm going to mash up a meatball. Delicious," she says. She's serious. "I can take care of you by myself," she says, leaning into him. A half hour ago I changed his diaper because she couldn't hoist herself up from the couch. She told me to "powder him up, good." When I told her that powder is kind of taboo she told me I was crazy. I smile down at her. Her gray hair is knotted in a low bun and her eyes are tired.

"Oh, I love his hands," she says. "Look at these little hands, Chris!"

I look down at Jack's chubby pink hand wrapped around her crooked, bony finger. Sometimes her hands are so stricken with arthritis flare-ups she can't even unfold them and they look like penguin hands. They're the hands of a hard worker. They permanently smell like warm bread, as if she dips them in flour every single day. Beautiful hands, they are. Kind, gentle ones.

"See, he's not hungry, Nan," I say. "Look how relaxed and happy he is in your lap." She smiles at him, then looks up at me.

"He's freezing, is what he is!" she says.

23

Present

Uncle Brian and I are taking Jack to buy a pumpkin to-day. It's a weird autumn day—not how I imagined Jack's first trip to the pumpkin patch. I'm starting to realize the small things, like the big ones, are not always how you imagine they'll be. Sometimes life erupts; you wake up on a fall day thinking it might be cool enough for a fuzzy sweater, but then you realize it's time to turn the air conditioner back on. We seem to be in the midst of an Indian summer. It's a little magical, actually. The air is thick and humid. I'm wearing denim maternity shorts because my ass and thighs don't fit into regular ones, and a floppy, tent shirt from Urban Outfitters I passed off as a maternity shirt when I was pregnant. It's so warm Jack doesn't even have socks on. I have him in one of those T-shirt onesie numbers. He looks like a scrawny little frog today. All week I imagined shuffling through the leaves with Jack pinned against me in a little corduroy jacket. We pull up to the farm. It's crowded. I hope I don't see anyone I know—I'm not exactly ready to "chat." I don't even have makeup on.

"Do you think we'll run into people here?" I ask Brian, lifting Jack from his car seat.

"Like who?" he asks. "Old friends or something?"

"I dunno," I say, scanning the open field.

"Doubt it," he says. "This place is infested with moms!" I stare at him, raising my eyebrows, baby cradled in my right arm, diaper bag crossed over my body, pacifier set like a ring on my index finger.

"You're not like those moms," he says. "You're a *cool* mom!" I roll my eyes at him and we walk through the gate.

"See," he leans in and whispers. "That lady has on jeans up to her boobs!" I burst out laughing and nudge my body into his, signaling him to stop.

"You have like a thousand-dollar Gucci bag for God's sake," he says, squinting his eyes at my head. "And DK sunglasses on! Dior?"

"Donna Karan," I say, matter of factly.

"Exactly," he says, taking Jack from me.

"Come on 'Mr. Turkey Boy,' let's go look at the horsies," he says. I don't know what is worse: "Mr. Turkey Head," via Carlo, or "Mr. Turkey Boy," via Bri. What happened to "Lil Sport," or "Champ," or "Buddy"—"Bud," even.

I lean on the wire fence, watching Brian and Jack. He's got him pressed against his chest with his legs flopped over his forearms. Brian is pointing to the horse and making Jack's hand wave at him. I search the farm, noticing fathers hoisting gigantic pumpkins onto their shoulders, then extending their free hands to little chubby ones, stained in dirt. I whirl around, suddenly overwhelmed by images like this. Another father is on his knees tying his daughter's shoelaces. There's a father and son duo in matching Mets caps feeding a gaggle of chickens; another standing over his four-year-old, laughing, as the little guy tries to lift a twenty-pound pumpkin by its stem. There's one with his back to me setting his baby on the produce scale—*What a cute picture that will make,* I think, walking toward them. *Oh. That's Brian. My brother. And . . . my baby.* I smile gently, tucking a strand of hair behind my ear.

As I walk over to them I hear someone—a guy—call out to me. I stop. Close my eyes. My heart races. I turn around slowly, wondering who I'm about to find.

"It *is* you!" Michael says, smiling. Michael, whom I dated briefly my junior year of high school. Ten years ago.

"Hi-ee," I hesitate in saying. "Hooooooow are you?"

"Great!" he says, opening his arms for a hug. "What are you doing here?" he asks, and I pull away from his chest.

"Just, you know, pumpkin picking," I say.

"Me too," he says, smiling, then pointing to the patch. "My nephews are running around here somewhere. There's one!"

"I'm here with my baby. I had a baby!" It just spits out from me. Michael smiles.

"Really?" he says. *No Michael, I'm lying. I'm just at a pumpkin patch in Wayne and not in my NYC apartment, drinking coffee, waiting on a text about where I'm meeting the ladies for brunch, for fun,* I think, then smile politely.

"I didn't know you were married," he says.

"I'm not and my boyfriend—ex-boyfriend—isn't involved." *Because he's a selfish son-of-a-bitch,* I think, and smile politely again.

Brian walks over with Jack and extends his hand to Michael.

"What's up, bro," he says. "Long time."

I take Jack from Brian and lean into Mike.

"Here he is." I whisper because Jack has fallen asleep.

"He's awesome!" Michael says.

"He's from heaven," I whisper. "I keep telling him he should have told someone up there he was coming down to me because they're probably looking for him up there. I'm so cheesy! I know." I shrug my shoulders, bringing Jack's cheek to my nose, nuzzling him gently.

"No you're not! Look at him!" Michael says, staring down at Jack.

"So, what's new with you?" I ask, realizing now that Jack is settled in my arms I am completely without reservation and ever so sure of myself. It's like I just tied my superhero cape around my neck. I feel I may have even grown an inch. Jack just makes me better.

"I'm a full-time magician," he says. "Have my own company!"

I smile. Michael used to pull quarters out of my ear in high school.

"You really did it!" I say.

"What about you?" he asks, now with Jack's hand wrapped around his finger.

"I write a blog for *Glamour* and I'm a full-time assistant editor at *First* magazine. So, I write—a lot! But I'm on maternity leave now," I say.

He looks down at Jack, then smiles up at me, nodding in assurance.

"You really did it, too!" he says.

Jack has a checkup with the ped today and I'm sitting in the waiting room with him in my arms and my mother next to me. He's sucking intently on his pacifier with his fists in signature balls, resting just under his chin. This morning when I was strategically dressing him in denim overalls, a punchy red and orange plaid shirt, red Converse sneakers, and a Yankees cap popped on backward, I tried to explain that he was getting a shot today and that it was not going to be fun, but it was something he had to do (despite the protests of mothers who refuse to vaccinate their babies), and sometimes in life we do things we don't want to do. I was trying to be metaphoric and poetic and lovely, too, but he fell asleep midspeech. There's a newborn across from us in her car seat with netting pulled over it looking like she's about to go on a safari. She's awake in there, too. Her mother is drumming her fingers on her knees. She seems like a nervous mom. I bet she doesn't let anyone hold her daughter.

"Jake Coppa," a nurse says, standing in the doorway wearing salmon scrubs and a tunic stamped with hearts.

"It's Jack," I say, rising up with him, then whispering, *Copa-Cabana, the music, the magic* in his ear (*Get used to it, little man*). I follow her into a hallway lined with exam rooms. A baby is screaming behind a closed door. It sounds like his mouth might be pushed into his mother's sweater. I curl my lip in sympathy and smile at the nurse.

"Ah, shots! What can I say? Not fun," she says.

I read online that some moms drug their babies with Tylenol before shots. However, this morning when Jack and I were talking seriously about his needing to calm down and stop smacking himself in the head with a plastic rattle I was letting him experiment with, I couldn't sedate him. He was just too animated and wondrous, digging his feet into the carpet, then in circles on his imaginary bicycle.

After the nurse weighs and measures him we come into the blue Cinderella room and I set him down on the papered exam table. He immediately starts pedaling his feet, then stops suddenly, trying to figure out the noise his body made against the paper.

"It sounds like we're pushing your stroller through the leaves, Jack!" I say, and he pedals again, furiously, then stops, trying to catch the sound, unaware it's him who's making that incredible, fast "shhh." The doctor comes in smiling and walks over to the sink.

"Hello! This is Grandma," I say, pointing to my mom.

"Hello, Grandma. I'm Dr. Z," he says, walking over to Jack. "How's Jack?" he says, leaning over him, making his stethoscope look like an elephant's nose. Jack makes the spout mouth and his eyes smile. Poor guy has no idea the cool doctor with the Versace glasses who turns his medical instruments into circus animals is about to sneak-attack him with a needle.

"Amazing! He slept through the night for two nights in a row now. I woke up like clockwork at around two a.m. and it was silent. I rushed over to his crib to find him . . . sound asleep," I said. "It was a little scary at first. I kept thinking, Why isn't my baby crying? Did someone take him?"

Dr. Z laughs. "Let's see, he's two . . . two-and-a-half months. That's about right," he says.

"Okay. Because I told one of my coworker/mom friends about it in an e-mail and she said sometimes babies sleep when they're hungry. I immediately blamed myself for starving my kid to sleep, thinking maybe my neurotic Nanny was right after all."

Dr. Z laughs again. "You'd know if Jack was hungry. He'd wake up crying!" he says.

"And another thing. He doesn't really smile at me. Do you think he likes me?" I ask, in all seriousness.

"You're his mom. He loves you. He'll start reacting more," he says. "Look at him now, wiggling away."

"It's Jazzercise!" I correct him. "We Jazzercise."

Dr. Z laughs again. Lots of laughing. God, I hope he doesn't think I'm crazy.

Jack is a happy, cooing little cherub during his examination. Dr. Z points light into his eyeballs and he coos even louder. He barely squirms when he gets his ears checked. He's content and so at ease he even pees on Dr. Z when he opens his diaper. We all laugh. *Ah, happens to the best of us,* I think. Jack is flailing his arms up and down, moving his legs like he's suspended in the air, poking them in and out of two holes. The nurse comes in with a tray. I look at it—the vile and silvery needle— and look down at Jack, who is sucking on his hand sideways, is now staring, engaged, at the bright blue ceiling. *Crap, this is it.*

"Okay, I want you to just slide Jack around so his legs are facing me—and maybe hold his arms down," Dr. Z says.

Uh, he wants me to participate in the torture. Jack's meaty thigh looks like it might develop a bull's-eye right about now.

"Hi, hi, Jack," I say, leaning over him. His eyes widen, responding to my voice.

"Hi-eeeee," I say again, not looking at Dr. Z. All of a sudden Jack erupts into the most outrageous yelp. It reminds me of the time when Brandy was a puppy and she got her paw stuck in the lock latch of her crate. Jack's eyes squint closed, wringing tears that are collecting on the corners of his open mouth. Dr. Z is applying a Band-Aid, when Jack's mouth suspends into a gummy half-circle, and now he's just reaching for a breath, unable to scream through his agony. Ah, there he goes.

"There, there," I say pulling him up to my chest. "All done."

"I know, little one. I'm sorry," Dr. Z says.

Little one? What about me? I think I hurt more than Jack. You made my baby cry. Can I get a cherry lollipop or something? I think, zipping Jack's jacket up to his chin.

Kateri walks through the door with a pile of magazines, a bottle of cheap wine, and Chinese takeout. I'm so tired. Jack didn't nap much today, which meant I didn't, either.

"Tired?" Kateri says. I extend Jack to her, even though her hands are full. She walks into the kitchen and plops the food and wine on the kitchen table, then takes Jack from me.

"How's my nephew?" she says, walking over to the couch. God, how I want someone to hold me and ask, "How's my Chrissy?" I shuffle through the magazines and settle on the couch with one, but I'm too tired to even open it. Kateri's heels are on the floor and I study them, convincing myself they are magic and if I step into them I could be transported to a fancy magazine meeting with a big round table and strategically placed pitchers of water no one dares to touch. My editor e-mailed me saying *Glamour* wants to extend my blog contract for another six months. I am both excited and terrified about the idea of continuing to write about my—I mean, our—lives for the world to pick at. The writing itself is actually kind of therapeutic, but some of the comments from people can be brutal. I can handle the trolls—no one takes a person calling a baby "Devil's Spawn" too seriously—but it's the pointed questions that are starting to piss me off. I realize I've half opened a window into my personal life, but people take it too far when they ask me probing questions about child support, Jack's "father," my financial situation. Sometimes I feel like I'm a never-ending talk show. I look over at Kateri, who is singing Jack the alphabet in Spanish. It's soothing him to sleep.

"Should I keep blogging?" I ask her, pulling my legs against my chest.

"Do you want to?" she asks.

"Yes. No. Yes," I say. "It's more, Do I need to? My blog

paycheck has been an incredible, unexpected second income," I say. "And I secretly love writing for *Glamour* every single day."

"You shouldn't have to work two jobs! What happens in January when you go back to *First*? You work a full day, then blog at night? It's called child support!" she says.

"Trust me. I know!" I say. "But A is so difficult. He told his lawyer he just wants to sign his parental rights away, but in New Jersey there is no such thing, unless, say, I get married and my husband wants to adopt Jack." I burst out laughing. "Like that's going to happen!"

"Yeah, actually it is," she says. "I'm going to put him down. Be right back."

"Make sure you tuck the blanket tight around him," I whisper loudly. "And put the Gloworm on my bed. And shut the window. It's drafty in there, no?" Did I just say *drafty*? I am a mom, but it's true and the Indian summer, thank God, has moved on. The air is crisp now and cool enough for Jack to wear these ridiculous mittens that are big enough to fit his head.

Kateri hands me a wineglass, filling it with red. This has become sort of a new thing Kateri and I do. Every Thursday for the past couple of weeks she has come over straight from work with food and wine. I get so excited when I realize it's Wednesday because I know I have a date the following evening. Sometimes when Jack is napping I'll surface-clean the bathroom with one of those fantastic Clorox wipes and chop up veggies for makeshift crudités, kick some stray toys under the couch. A far cry from how I used to prep for dates pre-baby. Back then, I hit the elliptical, then the steam room, then plastered my face with some goop, showered, tried on three different outfits, maybe had a drink. . . . Gone are those days.

"Do you ever think about dating?" Kateri says. I do, but then my stomach turns because I think how backward my life is, then it turns over again, because I don't think I could make it through a date right now. I'd miss Jack too much. This probably means I'm not ready to be away from him—especially on a series of first dates. The thought is so exhausting. I can't imagine sitting across from someone, realizing there is zero chemistry, but not being able to just bail. I can see myself daydreaming about something I'm missing that Jack is doing, like rolling over. I went on a blind date once where I walked into the wine bar, saw the lanky guy standing by the bar, and knew instantly it wasn't going to be a love connection, but I still had some cocktails and a meal with him—asked him a million questions—and then said good night.

Kateri and I polish off the bottle. I'm not drunk at all, but I definitely feel warm.

"Should I call A?" I ask her.

"Now? Uh, no," she says, plucking the glass from my loose grip.

"No, not now, but soon?" I say. "Maybe an e-mail?"

"For?" she says.

"I'm not sure. . . . Invite him into Jack's life?"

"Maybe you should," she says. "But, don't you think he can do the math?"

"Huh?"

"Christine. You found out you were pregnant in January. Whether or not A knew the exact due date—it's November now. You clearly gave birth."

"You're right," I say, half-nodding my head. "But . . ."

"What?" she says. I look at her, then at the clock. It's almost midnight.

"Never mind," I say, clanking the glasses between my fingers, walking into the kitchen.

This is the final straw. I'm trading automobiles. My two-door Accord is too small. It takes me seven minutes to figure out what angle worked the last time when I'm trying to get the Bugaboo in the trunk. I've also become increasingly aware of the fact that I stick half of my body into the backseat when I clip Jack in and out of his car seat and that a psychotic person might take advantage of my guard being down and force me in, or worse, out, then drive off with my baby. I am ridiculous, but still, it's time for a new ride.

So Carlo, Jack, and I are headed to Jeep today. It's raining, so Carlo lets me off in front with Jack. I walk in, pulling Jack's hood down. His owl eyes find the light.

"Hi, Buggy-Bug!" I say, then air-kiss nothing, make my lips squeak. "Let's get something red. To match your stroller." First mistake, saying that out loud—three men pounce on us, likely thinking I'm a twit who wants to color-coordinate at any cost.

"Husband parking the car?" a salesman with salt-and-pepper hair says.

"No, I'm a single mom," I say, completely unfazed, squinting at the window sticker on a compact, chubby truck.

"Well, let's get you something safe!" he says and introduces me to one of his employees. "This is Rex. He'll help you with anything you need." Rex is cute. We walk over to an oversize black truck.

"How old is your baby?" he asks.

"Almost three months," I say.

"My son is six," he says. "I'm a single parent, too." *Er, interesting,* I think. Rex starts telling me about the "souped up" Commander because it's "so safe." The lease is also about half my rent. Carlo walks in, shaking his umbrella out. He extends his hand over my shoulder, shaking Rex's hand and announcing, "She doesn't need a Commander."

"This is my brother Carlo," I say.

"How's the gas mileage on the Patriot?" Carlo asks. Jack burps and a small eruption of spit-up pops from his little mouth, which then dissolves into a smile.

"Aw, you feel better now?" I say. "Has that been stuck in there since breakfast, lovebug?" When I look up five men are staring at me over their desks. It occurs to me I'm in the middle of a dealership.

"I'll be right back," I tell Carlo and disappear into the bathroom.

I press Jack against my chest with one hand and turn the water on, wetting a piece of paper towel.

"Let me see." I dab his mouth clean. He makes a happy noise. He sounds like a yawning puppy.

"All clean!" I say, looking up, catching my reflection in the mirror. Jack is mesmerized by the image. He's staring at us in the cloudy mirror, wondering how we got in there. I look down at him, kiss his head, and look back up at us. *I have no idea, either, pal,* I think. Here we are, in Jersey, in a Jeep dealership.

"At least we're not leasing a minivan!" I say, exiting the bathroom.

Back on the floor Carlo takes Jack from me and I fill out some paperwork and sit through a credit check.

"Do you need a co-signer?" Rex asks.

"Nope," I say, smiling as I watch Carlo cart Jack around the floor dotted with trucks.

I write out a down payment check, subtracting the amount from what I know is stashed in my savings, feeling a slight twinge of anxiety, but then it goes away. What an empowering thing to do—lease this vehicle all on my own. Suddenly all the work I've done over the months doesn't seem so tedious and exhausting. It seems ever more worth it. That's one impractical NYC apartment and one impractical sporty car down. Change. It's fine. I gave up a few things . . . but I gained more—so much more.

24

Future

My girlfriends from New York City are coming over today. They're caravanning in Stef's mom's car. They're calling it a road trip. I live twenty minutes from the city. Jack is sleeping on his tummy in his crib, even though the ped said he shouldn't. It's not like I'm sound asleep and I'm not checking him every three minutes. It's not like it's a law. I've been dipping my head into the bedroom, in between slicing up a long roll of French bread for the cheese plate. He's completely fine, sucking his thumb, with his warm, flushed cheek pressed against the mattress. I nibble on a piece of cheese as I unload a bag of baby carrots into a dish. I managed a shower this morning when my mother came over to see Jack. It was a long, exaggerated event. I used papaya *and* citrus-mango body wash. I deep-conditioned my hair and shaved my legs. I was behind the curtain, just me, for a good twenty minutes. I felt like I was on vacation. I look somewhat presentable, in black yoga pants and a long-sleeved Ed Hardy T-shirt. When I pulled it over my head this morning, I laughed, thinking: *Who in their right mind spends seventy bucks on a T-shirt?* It was a "PPP" (pre-pregnant purchase). I slide my hand into a mitt and open the oven to check on the shrimp toast. I've morphed into Susie Homemaker. It's a little bizarre. I don't know if I like it. I might.

My apartment has become a cross between then and now. Thick art books anchor the coffee table down and my *Vogue*s and *Glamour*s for this year line the bookshelf—next to Dr. Seuss, of course. My heels, three months later, are still in boxes somewhere (I think in the ones pushed up against the wall, next to the couch), but my sneakers sit waiting for me at the front door, untied. Jack's toys dot the living room, like they fell from the sky, and my pretty L'Occitane candles make the apartment smell like lavender—and, okay, sometimes lavender-scented dirty diapers. The plant is still alive, too. I turn it on the windowsill so it can sun itself and lift its leaves carefully as I water it every Sunday morning with one of Jack's long, skinny Playtex bottles. *I wonder if I bought enough wine*, I think, looking at three extra-large bottles, scooping a hunk of hummus into a chubby soup bowl.

The doorbell buzzes and I jump, dropping the spoon of hummus on the floor—"fuc"—"fudge," I whisper loudly. *Sleeping baby!* I think as I run to the door on my tiptoes like a ballerina late for a curtain call. Kateri, Lo, Rachel, Sherri, and Stef are standing at the door with some sort of apparatus between them.

"Hi," I loud-whisper.

"What's up, mommy!" Kateri says, not loud-whispering at all.

They shuffle in sideways. Lo blows hair out of her face and Stef trips into Rachel.

"Hello!" Rachel says to Stef. "Shoes!"

Once inside they plop the thing on the floor and stand around it like it's a tent they don't know how to put together.

"My aunt said this is all yours!" says Stef, unfolding the structure mid-living room. *Great,* I think. *What the hell is it?* As the thing unfolds open, locking into place, I realize there is a bucket-seat cradle dangling from it. It's a swing. Stef's aunt took procreating into her own hands. She went to a sperm bank, bought some sperm, and had some twins. She is not married. It's just her and the babies and her family and friends. She is my hero. I can't imagine having two Jacks.

"Voilà!" Stef says, turning it on. The five of us stand around it, watching it sway, lazily, side to side.

"Awesome," Lo says. "I kind of want to test it out."

"Wait," says Stef, and she twists a dial and steps back. Suddenly the living room sounds like midnight in a rainforest. Crickets and birds chirp on a never-ending loop behind the ripple of a waterfall.

"Let's put Jack in," says Kateri, looking around the room. "Where's Jack?"

"Shh. Sleeping," I say, setting a bear in the seat, then stepping back. The girls cock their heads and "aw" in unison. They're armed with their purses, wearing jeans with rips on purpose and designer boots they probably scored at DSW. Here we all are standing around in my Jersey apartment fascinated by a singing swing, baby sound asleep in the bedroom, appetizers I cooked waiting in the kitchen. Oh how things change. And stay the same.

"Wine anyone?" I ask, and they all look up like hungry

puppies. *Ah, that's my girls,* I think, walking into the kitchen.

It's raining the next day. It looks like nighttime even though it's only two in the afternoon. I love the rain. It makes me feel okay about being lazy and watching television—letting Jack exist in the same clothes he went to bed in, and me too, for that matter. My mother was supposed to come over and hang out with us so I could unpack the last of the boxes that have sort of become impromptu seating when friends come over, but I tell her to stay put because sheets of rain are heaving down at an angry angle now. In fact the sky just lit up in a pulse of lightning. *Come on, Mr. Magoo, let's go sit on the couch,* I say to Jack, pushing up from the rocker and away from the picture window. *Mr. Magoo—I don't know where it came from, either,* I think, looking down at my son, who looks confused.

I spread a blue blanket on the middle cushion and set Jack down. He immediately starts Jazzercising, popping his arms in and out at the elbow. His movements are more in sync now. Sometimes it looks like he's swimming under water. I rest my nose on his belly. *Mmm.* The formula seeps from his skin. He smells like warm oatmeal all the time. I want to bottle this. It's the most amazing thing I've ever smelled. This time last year, I would have been declaring this at a Saks counter while Nic and I touched up our faces with ridiculously overpriced lip gloss and bronzer after charging three-hundred-dollar jeans.

"Jack, Jack," I say. "Mama loves you. You smell like toasted marshmallows, a little, right now. Must be mama's vanilla hand lotion, huh?" His mouth moves as if he has something under his tongue, then it happens—it's like someone pulled the sides of his mouth into a smile. He holds it there and does not spit up or fart, even. This is a real smile.

"You're smiling at Mama?" I ask, and his mouth hangs open, revealing a set of pink gums. I pull my hands over my mouth, excited. *You do like me, huh?* I whisper.

"You are," I say, lifting him up to me.

"Yeah, that's it. You're smiling now," I say, tears filling my eyes, then searching for my camera, which is not right here on the coffee table. I look to the left and to the right, realizing we are alone in this apartment. There is no one else here to take a picture of his first smile, or even fetch the camera. It's just us. I suppose I realized I'd have to learn how to brush my teeth with a baby pressed against my chest, manage a wet diaper/hungry cry simultaneously, but with all that conquered, I haven't quite examined that there is no quick fix for rainy days when all I hear is the ting on the windowpane and a distant wave of thunder rumbling in. I wipe a tear from my cheek and close in on Jack. I coax him with a smile and he responds, again, letting his mouth open into a tiny half-moon. It's radiant and brings a whole new set of tears, but these are because for the rest of my life I know I'll never forget this moment and how it made me feel. *We're a team, Jack,* I think. *From the very beginning it was just me and you.* I feel so lucky and a little mystified because I don't think I can ever love anyone, even another child, the way I love my Jack. I nuzzle his cheek with my nose. "Do it again, Jack, smile." The rain is starting to echo in the open space. My living room seems bigger than before. I pull Jack into me, tugging a big red blanket over us. He and I fall asleep to the sound of the rain tapping on the windows.

The next day, while Jack is in the middle of a morning nap, I e-mail A. I ask him if he's changed his mind and what he wants to do. Do, as in meet his son, start paying child support—something. My hands shake as I type the e-mail. Part of me believes I am going to hit Send and immediately find one of those "Mailer Daemon" alerts in my inbox, because he probably changed his e-mail, like he did his phone number. After I send my note into cyberspace I smack my computer shut and forget about it. Brian and his friend Jay are coming over to watch Jack so I can go to the gym. I'm about 90 percent confident they can handle it and 10 percent ready to strap Jack to my chest and hit the elliptical. They arrive, looking a bit scared. This is not a good sign.

"Where is he?" Brian whispers, leaning into the living room like there might be a lion in there.

"Sleeping," I say, and Brian puts his finger to his mouth.

"What do I do when he wakes up?" he asks.

"Change him. He'll be wet. Then warm his bottle in the

bottle warmer and feed him. Then burp him," I say. "That's all."

"What else?" Jay asks, looking concerned and about ready to pull pen and paper from my desk to write down exactly what I say.

I stand back, surveying the two guys. They're both wearing polo shirts with the collars popped up. Jay has a bandana tied around his head and his hair is spiked like a Backstreet Boy.

"Just engage him," I say. "Lay him under the baby gym." I grab my gym bag. "I'll be back in one hour."

"Okay," Brian says.

"Okay," Jay says.

"Okay," I say.

I return forty-seven minutes later because I miss Jack and keep picturing Bri and Jay not knowing how to diaper him so Jay twirls him midair while Bri works a roll of toilet paper around his butt. I walk through the front door and find my father in the rocking chair by the window and Jack sound asleep in his arms, wearing no pants and just a diaper.

"Where are Bri and Jay?" I say, looking around the apartment.

"Brian called me because Jack was crying," my father says, smirking.

"They left?" I say, pulling the blanket down from Jack's chin. He's so beautiful. He morphed into something more beautiful while I was on the treadmill and wrestling with a Pilates machine.

"They both looked really beat when I got here," he says.

I roll my eyes. "I wasn't even gone for an hour."

"I've been here for about twenty-five minutes," he says.

"Where are his pants?" I say.

"Brian changed—tried to change—his diaper, but couldn't get his pants back on because he was 'wiggling' too much," my dad says. My nine-pound baby defeated my twenty-four-year-old brother. Amazing.

The following Sunday I'm walking up Lafayette Street in the city. Jack is at home with my mother. I keep checking my purse like I forgot my wallet or the parking ticket, but it's all there, tucked in the Marc Jacobs I've carried one hundred times but feels brand new right now. These days I just throw my wallet in my fabulous Gucci diaper bag and try to leave my apartment, only to get Jack strapped into the car seat, then realize I may have the hot, nine-hundred-dollar bag crossed across my body and a magazine tucked inside to read, but the bottles are in the fridge. Back in we go. And then when we get inside, my baby, bundled in a tiny bomber jacket, smells like poo all of a sudden. Sometimes I think it's easier to just stay home, so when Nic called, summoning Jack and me to brunch, I got a babysitter.

I sit down and wait for Nic. The waitress comes over and asks if I'd like a drink. *Yes, please!* I think, especially after the morning I had. I checked my e-mail. A wants to continue as if Jack and I don't exist and he wants to make it official with an agreement our lawyers have discussed that says I will not ask him for child support and he'll never see Jack. I fantasized about what he would write back in the e-mail and part of it was "I'm so sorry." I would have forgiven him and forged a friendship because he is my son's father. The olive branch has been extended and it was denied. I'm mad that I even bothered to reach out to him now, but at least I know for sure. After I read his e-mail I felt my face flush with heat. It went away two minutes later because Jack discovered his feet. He was lying under his baby gym with his feet pointing to the ceiling when all of a sudden he grabbed them. He tried to stick his left foot in his mouth. It was extraordinary. I took twenty-seven pictures of the same thing.

I order a Bloody Mary and peel off my sweater. Under it, a svelte black T-shirt and jeans—okay, one size up from my "PPP" ones, but at least they have a zipper and a button. I sip my drink and peer around the restaurant. Nothing has changed. People are still wearing sunglasses indoors, eating fancy eggs, and throwing back flutes of champagne. I twirl the celery stalk around my glass, then look at my watch. But actually things have changed, because I think I would rather be home in slippers, drinking coffee from the little automatic pot, singing *Heaven must be missing Jackie, missing my Jackie boy, because he's here with me right now. . . .* Nic arrives in pencil jeans, a bedazzled T-shirt, and a cropped leather jacket. She's carrying a big rectangular clutch and wearing boots for horseback riding.

"Sorry I'm late. Subway di-sas-ter," she says, pushing her sunglasses over the crown of her head.

"It's fine," I say, passing her a menu.

"Water with lemon, please." She looks up at the waitress.

"What's up?" she says, running her finger down the menu. "How's the little worm?"—her new nickname for Jack since I sent her a photo of him wrapped up in a bath towel, with his hair stuck up with Vaseline in a little mohawk.

"Amazing," I say, admiring a toddler tucked into a high-chair at another table eating a piece of bread. "He smiles now. It's the most, the most"—I pause at a loss for words—"well, amazing thing, ever," I say, and I feel my mouth dissolve into a drunk smile as I remember the gummy half circle explicitly.

"Should we go shopping after?" Nic asks, closing the menu.

"Huh?" I say, breaking a piece of bread.

"Shopping," she says.

"I want to, but I have to write my blog for tomorrow and I have like four loads of baby laundry," I say. "He goes through three onesies a day!" She's looking at me like I just stood on the table and did a little dance. I actually already wrote my blog and my mom brought over a load of clean clothes this morning. I just want to get home to Jack. I don't make sense without him. I feel like I could burp Nic every time she sips her water. I didn't think I would feel like this— so in half. There's a delay when I try to answer the waitress when she asks what I'm having. It's like she asked me to solve for X. I order some eggs.

I step away from the table to call my mom to check on Jack. I hope I didn't miss anything good. I stand outside on the corner, wondering why I forced myself to come into the city today. I thought I needed to cling to my old rituals, but the truth is, I have new ones. Things changed, that's all. I'm still me at the core, just a different version—and doesn't that happen when you grow up? Things change and rearrange? This is clearer than ever as a cab pulls up and four girl-friends spill from it in what seem to be last night's outfits. I look away, plugging my ear. "Put Jack by the phone," I tell my mom. I stand on the corner singing *Jaaaa-ck* into the phone while the rest of the city turns round and round like a revolving door. On the way home I don't even notice the skyline disappearing in the rearview mirror and when I look up it's completely out of sight. I spend the rest of the day folded up on the couch with Jack, playing the staring game.

I love how church smells—all warm, like spicy, burning fire-wood. Jack is sleeping in my arms. It's his first mass and I have him dressed in a white-collared shirt and a navy cor-duroy vest and pants. He kicked one of his shoes off when we got here, so he has one red sock on and one brown, soft-leather bootie. Everyone is staring at him, then smiling up at me.

"He's so gorgeous," an elderly woman with a crumpled-up tissue in her hand says.

"Thank you so much," I say.

A toddler kneels on the bench in front of us and reaches for Jack's foot.

"Be-be," he says, and his mom smiles at me like I'm the Virgin mother holding baby Jesus on Christmas morning. I admittedly zone out during the readings. I find myself examining all of the families around me sitting side by side, holding hands during the Our Father. After the Eucharist the priest welcomes a young family to the altar to baptize their baby. The infant is wearing a billowy white dress and doesn't even startle when the priest drips water on his forehead. The parents are beaming, snapping photos at all angles. My father has been on my case about getting Jack baptized and I plan to, especially now when I see how lovely this little ceremony is. The priest is walking up the main aisle with the baby, then back down. Suddenly the congregation erupts into applause, waking the infant—and Jack. He startles in my arms. His owl eyes pop open, but he smiles easily when he sees me looking down at him. His eyes find the iridescent light streaming in through the stained-glass windows. He doesn't make a peep.

After mass we sit outside by the Mary statue and I give Jack his bottle. It's a beautiful day. The patio is carpeted with red and orange leaves and it smells like grass when the wind blows. Jack's palm is spread over my hand that's holding his bottle. He's examining the sky overhead, which is scraped gently with feather clouds. I look up to see the priest from mass approaching us.

"Are you alright?" he asks.

"Yes," I say, smiling. "Just having a bottle before we head home to avoid a meltdown in the car." I laugh.

"Are you from town?" he asks. I smile.

"I went to school here—K through 8, in fact. Father R. resided," I say. "I'm Christine Coppa."

"Aha. What's your maiden name, dear?" he asks. *What's my maiden name? I feel like my parents just caught me having sex on the couch, like I lied on my résumé and my employer found out. Like I stole gum from the supermarket.*

"I'm not married," I say, looking away from him, down at Jack. "I'm single."

There is a pause. I'm not looking at the priest but I feel on fire like my sins are glowing from me.

"Is the baby baptized?" he asks.

"Not yet, but I plan to soon," I say. "He's just about three months."

He leans into me. "I can work with you, privately, on a baptism, if you like," he says.

"Privately?"

"Only because you're not married," he says.

Oh, right. I forgot. *I'm bad.* I can barely contain my laughter as we walk to the car. I suppose this should really bother me, but it doesn't. I was planning on having him baptized at my favorite church in Paterson, anyway. The dome ceiling is painted with gold angels. I would have gone to mass there today, but when I realized it was almost noon I just drove straight down the block to the church I made all my sacraments in. On the way home Jack blows bubbles and chews on his hand sideways. I smile at him in the rearview mirror, turning around in awe of him at every red light until horns beep from behind.

25

Forever

The weekend is here again. It's barely seven p.m. and Jack is sleeping like an angel baby and will sleep for a good stretch, probably until midnight. He'll take a bottle then and fall asleep in my arms, not even realizing when I lay him back in the crib. I read horror stories about colic and how parents had to run the vacuum at all hours because the whir soothed the baby. I hardly ever vacuum, and when I do I have Jack in the sling, pressed against my chest. It's the picture of the 1950s housewife I hardly am. I set my fingertips on the railing of the crib. He's on his side, a position he managed all on his own. *How'd ya do that?* I think. His cheek is smushed on his arm, making his lips pout. He looks like a cherub hanging on a cloud.

I tiptoe out of our bedroom, collecting a bear, a pacifier, and a blue rattle with a little bell in it from the floor, gently easing them onto the changing table in the hallway leading to the bathroom, where I find a soggy diaper, probably from this afternoon. I steady my hands on the table, feeling like the room is spinning around and all I can see is the crib. I take an easy breath, collecting the diaper with two pinched fingers, like a clothespin.

Something has happened over these past months. The anxiety, even those lulls of heaviness have lifted. When they do surface (because they do), something returns me. I haven't taken the little yellow pill in weeks. It occurred to me the other day that I hadn't in some time. It just popped in my head like a random memory bleeping around, like the one of when I was three and I got my foot stuck in a hole by the duck pond. My Poppy had to fetch my Velcro shoe with his hand. My sock got dirty with mud.

I checked myself for panic or sadness when I realized I had gone weeks without the medicine. I was fine and I think I was looking for fear, but there was none. This new feeling is like seeing light through the cracks. It reminds me how afraid I was when I was pregnant and how I spent a great deal of time worrying. I could hardly believe the wave of relief I was feeling until I found the bottle and opened it up. It was full, full of the little magic pills that used to make me feel easy or happy—I can't remember. I pushed the bottle to the back of the shelf in the closet with two fingers and closed the door. The thing is, I do get overwhelmed, incredibly so, and I do panic, wondering if this is, in fact, it—a small apartment, a steady but not excellent paycheck, a beautiful baby. And it should all be enough. I am blessed a thousand times over and I know it, I really do, but sometimes when I'm in my bed, I just want to turn over and nuzzle someone to wake up, ask them if things are going to always be okay. Time and time again, no one is there, and the panic begins to boil, riding up my insides with a slow churn. But then something else happens—I realize there is no time for this. I think of

Jack, of all the joy he has brought me, and I find myself easing into calm. It's like he saved me from everything I was
ever afraid of and then I'm smiling and thanking God out
loud for bringing him into my life. I take a breath and push
off from the changing table, settling onto the living room
floor with a few envelopes, all stacked with pictures of these
past three months and a new leather-bound album. Most
nights, like tonight, are incurably lonely. I hoist up onto the
couch and start to drift to sleep on its arm when all of a sudden Jack cries out, reminding me I'm not alone after all. I'm
needed and loved.

"Should I maybe"—and I lower my voice—"drug him?" I ask
Katie, biting my lip. We're dressing Jack for his baptism today and he is not liking it at all. He's beside himself at the
moment, in fact—won't even take a bottle. *Did he poop today?* I try to remember. *Did he poop yesterday?* Pooping is
very important, I've learned.

"Shhh, shh, sweet Jack," I say, leaning over him on my
bed—my left foot slipping out from a fuzzy red slipper.
"Mama's here." His eyes squeeze tighter together and he lets
out another incredible screech. It only goes away when he
realizes he has no breath left. Feeling defeated, I look over
to the mirror pressed against the wall, finding myself half-
dressed in black tights and a fitted black dress, my hair tied
back in a half-bun. Katie returns and hands me the bottle of

Tylenol and I pop a drop on his tongue. I hear the front door open, then close. Carlo walks into my room. His tie is hanging undone around his neck and his suit jacket is flung over his shoulder, resting on a finger.

"What's up?" he says to Katie and me. We look at each other as if we have a secret.

"Nothing," we say in unison. Carlo dips his arm around Katie's shoulder and says: "One day I might ask you for a favor, godmother Katie," imitating Marlon Brando's iconic raspy voice from *The Godfather*. I roll my eyes at him and Katie twists out from his arm.

"Your godfather is cuckoo, Jack," I say, buttoning his vest. "Cuckoo." Jack smiles and kicks at me.

Carlo and Katie finish dressing Jack, snapping buttons and tying strings. I hold up a little silk bonnet, smiling. Jack is being baptized today in the same outfit Carlo and Brian wore. It's a white three-piece short suit meant for spring baptisms—not winter ones. *Uh, especially ones like this,* I agonize, squinting my eyes at the whiteness whirling around outside.

"Do you think the storm is going to keep people from coming?" I ask, dabbing my lips with gloss.

"Maybe your friends from the city," Carlo says.

"Ha! They already left," I say over a gurgle of laughter, imagining all of them squished in a car together with fur-trimmed hoods on, their palms pressed against the windows.

"All the girls are coming, too," Katie says.

"And their boyfriends, husbands, whatever. It's okay, you know, to mention the guys," I say. Sometimes I feel like there is something wrong with me because I couldn't get a husband or even a boyfriend. I wonder exactly when A and I ended and I can't pinpoint it. I look at my friends' lives and I wonder how I veered off track, but then Jack calls out to me in an incredible yelp and I suppose I am on track—mine. I pull a comb through my hair, yanking at the knots, then toss the comb on the bed.

"Your grandparents brought me home from the hospital almost twenty-seven years ago in the snow, Jack," I say, curling my eyelashes in the mirror. "We'll be fine today."

Jack is dressed now and Katie is cuddling him on my bed, feeding him a warm bottle. Carlo is explaining to our friend George, over the cell, that he absolutely has to come to the church and not just the party, reminding him trucks are made for snow. "You have a Jeep," he yells into the phone, walking into the living room. "I can't believe this weather!" he yells to us. "It's like a blizzard out there."

I pull the curtain to the side, peering out at the whiteness everywhere. It's snowing hard now. There are perfect lines of snow collected on the tree branches. The lawn is unscathed, just a thick, powdery white covering. The roads were plowed once, but the streets are now covered in snow all over again. The wind picks up, howling like a little dog, and I feel a subtle chill push in through the glass on my face and neck. *It's snowing again*, I think, pushing my palms against the windowpane, feeling the chill, staring out into the whitewash. It feels like yesterday I was in my car willing the snow to hold me still in its wrath, keep the minute hand from ticking into my future. How I willed it to suspend me in that moment. I turn around to find Katie bouncing Jack in her arms. He's smiling at her, his owl eyes blinking at the sound of her tongue clucking. These are the new moments I want to be suspended in. I plop next to Katie, taking Jack from her.

"Don't you want to finish getting dressed?" she says.

I wake up with a start. It's quiet and it's starting to get light outside. I rub my eyes and find the clock. Quarter to six, I see. I lay back down. Today is my birthday. I'm twenty-seven now. I pull the covers back up to my chest and lie here, peering over at the crib. *Twenty-seven and a mom—and a writer. Not so bad, Christine. This is pretty good. But what an unpredictable year,* I think, turning over to the crib, anticipating a wind-up of tears any minute now. There's no cake in front of me but I make a wish anyway, one for Jack. I quite simply wish that he'll grow up feeling complete and happy. I just want a happy child. A tear passes from my eye and I catch it on my finger. Like clockwork Jack wakes, suddenly demanding a bottle. I pull him up to my chest.

"It's Mama's birthday," I say, sweeping my lips across his cheek. "Do you remember this time last year?" I hold him out from me.

"You had big plans for mama, huh?" I say, laughing at the lull of nausea that toppled me over this time last year, which I immediately wrote off as the flu. *I was so naive.* I laugh to myself. "Yes, you did."

I lay him down on the changing table, peeling open his diaper. "What a surprise you were," I say. He kicks at the mattress.

We sit in the rocker by the window and I feed Jack his bottle. It's gray out, threatening rain because I don't think it's cold enough to snow today. I teeter back and forth in the chair, thinking that for the first time in years I don't have any birthday plans. I sit Jack up and pat his back, then pull him up to my eyes.

"We need to celebrate, Jack," I say. He looks at me sleepily.

Two hours later I'm pushing Jack up Fifth Avenue.

"This is New York City, Jack," I say, pushing the red canopy to his stroller back like an accordion.

"Mama used to live here," I say, taking a breath, whirling around.

Jack's mittens are too big on him and his face is almost entirely covered by a wool hat with earflaps and the fuzzy collar of his jacket. He looks like he wants to move but can't. We push past a cart selling coffee and bagels. The warm, burned smell wafts through the cold air. A rush of yellow cabs speed past, changing lanes without their blinkers on. I smile at the routine chaos all around us. We stop at a traffic light. A woman wrapped in cashmere is scrolling through her Palm Pilot with a gloved finger. She smells like roses and her face is made up. We cross the street, passing men with briefcases and a woman walking a bundle of dogs. The Metropolitan Museum is set out before us now.

"You'll like it here, Jack," I say. "Mama came here a lot when she lived here."

I whirl the stroller around and set it before the grand cascading steps. I did it—here I am, back in New York City, with my baby. I smile up at the sky, feeling satisfied. I reach for my camera in the pocket of my diaper bag that's stuffed under the seat of the stroller. I pull it out and bite my left glove off. When I focus the picture I see that Jack is perfectly sound asleep and content; his mitten pulled up to his mouth. I kneel down to him, pulling his hands down and he startles.

"Jack, this is New York City," I whisper loudly into the stroller. He smiles at me, then up at the dizzying line of buildings. I look up with him, fixed in the moment, while people rush past us with newspapers under their arms, lattes in their hands. The sky is still gray but dazzling with light, like the sun might reveal itself just about now. I look back down to Jack. His mouth is hung open in a little circle.

"It's beautiful," I say to him. "Yes?" His eyes switch to me. I feel myself close in on him, everything else fading away.

"The most beautiful thing I ever saw," I say.

Acknowledgments

This book would not be possible without the support of *Glamour* magazine and Glamour.com. My sincere gratitude to editor-in-chief Cindi Leive—thank you for believing in me and standing proudly behind Storked! Many thanks to Susan Goodall, Jill Herzig, Ellen Seidman, Genevieve Field, Ayana Byrd, Anne Sachs, and everyone at *Glamour* for their continued support and faith in me. I'll *always* consider Storked! my second baby of 2007.

Thank you to Carol Brooks at *First* for welcoming me back to her staff in July '07 and for her support when I chose to pursue a full-time freelance career; Maria Lissandrello at *Woman's World* for being a boss and a friend; Matt Sullivan at *In Touch* for always coming to my rescue with a humorous guest blog; and Deb Baer at *In Touch* for encouraging me to pitch *Glamour* back in '06 after the Scratch It reading.

To my Storked! readers at Glamour.com—thank you for coming back, for championing me. You are my friends.

A warm thanks to my agent Brettne Bloom at Kneerim & Williams at Fish & Richardson who among *many* things reminds me daily I am a "warrior single mama." To my lawyer, Elaine Rogers, thank you for all of your time and dedication (and for answering all of my e-mails). I am deeply grateful to my editor at Broadway, Christine Pride, for her time and guidance (and superior notes), and to everyone at Broadway for making this experience so pleasurable and exciting.

To the NYC and NJ aunts (and Aunt T in LA)—I don't have any sisters, but my son sure does have a lot of aunts. Kateri Lopez, thank you for *always* being excited and positive; Nicole Anello, thank you for *always* answering the phone (and for the Gucci diaper bag); Lauren Matthews, you're a stellar baby handler; Sherri O'Connor, thank you for shooting this jacket portrait—two times; Katie Ferrara, thanks for the free baby haircuts.

To Theresa Williams and the Imbruglia family, thank you for loving Jack when I was on scary book deadlines. I never felt like I was bringing Jack to day care and I will always remember your kindness and support.

To my parents, thank you for twenty-eight years of unconditional love and support. To my older brother, Carlo Jr., thanks for being the man that you are. I don't know what I would have done without you. To my younger brother, Brian, thanks for cooking me dinner and sort of learning how to change a diaper.

To my sweet Jack Domenic, thank you for coming into my life and completing it to infinite ends. No one will ever love you like I do. I'm honored to be your mother.

Jack Domenic's Great-Nanny, Antoinette Coppa, passed away on May 19, 2008. This book is in memory of her and her words: "You're going to have a beautiful baby."

1. When Christine first learns that she's pregnant, how does A's reaction differ from her own? How do their feelings change over the next few months? Can you think of a time in your own life when everything changed in a split second, like when Christine saw her baby's heartbeat and knew her pregnancy was real? How did you feel?

2. Were you surprised by A's decision not to be involved at all? Given that women have the right to an abortion and Plan B, do you think a man should have the right to walk away if he doesn't want to be a parent?

3. Has anyone you loved ever been injured in an accident, like Christine's ex-boyfriend Keith? How did it affect you? Do you think Christine was wrong to leave him?

4. Christine grapples with how to share her pregnancy ne~ with her family and friends. Did her parents' reactio~ prise you? How did Christine's girlfriends differ responses? How did you react when a girlf~ something surprising with you?

5. What do you think of Christine's solo trip to Palm Springs, California? What does her "babymoon" teach her about herself? Have you or would you ever travel solo? Why or why not?

6. Christine remarks that moving to New Jersey seems, at times, "more impossible" than being pregnant. What do you think she misses most about city life? How does her move affect her relationship with her girlfriends? What are the advantages and disadvantages of raising a child in the city? In the suburbs?

7. What do you make of Christine's relationship with her brother Carlo? Do you think he helps or hinders her ability to become independent and ready for her baby?

8. Christine's work as a blogger often makes her private life open to the public. Do you think readers have the right to critique her decisions? Have her readers crossed a line by asking questions about child support, Jack's father, and her financial situation? Do you think A ever read(s) her blog?

9. How do Christine's feelings about being a single-parent family change as her pregnancy progresses? How does she overcome concerns about raising her son without a father? Do you think American society still views a nuclear family as the ideal?

10. What is the significance of Christine's return to New York City with her son to celebrate her twenty-seventh birthday? How has she changed since the beginning of the book?